A Pocket Guide to
Suffolk Parish Churches

A POCKET GUIDE TO SUFFOLK PARISH CHURCHES
© RICHARD CASTELL PUBLISHING LIMITED

A Castell Pocket Guide to
SUFFOLK PARISH CHURCHES

ISBN 0 948134 48 8

Published by Richard Castell Publishing Limited
Thwaite Eye Suffolk IP23 7EE

Printed by Gipping Press Limited
Lion Barn Industrial Estate Needham Market Suffolk IP6 8NZ

INTRODUCTION

SUFFOLK HAS AROUND FIVE HUNDRED MEDIEVAL CHURCHES, one twenty-fourth of the total for the whole of England and, whilst the fifteenth century provided the peak in church building and beautifying, no less than four hundred and seventeen of these were mentioned in Domesday Book in 1086.

THE earliest missionary bringing the Christian faith to East Anglia was St Felix. It was he who converted Sigebert before the latter had been elected to the East Anglian throne as Raedwald's successor. Raedwald had himself already taken on the Christian faith, but through pressure from his recusant wife decided to keep a foot in both camps and worship Woden as well. Surprisingly, when Sigebert, the Queen's son by a previous marriage, clashed with Raedwald's own two sons, it was Sigbert who was banished to France. Here he met Felix, a religious Burgundian ecclesiastic, who accompanied him when he was called back to England. After being consecrated by Honorius II, Archbishop of Canterbury in 630, and made a bishop, Felix set up his seat at Dunmoc. He died in 647 and such had been his success that he was buried in Bury Abbey and canonised as a saint. Where was Dunmoc? It was likely to have been Dunwich where the site of his monastery will have long been lost to the merciless North Sea, but there are also claims for it being at Walton, where the neighbouring hamlet of Felixstowe took on his name - 'Felix' from St Felix, and 'stowe' being Anglo-Saxon for 'holy place'. Any evidence has again unfortunately been removed, as the possible site - the Roman Saxon Shore fort - is itself now submerged.

Another mission was established by the Irish monk St Fursey (or Fursa), who set himself up within another abandoned Roman shore fort, that of Gariannonum (Burgh Castle, just south of Great Yarmouth). Luckily this ancient monument still survives intact.

A third, St Botolph, founded an orthodox monastery, famous throughout the country, at Icanhoe in 670. This we can confidently identify as Iken, a beautifully atmospheric spot at the deserted marshy southern shore of the Alde estuary. It most likely stood on the site of Iken Church which keeps his dedication, or may even have been the strange round earthwork of Yarn Hill close by, which would at that time have been surrounded by water. The monastery survived for 200 years until 870.

Very few of these four hundred or so Saxon churches which the Normans inherited have survived. Most were of wood or had a wooden building attached to the flint and stone round tower. The chancel at Crowfield is the only original part of a Suffolk timber church which survives, but Essex still retains a complete wooden Saxon church at Greenstead, the nave made up from split trunks of oak trees. Saxon remains in Suffolk are generally restricted to round towers and meagre traces of long and short work on the corners of the buildings. It is not always easy to identify whether a tower is Saxon or early Norman and a conflict of opinion emanates over the origin of several churches.

Why does Suffolk, and particularly Norfolk, possess virtually all the round church towers in the country? Is the reason, as has been confidently suggested, the

The wonderful tower of St Peter & St Paul, Eye, 'panelled in flushwork from foot to parapet'

lack of natural building material which makes it difficult to work flint corners into a square building; if so, why are the majority of round towered churches situated along the coast where alternative materials are available, and why did the style die out soon after the Normans established themselves here? It surely relates more to the country's political state at the time. When conflict threatened, a tall round tower, with no access or windows on the ground floor, provided a double use: a look-out tower and a defence against attackers - entry only being gained by ladders to the first floor which could be pulled up. Their religious houses were usually constructed in wood, attached to or even standing alone from, the tower; in many cases these were put to the torch by the attackers to be rebuilt again - probably several times. Initially the Normans too had a need for defence, but when their conquest was complete and the countryside finally subdued they reverted to conventional square towers with attached nave and chancel built in whatever stone was available.

Although flint was the most widely used, it was not the only building material; along the coast two other materials found favour, the buff-coloured shelly Coralline Crag, and septaria, a clay limestone seen at its best in the walls of Orford Castle keep, still perfectly preserved after over 900 years. Roman brick found its way into many early buildings scavenged from some nearby ruined site and, one thousand years later, Tudor red brick began to replace the flint. The Victorians, who were responsible for resurrecting church building and restoration - well-intentioned but sometimes with horrendous results - occasionally used the locally manufactured Woolpit whites which, in their original form, were a warm cream colour but weathering to an unfortunate dirty white; many public buildings were constructed using them and a recent purge to beautify the town centres has seen them pressure-cleaned back to their original attractive colour.

As previously stated, the 15th century brought about the biggest rush of church building and restoration in the county, with the emphasis on spectacular towers. Two very diverse industries financed this explosion. Inland, along the Stour valley, the Wool trade made fortunes for clothiers like the Shillings of Lavenham who assisted their passage to Heaven with massive endowments to the local church, where they would later be buried in isolated splendour in their own richly-ornamented chapels. And along the coast, medieval ports like Blythburgh, Walberswick and Covehithe flourished and built monuments in flint and stone to their wealth. Sadly when these harbours silted up and trade floundered, so too did the towns they supported, and they returned to what they are today - pretty, isolated villages, the churches abandoned and in ruins (except thankfully for Blythburgh which remains one of the most memorable sights to travellers on the road to Lowestoft).

After the Reformation the great era of church-building came to an end and it was not until Victorian times that these great shrines again received any real attention.

While these great churches remain to remind us of our important past, many of the wonders they contained within do not. Appointed by the Earl of Manchester in 1643, during Cromwell's 'reign', to remove all superstitious things in Suffolk's churches, William Dowsing, locally born at Stratford St Mary and buried in Laxfield churchyard, took to his task with an egotistic enthusiasm and will be forever remembered for his rape of much of the beauties created by our forefathers.

The churches are probably Suffolk's greatest treasure, providing a continuing link with its past. They are great in number - there are few paths or roads from which you cannot spot at least one - yet provide an unobtrusive and indelible part of the county's unique and expansive landscape. In the following pages, details of some 500 Suffolk parish churches, both past and present, are included, providing enough information for the average enthusiast. For the more serious student I would suggest for your further reading, *Suffolk Churches and their Treasures* by H. Munro Cautley, Nikolaus Pevsner's *Suffolk* (part of the 'Buildings of England' series), and E. Farrer's *Monumental Brasses of Suffolk*.

Selected Bibliography:

The Buildings of England: Suffolk - Nikolaus Pevsner

The Little Guide: Suffolk - P. G. M. Dickinson

The Making of the English Landscape: The Suffolk Landscape - Norman Scarfe

The East Anglian Miscellany: various

Suffolk Churches and Their Treasures - H. M. Cautley

Men of Dunwich - Rowland Parker

History, Gazetteer & Directory of Suffolk - William White

Suffolk - Norman Scarfe

The King's England: Suffolk - Arthur Mee

Victoria County History of Suffolk: Vol II

Proceedings of the Suffolk Institute of Archaeology: various

Please note that a fully illustrated, larger format hardback edition of this guide will be available under ISBN 0 948134 49 6.

Other Church Guides in the Series:

A Pocket Guide to Norfolk Parish Churches

A Pocket Guide to Essex Parish Curches

ACTON

Location: 3 miles NE of Sudbury.
Dedication: All Saints.
Description: Comprises aisled nave, chancel with N and S chapels, porch and low W tower.
Periods: The W tower, which became unsafe, was taken down in 1885 and rebuilt to a less ambitious height. The base is of c1300, the same period as the S aisle and S chapel. The N doorway and N chapel are 14c Dec.
Features: Carved bench-ends; carved wooden Hanoverian Royal Arms; 17c communion rail; famous brass to Sir Robert de Bures 1302 - one of the best in England, a brass to Alyce de Bryon, daughter of Sir Robert c1435, and another to Henry Bures, Knight 1528; canopied and pinnacled alter-tomb and a monument to Robert Jennens 1725 in chapel at E end of S aisle. The church Register dates from 1564.

AKENHAM

Location: 3 miles NW of Ipswich.
Dedication: St Mary.
Description: Small church of flint with Caen stone dressing, consisting of a nave, chancel, chapel and S tower. The church suffered bomb damage in World War II and was rescued by Friends of Friendless Churches.
Periods: Small Norman window in N wall of nave; restored 14c tower; remains of Early English work in chancel; S aisle of 16c brick.
Features: Octagonal font; cup and paten 1751; brass inscription of c1500 to Sissile Joiy; several 17c memorial slabs.

ALDEBURGH

Dedication: St Peter & St Paul.
Description: The church stands on a hill to the west of town. Built of flint and freestone it consists of nave and chancel, with full length aisles to both, W tower and large S porch.
Periods: The church was rebuilt in 16c, but the W tower is 14c. The chancel was restored in 1853.
Features: 15c font; piscina in N chancel chapel; 2 ancient chests, one dated 1632; 17c pulpit; old bench ends and panelling from rood-screen; Royal Arms of Charles II; matrices and brasses dating from 1519 to 1635; three 17c coffin-shaped wooden slabs; marble bust of poet George Crabbe - born here in 1754, a monument to Lady Henrietta Vernon, 1786, and memorials to victims of 1899 lifeboat disaster.

ALDERTON

Location: 8 miles SE of Woodbridge.
Dedication: St Andrew.
Description: Nave, chancel, N porch and ruined W tower.
Periods: The oldest parts of the nave are Dec and the N porch is Perp. The chancel was rebuilt and the church restored 1864-5.
Features: 14c piscina in S wall of nave; Royal Arms of George III; paten 1715, cup and paten 1733; memorial tablet on chancel wall to Charles Goodwyn

Archer, rector here 54 years, who rebuilt chancel and restored nave.

ALDHAM

Location: 2 miles NE of Hadleigh.
Dedication: St Mary.
Description: Standing beside the Hall with earthwork traces of a deserted settlement to the west, the church is on a mound partly surrounded by a dry moat and has a round flint tower, nave and chancel.
Periods: The S wall of the nave contains pre-Conquest remains in window jamb; the W tower is probably Norman, and the nave and chancel Dec., though much restored.
Features: 13c piscina, oak lectern, the base original 15c; some 15c carved bench-ends; 17c communion rails; Royal Arms of George III, paten 1735, cup and cover 1785.

ALDRINGHAM-cum-Thorpe

Location: 5 miles SE of Saxmundham.
Dedication: St Andrew.
Description: Situated some distance from the road, the church consists of a nave and chancel, under one roof with no chancel arch, and a bellcote.
Periods: The tower, which had been in ruins for many years, was removed in 1843 when the mainly 13c church was restored and a bellcote added.
Features: Very fine Perp octagonal font; shaft of 13c pillar-piscina.

ALPHETON

Location: 6 miles N of Sudbury.
Dedication: St Peter & St Paul.
Description: Church and Hall stand remote among farm buildings at end of half mile long lane W of the main road. It consists of a nave, chancel, wooden S porch and substantial W tower.
Periods: Mainly 13c and 14c, with a 15c porch.
Features: 15c font; 14c piscina and remains of very fine 14c triple sedilia; traces of original colouring on canopied niches either side of chancel arch; some old stained glass; traces of a late 14c painting of St Christopher on N wall of nave; choir stall, the back comprising two misericords; some old carved bench-ends; part of rood-screen; small Jacobean pulpit; box pews; Royal Arms of Charles II. The Register dates from 1571.

AMPTON

Location: 5 miles N of Bury St Edmunds.
Dedication: St Peter.
Description: Interesting small church with nave, chancel, N chapel, W tower.
Periods: Mainly 14c, but much restored about 1848. The unusually designed chantry chapel was built in 1479 by John Coket.
Features: Good painted chancel roof, re-discovered in 1889; remains of two large consecration crosses at W end of nave; old armorial glass in windows of N chapel; ancient iron-bound chest; Royal Arms of Charles I; 17c paten, cup, flagon and almsdish; very rare Prayer Book of 1661; late 15c brasses, mainly of Coket family; 17c monuments of Calthorpes, including that of

Dorothy Calthorpe, who had founded the picturesque almshouses in 1692, inscribed 'A Virgin votary is oft in snares; this safely vowed and made ye poor her heirs'; The Register dates from 1562.

ASHBOCKING

Location: 7 miles N of Ipswich.
Dedication: All Saints.
Description: Beside Hall, with nave, chancel, S porch and W tower.
Periods: A rebuilt Domesday church with surviving Late 13c chancel, a Dec nave and Tudor brick W tower. The S porch is modern.
Features: Norman font on modern shaft with 15c cover; tomb recess in nave; 13c chancel windows with plate tracery; fine 14c iron-bound chest; Royal Arms of Charles I dated 1640; Elizabethan cup; brass of Edmund Bockinge 1585 with his two wives and two daughters and an epitaph brass to Thomas Horseman 1619.

ASHBY

Location: 6 miles NW of Lowestoft.
Dedication: St Mary.
Description: Isolated and approached through farmyard, this thatched church has a curious tower, the first third round and flint, the upper section octagonal and brick.
Periods: Norman round tower with Tudor later stage; late 13c thatched nave and chancel.
Features: Damaged 12c font of Purbeck marble; 13c piscina and credence in chancel; two painted consecration crosses in nave; cup 1568 inscribed 'For the Towne of Asbe'.

ASHFIELD-cum-Thorpe

Location: 3 miles E of Debenham.
Dedication: St Mary.
Description: Nave and chancel with weatherboarded bell-turret.
Periods: Rebuilt in red brick 1853 by Lord Henniker after being in ruins for over a century.
Features: Only remains from earlier building are some fragments of 17c woodwork incorporated in the modern altar and prayer desk and an Elizabethan cup and paten.

Dedication: St Peter.
Description: Only the ruined Norman round tower of the church is standing, along with a fragment of nave wall now forming a feature in a rock garden of Thorpe Hall. Thorpe Chapel had been rebuilt in 1739 to provide the parish church of Ashfield, but following Lord Henniker's rebuilding of St Marys in 1853, St Peters was abandoned.

ASPALL

Location: 6 miles S of Eye.
Dedication: St Mary of Grace.
Situation & Description: W tower, nave and chancel, with a wooden porch.

Periods: Principally Dec with a Perp W tower.
Features: Octagonal 15c font; fragments of the rood-screen in front of the choir stalls; new seating carved in traditional style; cup and paten 1634, almsdish 1794; memorial to Lord Kitchener, whose Suffolk mother was the daughter of Rev. Dr. Chevallier of Aspall Hall, a residence the family still hold.

ASSINGTON

Location: 5 miles SE of Sudbury.
Dedication: St Edmund.
Description: Situated close by the Hall and comprising aisled nave, chancel, N and S porches and W tower, 75' tall. Tradition says it stands on the site of the Battle of Ethandune between the English and Danes, though this is disputed in Essex.
Period: Much restored in 1863 when the Dec chancel was rebuilt. The tower is also Dec, though it is suggested that the interior includes some reworked Saxon material. The nave and aisles are Perp and S porch also 15c.
Features: Fine S door with tracery; Perp font; Some panels from the rood-screen incorporated in the choir stalls; set of plate 1843-4; brass of Knight and Lady c1500 thought to be members of the Wingfield family; monuments to the Gurdon family who rose to wealth and influence when Sir Adam Gurdon was befriended by Edward I after losing to him in single combat during the Barons War. They comprise: Robert Gurdon 1577 and wife, John Gurdon 1623 and wife, double memorial of c1625, Brampton Gurdon 1648, John Gurdon 1758 and his wife 1710, and Philip Gurdon 1817 and wife. The Register dates from 1558.

ATHELINGTON

Location: 4 miles SE of Eye.
Dedication: St Peter.
Description: Small, with chancel and nave under one roof. Flint and red Tudor brick W tower with stair turret.
Periods: Early English.
Features: Octagonal 15c font; dainty trefoiled piscina in chancel; beautifully carved benches - among the best in Suffolk; cup and two patens 1706, flagon 1708; three interesting 15c bells in the tower. The Register dates from 1694.

BACTON

Location: 6 miles N of Stowmarket.
Dedication: St Mary.
Description: Large church of great interest. It consists of an aisled nave, stone and flint panelled clerestory, chancel, S porch and W tower with brick stair-turret.
Period: Chancel, nave, aisles and tower are Dec. Perp windows have been inserted in the chancel, while the clerestory, S aisle and S porch are also of this period. The tower was once crowned by a tall spire but this was taken down in 1935. The stair-turret is 15c.
Features: Latin inscriptions under the eaves of the aisles; sanctus bell-cote over the nave gable; very fine double hammer-beam roof to nave and painted roof of chancel; repainted Canopy of Honour over eastern bay of

nave; early 16c font; remains of 'Doom' painting over chancel arch; painted memorial to Thomas Smyth 1702; inscription to James Hobart, Attorney-General under Henry VII in S aisle; some interesting bench-ends; Elizabethan cup, paten 1682, almsdish 1729, flagon 1756; tablet memorial to George Pretyman 1732 and his wife 1738 in the nave.

BADINGHAM

Location: 4 miles NE of Framlingham.
Dedication: St John the Baptist.
Description: Situated on the slope of a hill known as Burstonhaugh, and later as Derhaugh, with chancel, nave, S porch and W tower.
Periods: There are remains of the former Norman church in the western corners of the building and in the tower. 13c nave, 15c tower and S porch. The chancel was rebuilt in 1873.
Features: Excellent single hammer-beam roof to nave; richly carved Seven Sacraments' font; remains of 15c rood-screen; 17c pulpit; small iron-bound chest; Elizabethan cup and paten; canopied tombs of Sir Robert Carbonell 1397 and of Sir John Carbonell 1423, and an early 17c monument to William Cotton and wife. The Register dates from 1538. In the churchyard is the base of the old cross, found under the belfry floor.

BADLEY

Location: 2 miles NW of Needham Market.
Dedication: St Mary.
Description: Situated in a remote spot and left mainly unrestored. It comprises a nave, chancel; rough wooden S porch and W tower with brick top.
Periods: Norman S door; lancet window in chancel and the S nave doorway are both early 13c.
Features: King-post and tie-beam roof of nave; octagonal 13c font; rood-screen with traces of colour on lower part; old bench-ends and box-pews; 17c two-decker pulpit; iron communion rail dated 1830; cup and cover 1630, paten 1778; brass inscriptions to Edward Poley 1613; John Poley 1615 and Edmund Brewster 1633; monument to Sir Henry Poley 1707 and ledger-stone to Dorothy Poley 1625 with good inscription.

BADWELL ASH

Location: 4 miles N of Elmswell.
Dedication: St Mary.
Situation & Description: Impressive church with fine flushwork. Comprises nave with S aisle and fine clerestory, chancel, S porch and W tower. Inscription round parapet 'Pray for the good estate of John Fincham and Margaret hys wyf'.
Periods: Dec nave and chancel; Perp W tower, S porch and aisle.
Features: Hammerbeam roof to nave; fine porch with canopied niche and St George and the Dragon in spandrels of entrance arch; rood-stair with original carved narrow entrance door, only 16" wide; late 14c octagonal font; piscinas of c1300 in S aisle and chancel; carved 17c chest in tower; Elizabethan cup and paten.

BARDWELL

Location: 8 miles NE of Bury St Edmunds.
Dedication: St Peter & St Paul.
Description: Fine large building with good flushwork decoration. Lofty nave, chancel, tall S porch and embattled tower topped by short spire.
Period: Perp W tower and S porch. The nave has Dec windows and the chancel is of 1553. The nave and chancel were extensively restored in 1853.
Features: 15c hammerbeam roof to nave with fine carved angels; modern statues in the three niches of the S porch; 15c glass commemorating Sir William Berdewell 1367-1434; remarkable series of wall paintings discovered during restoration including 'Doom' over chancel arch and St Christopher on the N wall now covered over again; four panels of traceried rood-screen; Royal Arms of George II; two cups and paten 1650, two flagons 1678; 17c sword; fine memorial to Thomas Read and wife 1652 on chancel S wall.

BARHAM

Location: 5 miles NW of Ipswich.
Dedication: St Mary.
Description: Large building with aisleless nave, clerestory, long chancel, two-bay N chapel and S tower the basement of which forms a porch.
Period: Mainly 14c and 15c. The much restored S porch tower is c1300 as are the nave doorways. The chancel has Perp windows, and the nave clerestory is early 16c.
Features: Good single hammerbeam roof to nave; the Middleton Chapel has a vestry which contains a large window of terracotta made c1525; picture of the Ascension said to be the work of Carlo Maratti 1625-1713 and brought from Italy c1830; pulpit with three coloured panels from rood-screen; the chapel has a fine 15c screen (another part of the old rood-screen?); richly carved altar rails from Italy of 1700; brass of Robert Southwell and wife 1514; monument to Sir Richard Southwell 1640, Booth tomb in N of chancel and memorials to the Middleton and Bacon families 1618-29 in side chapel. William Kirby (1782-1850), the famous entomologist, was rector here.

BARKING

Location: 1 mile SW of Needham Market.
Dedication: St Mary.
Description: Needham Market was included in the parish with Barking its mother church until 1901, after which it became a parish in its own right and ecclesiastically independent; the next year severing a connection going back many centuries. It is a large, interesting building with fine medieval woodwork and consists of aisled nave, clerestory, chancel with two-storeyed vestry, S porch and W tower bearing inscription relating to the granting of a fair.
Period: The tower was largely rebuilt in 1870 but the nave arcades, chancel, S porch and S doorway (with early 16c doors) are late 13c. The aisles are 14c.
Features: Massive 14c nave roof of king-post construction; 15c font with contemporary tabernacled cover; piscinas in aisles; terracotta detail of a window in N aisle (brought from old Shrubland Hall); excellent parclose screens of 15c date at E end of both aisles which form chapels; carved panel

of the Annunciation on pulpit; 17c communion rails; Royal Arms of Charles II;
set of plate 1750; crested helmet in S aisle; two wrought-iron braziers -
formerly used to heat church; marble monument to Crowley family 1771.

BARNARDISTON

Location: 5 miles NW of Clare.
Dedication: All Saints.
Description: A small church of nave, chancel large N porch and W tower.
Periods: Chiefly Dec and Perp.
Features: Wicket door within 15c S door; large rood loft turret on N wall
with stairs complete; incised drawing of a post windmill in sill of SW window
of chancel; massive 14c font - broken and repaired with straps (in 17c?); 15c
piscina in chancel; 15c rood-screen; Jacobean pulpit with hour-glass stand;
reading desk; simple benches with tracery; 17c communion rail with
candlesticks; early 17c paten, cup 1663; tower contains two bells, one of
which is probably 14c.

BARNBY

Location: 4 miles SE of Beccles.
Dedication: St John the Baptist.
Description: Thatch roofed nave and chancel in one, N porch and W tower.
Periods: Early, with a chancel of c1300 and 14c W tower.
Features: 13c octagonal font of Purbeck marble; traces of 15c wall-
paintings on S wall discovered during 1882 restoration depicting Crucifixion
and St Christopher; Royal Arms of George IV; banner-stave locker in S nave
wall - the only one retaining its original door.

BARNHAM

Location: 9 miles N of Bury St Edmunds.
Dedication: St Gregory.
Description: There were formerly two parishes and two churches here. St
Gregory comprises nave, aisle, chancel and W tower.
Periods: 'Too restored to have an architectural story to tell' (Pevsner), but
a piece of carved Anglo-Saxon coffin lid is built into the wall of a flint
cottage N of churchyard according to Norman Scarfe. The aisle added 1864.
Features: Fine 13c piscina in chancel; late 16c chair; Royal Arms of William
III; Elizabethan cup, flagon 1755, almsdish c1756.

Dedication: St Martin
Description: At NW end of village. In ruins for over 200 years, only tower
remains with part of an adjoining wall, forming a picturesque ivy-clad ruin.

BARNINGHAM

Location: 6 miles W of Botesdale.
Dedication: St Andrew.
Description: Good W tower with typical Suffolk 3-stepped parapet, nave
and chancel. The woodwork in the church is particularly fine.
Periods: Principally 14c, but the tower appears to be mid 15c.
Features: Octagonal Dec font; piscina and window-sill sedilia in chancel;

fragments of old glass in window-heads; set of 15c benches with fine tracery on ends and backs; late 17c pulpit; beautiful screen with original colour - though varnished in 1933; modern carved oak reredos illustrating the Last Supper; Elizabethan cup and paten, flagon 1762; brass to William Goche 1499; Royal Arms of Queen Victoria; two pre-Reformation bells in tower.

BARROW

Location: 6 miles W of Bury St Edmunds.
Dedication: All Saints.
Description: A long, light church much restored.
Periods: Most of church is Dec and Perp but the earliest is a Norman window on the N side. The chancel of 13c date was renewed in 1848.
Features: 15c octagonal font carved with heraldic shields, one bearing the Royal Arms; 13c double piscina and triple sedilia in chancel; canopied tomb recess in S wall of S aisle to which is attached a double sedilia with a piscina in adjoining E wall; Norman window has traces of two painted figures on its jambs; canopied tomb in N side of chancel with brasses and inscriptions to Sir Clement Heigham 1570 - Speaker of Parliament and Chief Baron of the Exchequer to Queen Mary.

BARSHAM

Location: 2 miles W of Beccles.
Dedication: Holy Trinity.
Description: Norman church with round tower, possibly Saxon. The nave is thatched. The E wall has stone latticework decoration of uncertain date.
Periods: Late Saxon or early Norman tower and nave.
Features: Chancel roof erected by Rev. Robert Fleming 1633 and stuccoed in Jacobean style 1906; Norman font of Purbeck marble; Purbeck altar-stone with consecration crosses; indistinct wall painting of St Christopher on N wall; rood screen, partly Jacobean; 17c pulpit; carved bench-ends; early 16c processional cross, said to have come from Northern Italy; pretty rood canopy of 1919; cup 1568, cup and paten 1822; stoup inside S door with adjoining poor-box dated1691; brass of Sir Robert atte Tye 1415; terracotta tomb chest of Sir Edward Echingham 1527, one of only seven such tomb chests recorded in East Anglia. The Rev. Alfred Suckling, author of the History and Antiquities of Suffolk was rector here.

BARTON MILLS

Location: 1 mile SE of Mildenhall.
Dedication: St Mary.
Description: A small, ancient structure with attractively textured exterior of flint and tile. It comprises an aisled nave, chancel, S porch and W tower.
Periods: Chiefly Dec but the tower is probably Norman. Tracery in the windows is 14c.
Features: Octagonal Dec font; damaged double piscina in chancel; consecration crosses on chancel walls; some original 14c stained glass in S aisle; 14c iron-bound chest; 17c Jacobean pulpit; Mass-dial in S porch by doorway; modern E window c1866, chancel N window c1907 and SE window c1867; paten 1710, flagon 1746; monument of Civilian and wife c1480.

BATTISFORD

Location: 3 miles W of Needham Market.
Dedication: St Mary.
Description: Small church with nave, chancel and bell-turret with saddle-back roof. Two gargoyles which form the threshold of the S porch remain from the former W tower which has disappeared.
Periods: Nave, chancel and S porch probably c1300.
Features: 14c font; simple 18c pulpit; Royal Arms of Queen Anne; cup and paten cover 1634; brass to Mary Everton who died in 1608 aged 103, a remarkable age, if accurate, particularly in those days; identical monuments to Edward Salter and John Lewis who both died in 1724.

BAWDSEY

Location: 10 miles SE of Woodbidge.
Dedication: St Mary.
Description: The nave and aisles were burnt down on Guy Fawkes night 1842 as a result of discharging fireworks from the tower. It was rebuilt the next year in simpler style, less the aisles and chancel. Its broad W tower remains now reduced in height.
Periods: The tower is 14c. and the early 13c aisle arcades remain now as outer walls.
Features: The church now retains little of interest, but there is an 18c font and an early 19c pulpit; cup 1773.

BAYLHAM

Location: 3 miles SE of Needham Market.
Dedication: St Peter.
Description: The church, which was heavily restored in 1870 when the chancel was rebuilt and transepts added, has a W tower of knapped flint.
Periods: There is a blocked N door of Norman date and some Dec windows.
Features: Nave roof of king-posts and tie-beams; octagonal Perp font; Elizabethan cup, paten 1715; large 17c monument on the N chancel wall of John and Elizabeth Acton and their family.

BECCLES

Dedication: St Michael.
Description: The great church, 147' long and 65' wide, stands on a commanding position above the river Waveney, dominating the town centre and visible for miles around. It consists of a chancel, clerestoried nave of eight bays, N and S porches and an unfinished detached tower, 92' high, standing on the SE side of the churchyard. Aisles run the whole length of the building. The tower is without its parapet and corner pinnacles and could not be built in its normal position at the west end of the nave owing to the steep bank here which slopes down to the river. The magnificent early 15c S porch, 34' high of two-storeys, is one of the best in Suffolk.
Periods: The earliest remaining part may be the S doorway to the chancel, possibly 13c. The remainder of the church is mainly Perp - the town centre tower 1515-47- but the N side has Dec windows and may be of c1369.
Features: The church was much damaged by the great fire of 1586 when

the interior was burnt out. It now remains bland and rather an anticlimax to the impressive exterior. Octagonal 13c font of Purbeck marble; enormous E and W windows, both with fine traceried heads; beautiful modern chancel screen; Royal Arms of Charles II; cup 1567, cup and paten 1568, flagon 1704, credence dish 1727, spoon 1775, paten 1802; bell-ringers' 'gotch' or beer pitcher; a fine copy of the first Prayer Book of Edward IV dated 1549; brass to John Denny 1620, in W wall; table-tomb of John Rede, Mayor of Norwich, 1502.

Location: Ingate.
Dedication: St Mary.
Description: Beccles was formerly in two parishes, but that called St Mary Ingate at the south end of town was amalgamated with Beccles, and had its church demolished, in the reign of Elizabeth I 1558-1603, after a plea by the townspeople that 'the parishes of Beccles and Ingate had been for so many years blended together that the bounds and limits of them could not be known in 1419'.

BEDFIELD

Location: 4 miles NW of Framlingham.
Dedication: St Nicholas.
Description: The church was much altered in the 14c when the W tower was added and many of the windows enlarged. It consists of a nave, chancel, S porch and tower.
Periods: Norman N doorway; the mainly Perp nave and chancel both retain Norman work. 14c S porch.
Features: The S porch has a king-post roof; octagonal 14c font with interesting 17c cover over 6' tall; fragments of 14c glass in window-heads; simple 17c pulpit and some benches; lower part of 15c rood screen with panel paintings of Old testament prophets.

BEDINGFIELD

Location: 4 miles SE of Eye.
Dedication: St Mary.
Description: Tower, with flushwork arcading, nave and chancel.
Periods: Most of the church is 14c Dec, but the chancel has one lancet.
Features: Double hammerbeam roof to nave; stone benches in nave from 1612; 15c octagonal font on 13c base; carved benches dated 1612; iron-bound chest; Royal Arms of Queen Victoria; Elizabethan cup and paten c1520 engraved with the head of Christ; modern brass in chancel to 15 members of the Bedingfield family buried here and in the porch 1371 - 1872.

BELSTEAD

Location: SW of Ipswich.
Dedication: St Mary.
Description: Much renewed with a nave, chancel, brick N chapel and S tower, the base of which forms a porch.
Periods: The church is of Dec and Perp dates with a 16c chapel.
Features: 15c octagonal font; 17c Jacobean pulpit; remains of squire's pew in the vestry; rood screen c1500 with painted panels depicting various

saints including St. Sitha, St. Ursula, St. Margaret of Antioch, St. Mary Magdalene, St. Lawrence, St. Stephen, St. Edmund of Bury and St. Sebastian; Royal Arms of George III; brass in nave to John Goldingham 1518 and his two wives; memorials to the Harland family including Sir Robert Harland, Bart 1784, and mural monuments to Blosse family 1630-1727. The Register dates from 1539.

BELTON

Location: 5 miles SW of Great Yarmouth. Taken into Norfolk in 1974.
Dedication: All Saints.
Description: By the river Waveney with nave, chancel, S porch and rebuilt round tower.
Periods: The church dates from the middle of the 14c with much of the window tracery of good Dec. work. The tower was rebuilt on its Norman foundations in 1849 after being in ruins for many years.
Features: Broken Norman font (found beneath present font in 19c); piscina and sedilia in chancel; tomb recess - probably used for an Easter Sepulchre - in N wall; modern Kempe stained glass E window; 14c screen; good reredos 1887; number of mid-14c wall-paintings on N wall of nave, discovered in 1848 and now much faded, including St. James the Great, St Christopher, and, partially covering St Christopher, the popular legend of 'the Three Quick and the Three Dead'; cup dated 1568 and inscribed 'for the towne of Belton'.

BENACRE

Location: 7 miles SE of Beccles.
Dedication: St Michael.
Description: Impressive if much restored W tower and a nave and chancel in one. The nave and chancel contain much rebuilding and repair work carried out by Sir Thomas Gooch around 1769 following a serious fire.
Periods: Early 14c W tower and wide S aisle of similar period.
Features: 13c font of Purbeck marble; Gothic chancel screen; unusual and attractive box-pews; squire's pew; Royal Arms of George II; paten c1680, cup c1685, flagon 1767; monuments to Sir Edward North 1708, Sir Thomas Gooch 1781, his son Sir Thomas 1826, Louise Anna Marie Gooch 1838 and Sir Thomas Sherlock Gooch 1851.

BENHALL

Location: 2 miles SW of Saxmundham.
Dedication: St Mary.
Description: Isolated between Benhall Green and Benhall Street by the A12, the church has a nave, chancel with vestry on N side, N transept, S porch and W tower.
Periods: Extensively restored in 1842 when the transept and vestry were added. Where unrestored, mostly Perp, but a Norman S door still remains.
Features: Old glass in E window; 17c pulpit; 19c box-pews; Royal Arms of George III; cup, paten and flagon 1670, spoon 182-30; brasses to Edward Duke 1598 and his wife Dorothy, and to Ambrose Duke 1610 and his wife Elizabeth; monument to Sir Edward Duke 1732 and inscription to Edward Glemham and his wife Mary 1571.

BENTLEY

Location: 5 miles SW of Ipswich.
Dedication: St Mary.
Description: A restored church with Norman origins. It comprises nave, N aisle, chancel, S porch and W tower.
Periods: Renewed Norman window in chancel N wall and the S doorway is mock Norman work with traces of the original. The N aisle was added in 1858 and the tower restored 1883.
Features: Simple hammerbeam roof to nave; disused 13c font bowl of Purbeck marble; piscina, and windowsill sedilia in Early English chancel window; arch behind pulpit once forming entrance to rood-loft; paten and flagon 1699, cup 1700. The Register dates from 1678.

BEYTON

Location: 5 miles SE of Bury St Edmunds.
Dedication: All Saints.
Description: Nave, chancel and oval flint W tower which is unusual in having two massive buttresses rising to belfry stage; one of only two buttressed round towers in Suffolk.
Periods: Norman N door and probably tower (with belfry added in 18c), but the church received much rebuilding and enlarging in 1854 and 1885 including nave and chancel.
Features: Some old carved bench-ends; reredos with the Last Supper on a gold mosaic background. The Register dates from 1540.

BILDESTON

Location: 5 miles NW of Hadleigh.
Dedication: St Mary.
Description: Large and impressively situated on a hill outside the village. The church has a nave with aisles and beautiful arcades and clerestory, chancel with chapels, fine flint-panelled, two-storeyed S porch. and short weatherboarded bell tower.
Periods: The tall Dec W tower fell as recently as 1975. The chancel with its chapels is also Dec, and the rest Perp.
Features: Roof with alternating tiebeams and hammerbeams; finely decorated S doorway; wooden balcony from upper storey of porch to the aisle; 15c octagonal font; canopied piscina in S chapel; splendid windows throughout; stalls carved with misericords in chancel; 17c communion rails; Elizabethan cup, paten 1639, cup 1780; brass to William Wade's wife and family 1599 - his effigy has disappeared; memorial to Captain Edward Rotherham, commander of the Royal Sovereign at the Battle of Trafalgar. The Register dates from 1558.

BLAXHALL

Location: 4 miles SW of Saxmundham.
Dedication: St Peter.
Description: Church consists of a nave, aisle, chancel, S porch and tower.
Periods: 14c nave and chancel have windows of c1300; tower and porch 15c.
Features: Nave has an early 16c hammerbeam roof; font with pretty

tracery design; two piscinas, discovered during 1863 restoration; piece of Saxon interlace re-set in the W wall; good Elizabethan cup and cover. The church has been greatly enriched in the present century by the work of Dorothy and Ellen Mary Rope. The latter, who died in 1934, was responsible for the window paintings in the porch (more of her work is in Winchester and Salisbury cathedrals), whilst the E window, and the relief on the chancel wall with angel and child, is by Dorothy.

BLUNDESTON

Location: 3 miles NW of Lowestoft.
Dedication: St Mary.
Description: The church which has a nave (thatched until 1849) and chancel is dominated by its unusually tall round tower with an internal diameter of only 8' 9".
Periods: Norman round tower, the upper section of which may be 13c. The nave was rebuilt in the 14c to double its original width, hence the off-set tower arch. In the S wall are the rebuilt jambs of the orginal Norman S door, whilst the reworked N doorway was also Norman. Chancel rebuilt 1867.
Features: Curiously carved corbels at each corner of the nave and mid-way on its side walls, and a grotesque head beneath the stoup E of the S wall; uncommon font; several old bench-ends; lower panels of much restored 15c screen with painted figures; cup 1647, flagon 1721; brass inscriptions and shields to William Sydnor 1613 and his wife Bridgett and to another William Sydnor 1632 and his wife Ann and several 17c monument stones. The Register dates from 1588.

BLYFORD

Location: 3 miles SE of Halesworth.
Dedication: All Saints.
Description: Situated on the marshes by the river Blyth with fine views. It comprises nave and chancel in one, S porch and W tower.
Periods: Two Norman doorways highlight its origins, the N very fine and the S much simpler. The chancel is of c1300. The nave windows are Perp as are the S porch and W tower.
Features: 13c font; 13c angled piscina and windowsill sedilia in chancel; banner-stave locker in W end of N wall of nave; fine Elizabethan cup, paten 1807. Interesting 18c headstones in churchyard.

BLYTHBURGH

Location: 4 miles W of Southwold.
Dedication: Holy Trinity.
Description: One of the most splendid churches in Suffolk, memorably situated overlooking the moody creek by the river Blyth. 128' long, it has a tower 83' high which, until 1577, was adorned by a spire. In addition it comprises a chancel with shorter flanking chapels, aisled and clerestoried nave and a 2-storeyed S porch. There is no chancel arch, instead a beautiful 15c screen divides nave and chancel.
Periods: The church stands on the site of another, simpler building of wood, thatch and mud which, in 654 A.D., held the body of the East Anglian King Anna after he was defeated and killed by the heathen Penda in the battle of

Bulcamp close by. It was removed to Bury Abbey in the 11c. The present church was built through middle and second half of 15c., but the tower of c1330 formed a part of the previous building. The Hopton Chapel was founded in 1452.

Features: Wonderfully light and spacious interior; roof of nave and chancel featuring large angels with outstretched wings retaining much of the original colour - many said to be pitted by shot from Cromwell's men; large external holy-water stoup carved with angels in S Porch; very fine mid-15c font (damaged by fall of spire in 1577); much 15c glass in window-heads; 15c screen; Jacobean pulpit; interesting carved benches, those in the nave representing the Vices, and in the S aisle, the Seasons; 15c wooden lectern; original side screens in chancel arcades and choir stalls from the Hopton Chapel where they were used as school benches - they still retain inkwells; 15c poor men's box; 15c 'Jack o' the Clock' at W end of nave; 15c Purbeck marble tomb chest of Sir John Hopton 1489 on N side of chancel, and another tomb chest in N aisle to one of the Swillington family. It is said that tombs at the E end of the N aisle and another in the chancel held the bodies of King Anna and his son Firminus (also killed in the battle), prior to their removal to Bury.

BOTESDALE

Location: 6 miles SW of Diss.
Dedication: Church of St Botolph.
Description: Rebuilt as a chapel-of-ease to Redgrave. It was later endowed as a chantry by John Sherife and his wife Juliana, and Bridget Wykys - an inscription set into the wall in flint asks us to pray for their souls. In 1576 Sir Nicholas Bacon founded it as a free school and it later became a grammar school. In 1884 it completed full circle when it was purchased and conveyed to trustees and used for services of the Established Church.

BOULGE

Location: 2 miles N of Woodbridge.
Dedication: St Michael.
Description: The church stands in the grounds of the former Boulge Hall, burnt down in 1923. It consists of a nave, S aisle, chancel and W tower.
Periods: Rebuilt 'unfeelingly' (Scarfe) by the FitzGerald family of Boulge Hall. 13c origins with early 16c brick tower, but the rest appears all from the 1867 'Early English style' rebuild, when the S aisle was added.
Features: Massive 13c Tournai font; Royal Arms of William III, carved in wood; Edward FitzGerald, translator of the *Rubaiyat of Omar Khayyam*, buried here, and there are family monuments in the S aisle and S chapel.

BOXFORD

Location: 5 miles NW of Nayland.
Dedication: St Mary.
Description: Stately church with tower surmounted by a small picturesque spire stands beside the river Box, here little more than a stream. The 14c wooden N porch is probably the most interesting of this period still in existence. By contrast the over-elaborate N porch has now been totally 'vandalised' and defaced by recent brash cream colour-washing. The church

comprises nave with aisles and clerestory, chancel, porches and W tower.
Periods: The body of the church is 15c, but the tower dates from the 14c and the wooden N porch from the same period; the S porch is Perp.
Features: 15c font with 17c cover which opens to display various painted texts; Elizabethan inscription on N aisle wall; traces of a 'Doom' over chancel arch; early 16c gallery in tower; 17c communion rails; 14c iron-bound chest; curious pulpit which appears to have been made from an 18c reredos; touching small brass in the S chapel to son of a rector who died in 1606; memorial slab in N chapel to William Doggett, bearing arms of the Merchant Adventurers and a mural tablet inscription commemorating Elizabeth Hyam who 'hastened to her end' in 1748 after a fall in her 113th year!

BOXTED

Location: 7 miles NW of Sudbury.
Dedication: Holy Trinity.
Description: The church of flint and stone stands near the top of the hill in the grounds of the ancient timber-framed hall. It comprises nave, chancel with Poley Chapel; S porch and W tower.
Periods: Mainly of 15c but much restored over the years.
Features: Interesting Jacobean hammerbeam roof to chancel; some original glass (the figure of a king) in the E window of the Poley Chapel; elevated Poley pew occupies most of the N aisle of the nave and is entered from the chapel; three-sided 17c communion rails; 17c pulpit, with sounding-board dated 1618; almdish 1674, cup, paten and flagon 1708; brass inscription to 'Recherd Poly Esquyer' 1546 and his wife Anne and to Sir John Poley of Wormegay in Norfolk and his wife Abigail; memorials to the Poley family, whose chapel is on the N side of the chancel, include two interesting life-size recumbent effigies in wood (which is rare) commemorating William Poley 1587 and his wife Alice on the S side of the chancel, another life-size figure in alabaster to Thomas Poley 1638 in the N chapel. The Register dates from 1538.

BOYTON

Location: 7 miles SE of Woodbridge.
Dedication: St Andrew.
Description: The church has nave, aisle, chancel, S porch and short W tower.
Periods: Rebuilt in 1870 except for the 14c tower, but the original nave was Norman and the NW quoin with remains of a shaft may yet be seen. The external doorway of the N transept is made up from what must have been a fine Norman door.
Features: Elizabethan cup; the vestry has a Book of Rules, with forfeits for strolling to Bawdsey Star and tippling, etc. (Scarfe).

BRADFIELD COMBUST

Location: 5 miles SE of Bury St Edmunds.
Dedication: All Saints.
Description: Small church with nave, chancel, S aisle, S porch and bellcote. The nave has been shortened at W end where perhaps a tower once stood.
Periods: Mostly Dec though a Norman door remains on the N of the nave. The church had major restoration in 1869.

Features: Norman font; double piscina in S wall of chancel; interesting wall-paintings of c1400, uncovered 1869, on N wall of nave, one St Christopher, the other St George and the Dragon; fragments of panels of rood-screen form back of organist's seat; cup 1570, paten 1748; memorial in S aisle to Arthur Young (1741-1820), the agriculturalist and writer, born in Bradfield - his tomb is in the churchyard, and in the vestry, a tablet to Martha Anne Young, only 14 when she passed away in 1797, with her last pathetic words: 'Play for me, Papa. Now! Amen.' The Register dates from 1540.

BRADFIELD ST CLARE

Location: 5 miles SE of Bury St Edmunds.
Dedication: St Clare.
Description: The dedication probably initially refers to the knightly family which first held the parish from St Clair-sur-Epte, although their allegiance was later transferred to the canonised Clare, St Francis's friend. The church, which comprises nave, chancel and W tower is generally dismissed as being of little or no architectural interest.
Periods: Dates from the 13c but was practically rebuilt in the 15c.
Features: The arch-braced roof has pierced tracery above the collars; Holy-water stoup inside S door; some simple bench-ends; cup 1668. The Register dates from the 16c.

BRADFIELD ST GEORGE

Location: 4 miles SE of Bury St Edmunds.
Dedication: St George.
Description: The church stands on high ground and consists of a nave, S aisle, clerestory, chancel, S porch and W tower 66' tall, from the summit of which sixteen churches can be seen in four counties!
Periods: The church is of various dates. Earliest is a small Norman window in the S wall of the nave, the chancel is a little later, the nave Dec and the N aisle, S porch, W tower and clerestory Perp.
Features: Large lettered inscriptions on western buttresses of tower recording the name of its builder John Bacon; good 16c nave roof; fine 14c S doorway with ogee arch; 14c font; old stained glass in S chancel window shows figure of a Knight c1500; old carved bench-ends in N aisle; Jacobean pulpit; cup 1661, paten 1686, flagon and almsdish 1720.

BRADWELL

Location: 3 miles SW of Great Yarmouth. (Taken into Norfolk in the 1974 boundary changes).
Dedication: St Nicholas.
Description: The church consists of an aisled nave, clerestory, chancel and, like so many in this part of East Anglia, a round W tower.
Periods: Norman round tower, and 14c chancel, nave and clerestory but the church has suffered from over-restoration in the second half of the 19c.
Features: Rood-loft stairs on S of chancel arch; niches on either side of E window; 14c octagonal font; sedilia and piscina in chancel; 14c rose window at W end of N aisle; late 17c communion rail; two 15c bells; cup 1668; richly sculptured monument in N wall of chancel to William Vesey and family 1644.

BRAISEWORTH

Location: 2 miles SW of Eye.
Dedication: St Mary.
Description: The present church was built in 1857 'on a more central site than the old one' by E.B.Lambe and duly damned for its neo-Norman style.
Periods: A fine Norman S doorway from the old church has been built into the S wall and the outer doorway of the porch is the old Norman N doorway.
Features: 17c pulpit, also from old church.

Dedication: St Mary (Old Church)
Description: The old Norman nave was unsympathetically demolished and the chancel left to serve as a mortuary chapel.
Periods: Norman window remains in the chancel N wall.
Features: 14c Piscina with credence shelf; early 17c painting of the Lord's Prayer and Creed on the E wall; Royal Arms of George III; brass on floor with effigy to Alexander Newton 1569.

BRAMFIELD

Location: 2 miles S of Halesworth.
Dedication: St Andrew.
Description: The massive round bell-tower is detached some 12 yards from the body of the church which comprises a thatched nave and chancel, S porch and modern N vestry.
Periods: Norman round tower has an E arch of c1300 into a former nave. The main church is all 14c Dec.
Features: In the belfry are five bells, three of them medieval; 14c piscina in chancel and another crocketed piscina; recess in N wall of nave has traces of a wall painting; the screen, with its original colouring virtually unrestored, is possibly the most beautiful in Suffolk and retains the vaulting on both sides; set of plate 1707; fine alabaster monument in chancel to Arthur Coke 1629 and his wife Elizabeth, by Nicholas Stone, the latter exquisitely carved, and another memorial to Bridget Applethwaite carrying the intriguing epitaph 'After the fatigues of a married life, borne by her with incredible patience... and after the enjoyment of a glorious freedom of an early and unblemished widowhood.... resolved to run the risk of a second marriage-bed, but death forbad the banns'.

BRAMFORD

Location: 2 miles NW of Ipswich.
Dedication: St Mary.
Description: Large attractive church by the river Gipping consisting of an aisled and clerestoried nave, chancel, N and S porches and a W tower with a tall spire.
Periods: Late S13c chancel and S porch, remainder of the church is mostly 14c, though the chancel arch is Victorian and the tower spire was erected in the 18c.
Features: Dowsing claimed to have destroyed 841 'superstitious pictures' (stained-glass windows) here in 1644; The elaborate parapets of the aisles and nave are enriched with carvings of figures; good 15c N porch; remains of vaulting in the tower; hammer-beam roofs to nave and chancel; 15c font

with late 16c cover; 13c piscina and sedelia in chancel, and a piscina in S aisle; stone rood-screen of c1300; Elizabethan pulpit with linen-fold panelling; modern alms box in traditional design with inscription; cup and flagon 1759.

BRAMPTON

Location: 5 miles NE of Halesworth.
Dedication: St Peter.
Description: May once have been cruciform in plan but has been much altered. The fine tower has flushwork panelling.
Periods: The chancel is 3c Early English in origin and the nave Transitional. The remainder is mostly Perp.
Features: Nave has simple blank tracery; 15c octagonal font; piscina in chancel with stone credence shelf and window-sill sedilia; Royal Arms of George III dated 1797; cup c1723, cup and paten 1801, almsdish 1802; brasses and three marble monuments to Leman family, Robert was Lord Mayor of London in the 18c.

BRANDESTON

Location: 4 miles SW of Framlingham.
Dedication: All Saints.
Description: Comprises nave, chancel, porch and W tower. The chancel was described as ruinous in 1602 and, like the rest of the church, has witnessed major restoration.
Periods: Chancel of c1300 though much renewed, Dec tower, Perp nave.
Features: Traceried W door; 13c octagonal font; interesting late 15c glass in SW window of chancel; 17c pulpit; carved benches; communion rail 1711; set of plate 1710-11; brasses to Jane Stebbing 1616 and Elizabeth Stebbing 1621; monument to John Revett 1671; . The Register dates from 1559. John Lowes preached here for nearly fifty years from 1596, but was later accused by Matthew Hopkin, the Witchfinder-General, on a visit to the parish, of employing two imps to sink ships at sea. He was hanged at Bury in 1646 on his anniversary after first being compelled to read his own burial service.

BRANDON

Dedication: St Peter.
Description: The church is an early work, standing some distance away from the town centre on its pre-Norman site. It consisted originally of a nave built around 1050, to which was added, at various periods, a chancel, S aisle - extending the length of the building, a N porch, and a massive W tower.
Periods: The chancel is c1300 with two pretty E turrets and fine window-tracery; the W tower and S arcade of the nave are early 14c with the rest of the church c1420. The chancel was reroofed in 1842, and the rest of the building in 1873 when the church was completely restored.
Features: Uncommon 14c tracery to E window; pillar-stoup in N porch with carved shaft; 13c octagonal font; lower part of painted rood-screen; some 15c bench-ends in nave and well-carved stalls; Elizabethan cup, paten 1776.

BRANTHAM

Location: 8 miles SW of Ipswich.
Dedication: St Michael.
Description: The church has a very wide nave, N aisle, Chancel, N porch and W tower; the chancel and upper part of the W tower have received considerable rebuilding.
Periods: That which was not part of the 1869 rebuild is mostly Dec.
Features: Octagonal font from St Mary-at-Quay church in Ipswich; Piscinas in chancel, nave and N aisle; 15c glass in SE nave window; altar-piece consists of a picture of 'Christ Blessing Little Children' given by John Constable in 1804 but not considered a good example of his work; almsdish 1701. The churchyard is entered through a modern, theatrical Lychgate by E. S. Prior.

BREDFIELD

Location: 3 miles N of Woodbridge.
Dedication: St Andrew.
Description: Nave, chancel and large flint decorated W tower.
Periods: Tower was built 1452-61. Rest of the church is also Perp with traces of Dec work. The church was thoroughly restored in 1875.
Features: Excellent hammerbeam roof to the nave with a Canopy of Honour over the two eastern bays retaining much original colouring; sanctus-bell aperture in ringing chamber giving a view of the high altar; 17c pulpit; cup 1581, paten 1706; small brass to Leonard Faringdon 1611 and his wife Elizabeth.

BRENT ELEIGH

Location: 2 miles SE of Lavenham.
Dedication: St Mary.
Description: Sited together with the Hall on hill above the village and stream, the church consists of a nave, chancel and W tower.
Periods: The building is mainly Dec, but has a Perp tower and some windows of same date.
Features: Rare early 14c S door with blank tracery; 13c octagonal font of Purbeck marble with 17c cover; mid-14c wall-paintings - to the left of the E window, two censing angels probably mid 14c, under the window a Crucifixion said to date from c1300 and to the right of the window, the remains of a Harrowing of Hell, early 16c?; 14c parclose screen in S aisle; 18c box-pews in nave enclosing 17c benches; 17c two-decker pulpit, and three-sided communion rails; early Georgian reredos with fluted pilasters; monument to 'that good man Edward Coleman who died in 1739, last of an ancient family'. A parochial library of 1,500 volumes, given by Dr. Coleman of Trinity College, Cambridge c1700, was housed in the church until 1859.

BRETTENHAM

Location: 7 miles SW of Stowmarket.
Dedication: St Mary.
Description: The church which comprises nave, chancel and S tower, the basement of which is used as a porch. From the top of the tower in 1882,

ordnance surveyors were able to discern fifty other church towers.
Periods: The church was disused in 1957, but thankfully resurrected and re-opened five years later. The tower and nave are Dec and the chancel of c1421.
Features: S door with foliage-trail border; fine 14c octagonal font with carved oak cover; angle piscina in the S wall of the chancel bearing the arms of the Earls of Buckingham and Stafford; 17c lectern;17c altar rails; Vinigar Bible of 1716; three coped coffin-lids with floriated crosses; brass to George Weniffe 1611 and his wife Mary; memorials to the Torkington and Wenyeve families in chancel floor. The Register dates from 1584.

BRIGHTWELL

Location: 5 miles SE of Ipswich.
Dedication: St John the Baptist.
Description: A picturesque little structure standing on a wooded slope and commonly known as 'Brightwell Chapel'. It has an ancient nave and chancel, S porch, and a brick tower added c1620 by Thomas Essington. He appears to have rescued the church which was 'almost ruined' according to a later 17c manuscript, and it is he who is doubtless responsible for the two massive round support pillars, and the three strange stumpy pinnacles added at the E end of the church.
Periods: Nave and chancel possibly from c1300.
Features: Dec octagonal font with carved panels and cover of c1656; 13c ring-handle on S door; the Barnardiston armour consisting of two crested helmets, gauntlets, spurs and sword; monuments to the Barnardiston and Essington families include memorials to two of Thomas Essington's children, Thomas who died in 1656 aged five and Anna in 1660 aged seventeen with pathetic inscriptions.

BROCKLEY

Location: 6 miles SW of Bury St Edmunds.
Dedication: St Andrew.
Description: Nave, chancel, wooden S porch and large W tower with flint panelling
Periods: Nave of c1300, chancel Dec (Pevsner suggests that it was originally much shorter than at present - see the string course and change in construction - and could possibly be of Norman origin), tower and wooden porch, 15c.
Features: 13c font; double 13c piscina and windowsill sedilia in chancel; two corbels in E wall of nave which formerly supported the rood-beam; large tomb recess in S wall of nave; S door has interesting knocker and lock of early 14c?; part of rood-screen; old chest; Elizabethan cup, flagon 1771, almsdish 1817.

BROME

Location: 2 miles N of Eye.
Dedication: St Mary.
Description: The church with its original Norman round tower was almost entirely rebuilt in 1863 when a new transept and N aisle were added using virtually every architectural style from the 12c to 16c. Even the tower failed to escape 19c beautification with a modern octagonal belfry.

Periods: Norman round tower with belfry of 1875; the remainder mostly 1863.
Features: 15c font with carved cover; modern reredos of the Crucifixion; modern stone pulpit; cup 1568-9, paten c1600; The interior is dominated by the Cornwallis tombs, the best being that of Sir John Cornwallis 1544 and his wife Mary, in the chancel. Another tomb, with effigies, commemorates Sir Thomas Cornwallis 1604 and his wife Anne; in the N aisle lies Henry Cornwallis 1598 and another memorial is to Elizabeth Lady Cornallis 1680. The family had settled here as early as the 15c. when John Cornwallis, son of a London merchant, married the heiress of Brome.

BROMESWELL

Location: 2 miles NE of Woodbridge.
Dedication: St Edmund.
Description: Nave, brick chancel and S porch, and stone W tower.
Periods: Norman origins highlighted by 12c S doorway and blocked 11c N window (obscured by War memorial). All the rest is Perp except the chancel which was rebuilt in 1853 in Victorian brick.
Features: Hammer-beam roof to nave; 15c octagonal font; carved bench-ends; 17c communion rails and pulpit; Elizabethan cup; two ancient bells in the tower, one dated 1530.

BRUISYARD

Location: 4 miles NE of Framlingham.
Dedication: St Peter.
Description: Simple flint church with round tower, nave, chancel, S transept and S porch.
Periods: The tower is Norman and there is a good 13c door in the S chapel.
Features: 15c octagonal font; piscinas in chancel; painted set of the Ten Commandments 1794; 18c pulpit with tester; early 17c screen in S chapel; Hanoverian Royal Arms; 17c communion rails; Elizabethan cup, paten 1568; brass to Michael Hare 1611, Lord of the Manor, and his two wives (his effigy is missing). The Register dates from 1566.

BRUNDISH

Location: 5 miles NW of Framlingham.
Dedication: St Lawrence.
Description: Ancient church with square tower, nave, with some excellent windows, chancel and S porch with fine flint panelling.
Periods: Unlike many, this square tower is Norman. There is also a blocked Norman arch into the nave and a 12c window in the E side of the belfry; otherwise the church is principally Perp.
Features: Stoup in S Porch; 14c font; 14c piscina in chancel (adjoining small recesses possibly for cruets; old glass in many window-heads; several 15c benches in the nave, some incorporated in box-pews; 17c pulpit with pulpit canopy hanging from former Norman doorway now set into wall; Royal Arms of George III, 1765; brass of Sir Edmond de Burnedish 1360 is earliest Suffolk effigy of a parson, also brasses to the Colby family - John Colby 1540 and wife Alice 1560, John Colby 1559, Margaret, wife of Francis Colby c1570, and another brass of similar date is to the young Thomas Glemham.

BUCKLESHAM

Location: 6 miles SE of Ipswich.
Dedication: St Mary.
Description: Towerless church of nave and chancel in one with a wooden bell-turret with shingled broach-spire.
Periods: Almost entirely rebuilt in 1878.
Features: Stoup outside N door; 14c octagonal font; stoup outside the N door. The Register dates from 1678.

BUNGAY

Dedication: St Mary.
Description: The principal parish church of the town was originally the church of the Benedictine Nunnery founded here by Gundreda, wife of Roger de Glanville c1160. The Priory Church was originally both conventional and parochial, consisting of a long aisleless 13c chancel occupied by the nuns, quasi-transepts forming a kind of vestibule, and a wide aisled nave which was used as a parish church. The monastic buildings were on the S side of the nave and their ruins form part of the present churchyard. The nave still forms the body of the present church, 6-bays long with N and S aisles. There is no structural chancel, this was formed by a screen. There is a N porch and a large, graceful SW embattled tower with pinnacles 90' tall, which can be seen for many miles around and features some of the best flint panelling in Suffolk. Entrance to the church is by a beautiful N porch.
Periods: Earliest parts are the early 14c arcades; the N aisle, known as the Holy Cross aisle, is of late 14c date; the S aisle 1450 and the tower c1470.
Features: The great fire of 1688 which destroyed most of the priory buildings also decimated the interior of the church - a beam in the belfry is cut with the words 'The fire was mighty', but it still retains one of the most remarkable sets of church-warden's accounts in England from 1523-1853. Remaining are a late 17c font; an attractively-carved 15c piscina in the S aisle; an oak dole-cupboard of 1675; cup 1722, paten 1727, flagon 1728, cover 1729, cup 1822; monument to Robert Scales 1728, others to the Browne families, and a tablet to the artist Thomas Bardwell 1767, outside W door.

Dedication: Holy Trinity.
Description: Situated across the street from St Marys, Holy Trinity comprises a nave, S aisle, chancel, porch and round tower, and originally shared a churchyard with the former, and the church of St Thomas.
Periods: Its round tower is said to date from 1041, which would make it one of the oldest in England, and it still contains a Saxon window. Norman N window in nave; the nave itself, S aisle and porch are 15c. The chancel was in ruins from 1558 until 1754 when it was first restored and the present chancel, although panelled in old oak, only dates from 1926.
Features: Seven old armorial shields built into the tower parapet include those of Thomas de Brotherton, Earl of Norfolk and son of Edward I, and the Montacute, Bigod and Beauchamp families; font, possibly of c1700, recarved 19c; fine pulpit 1558; communion rail c1600; cup and paten 1561, flagon 1762, almsdish 1766; brass to Lionel Throckmorton 1599, and one to Dame Margaret Dalenger, the prioress of the nunnery from 1465 to 1490, who died in 1497; monument to Thomas Wilson 1774.

Dedication: St Thomas.
Description: As previously stated, the church, which was appropriated to the nunnery, once shared a churchyard with St Mary and Holy Trinity. It was still in use after 1500 but no traces of it now remain.

BURES ST MARY

Location: 5 miles SE of Sudbury.
Dedication: St Mary.
Description: Stately church overlooks the Stour with W tower, wide nave and aisles, clerestory, chancel and two fine porches, one in wood, the other brick. The Waldergrave Chantry Chapel on the S side of the chancel has some excellent traceried windows.
Periods: The flint tower dates from the late 13c to the early 14c. It was formerly surmounted by a handsome spire, which was struck by lightning in 1733 and burnt down together with all the woodwork in the tower - the heat, it is said, was so intense that it melted the bells. The chancel, N porch and arcades are both 14c, with the aisles and clerestory Perp. The chapel was built in 1514 by Sir William Waldergrave. The N porch is contemporary with the main church, whilst the S porch is Tudor.
Features: Remains of vaulting on inside of tower; curious tomb recess on exterior of N side of tower; stoup with carved bowl inside S porch; 15c octagonal font; vestry door with Tudor roses; almsdish 1734, cup and paten 1740; monument to 14c Knight (Cornard family?) in oak on the sill of a N window, tomb of Sir William Waldergrave, tomb in S chapel to another Sir William Waldergrave 1581, and a monument to William Waldergrave 1613 and his wife Elizabeth 1581. The Register dates from 1538.

BURGATE

Location: 5 miles NW of Eye.
Dedication: St Mary.
Description: Imposing flint church comprising W tower and combined nave and chancel. A corner of the nave is set apart to create a little chapel to the memory of King Edmund, whose body is said to have rested here on its way from Hoxne to Bury St Edmunds.
Periods: Main church from c1350 with large E and side windows belonging to the 19c restoration.
Features: Fine octagonal 14c font; piscina with canopy in S wall; lofty pointed arch on N side of chancel enclosing a shallow recess, probably for Easter Sepulchre; some stained glass in N window; 17c square pulpit; mid-17c communion rail; a 15c chest still retains traces of a painting of two knights in the tilting field; Royal Arms of George II 1735; magnificent altar-tomb in the centre of the chancel to Sir William de Burgate 1409, which includes the best brasses of their date in Suffolk.

BURGH

Location: 3 miles NW of Woodbridge.
Dedication: St Botolph.
Description: The church comprises nave, chancel, and S tower, the base of which forms a porch. It stands atop a steep bank in the corner of Castle Field, a rectangular banked and ditched Roman settlement site. The body of

St Botolph is said to have lain in a chapel on the site of the present church from 680 A.D. until taken by Bury monks.
Periods: Though the present Tower is Dec and the nave and chancel Perp, the church obviously has ancient origins.
Features: The chancel has a good timber roof; 15c font; windows have fine modern stained glass by Kemp of 1903-6; 17c Jacobean pulpit; 13c ring-handle in S door; iron-bound chest; cup and paten 1637.

BURGH CASTLE

Location: 4 miles SW of Great Yarmouth. (Taken into Norfolk in 1974).
Dedication: St Peter and St Paul.
Description: Standing on the banks of the Waveney, the church features a round tower, nave, N aisle, chancel and S porch. S of the church lies one of the best preserved of the Roman Saxon Shore forts. Restoration work over the years has incorporated much of the tile and brick material from the fort.
Periods: While the round tower is Norman, the remainder is Dec with a N aisle of 1847, and a S porch erected in 1858.
Features: Remains of two arches on either side of chancel; late 14c octagonal font; piscina and curious wall paintings discovered during 1846 restoration; stoup inside entrance to nave; modern chancel E window; rood stairs; some old carved benches; 13c sepulchral slab.

BURSTALL

Location: 4 miles NW of Ipswich.
Dedication: St Mary.
Description: Good Dec church comprising nave, with impressive N arcade and aisle, chancel, timber S porch and W tower.
Periods: Mostly early 14c, with 15c S porch.
Features: Fine 15c hammer-beam roof in nave and good roof to chancel; piscina and sedilia in chancel; niche in either side of E window of aisle; 14c N parclose screen; lower part of 15c rood-screen.

BURY ST EDMUNDS

Dedication: St James. (now the Cathedral)
Description: Tall, spacious and well-lit by an array of great windows and with a beautiful W front, the church, 195' long and towerless - the old Norman tower stands immediately S - has, since 1914, become the new Cathedral, on the site of the great Benedictine Abbey, founded in 1020. Enlargements were made in 1960-70 to endorse its role as a cathedral. These included a new porch at the NW corner of the nave - with a room over to house the cathedral library, eight (out of a planned twelve) bays of the cloister were built along the N side of the nave, and a new choir, with its flanking chapels, started from the E end and finished in 1967, after which the crossings and transepts were undertaken to join the choir with the nave. Further work will be undertaken when finances allow: including continuing the new tower, now being raised, above the ridge line of the roofs.
Periods: The chancel was rebuilt in 1865-9 by Scott when excavations revealed remains of the earlier chancel of c1390-1402. The rest of the building dates mostly from c1510-30, possibly to the designs of John

Wastell, although it was not completed until Edward VI's time.
Features: Much remains to be done, but earlier furnishings include the hammerbeam roof over nave erected by Sir Gilbert Scott and good Perp roofs over the aisles; a 19c font and pulpit, both designed by Scott, who is also responsible for the mosaic in the chancel; beautiful modern woodwork in bishop's throne and font cover; excellent glass in N window depicting a Doom, and the Flemish and other glass in the westernmost window of the S aisle, known as the 'Susanna Window'; painting in S chapel c1500; monument to James Reynolds, Chief Justice of the Exchequer 1738, and his wife; flagons and almsdish 1685, cup and two patens 1686, cup 1729 and almsdish 1807; and a cathedral library of 500 printed books of the 16c and 17c and six early manuscripts, established between 1547 and 1574.

Location: At SW corner of Abbey precinct.
Dedication: St Mary.
Description: 213' long, and even more impressive with a proud history going back to the 7c, St Mary's stands in the SW corner of the abbey precincts. It consists of a chancel of five bays with side chapels, an aisled and clerestoried nave of ten bays with a tower on the N side and a porch to the E of it.
Periods: The first church was built on this site about 633 and destroyed by the Danes. The second was erected in 903 to receive the body of St Edmund and a third replaced the wooden with one of stone in 1032. This is the fifth church on the site and dates back to 1433, although the tower pre-dates it.
Features: The glorious painted and gilded hammerbeam roof of the nave is one of the finest ever erected, and equally interesting is the boarded and panelled roof in the chancel and in the aisles and chapel; the bay over the high altar was originally a Canopy of Honour and bears traces of special colouring; below the sanctuary is a crypt or bone-hole; Notyngham porch, built c1437, has two external stoups, three canopied niches and an inscription to John Notyngham and his wife Isabelle; Purbeck marble font 1506; piscina and sedilia in S aisle with the adjoining chantry of John Baret 1467; great W window, one of largest of any parish church in England; a number of brasses and brass inscriptions including those to Jenkyn Smyth and Marion his wife 1481, Archdeacon Fynere 1509, Henry and Edmund Lucas, and an engraved brass tablet to Peter Gedge, who printed the first newspaper in the town, it reads 'like a worn-out type he is returned to the founder, in hope of being recast in a better and more perfect mould'; altar-tomb of Sir William Carewe 1501 and his wife on N side of sanctuary, and another to Sir Roger Drury 1536 and his wife Anne on the S side. In the N corner of the sanctuary is a tablet memorial erected in 1750 to Mary Tudor, Queen of France and brother of Henry VIII, who died at Westhorpe in 1533, and whose body was moved here from the abbey after the Dissolution - there is also a window of about 70 figures depicting scenes from her pathetic royal story, dedicated by Queen Victoria. The inscription of the memorial reads: "Sacred to the Memory of MARY TUDOR, Third daur. of Henry ye 7th King of England, and Queen of France, Who was first married in 1514, to Lewis ye 12th King of France, and afterwards in 1517, to Charles Brandon, Duke of Suffolk. She died in his life time in 1533, at ye manor of Westhorp in this county: and was interr'd in ye same year in ye Monastery of St Edmund's Bury, and was removed into this church, after ye Dissolution of

the Abbey." The tablet, some two or three yards W of her tomb, is below the floor and marked by a marble slab bearing five crosses. An appalling act of desecration took place in 1784, when her tomb was opened and nearly 2 feet of her beautiful golden hair, still in perfect condition, was cut off.

Location: St Johns Street.
Dedication: St John.
Description: In white brick with a very striking tower surmounted by a tall spire 178' high supported by flying buttresses.
Periods: Built in Early English style in 1840-1 by W Ranger. In 1871 the spire was struck by lightning and replaced the next year.
Features: Vaulted roof; original but renovated stained glass E window. represents the Last Supper, Crucifixion and Ascension. All fittings are 19c.

BUTLEY

Location: 7 miles E of Woodbridge.
Dedication: St John the Baptist.
Description: Situated three-quarters of a mile from the Priory, the little parish church, with walls of septaria, crag, flint and plaster, has a thatched nave, chancel and W tower
Periods: The church has a 13c tower containing Norman masonry and there are two Norman doorways and an early pointed arch in the porch. The chancel is c1300.
Features: Fine 15c octagonal font; 15c screen; modern oak chancel screen with Royal Arms; Elizabethan cup, paten 1716. Buried in the churchyard are five stone coffins from the Priory.

BUXHALL

Location: 3 miles SW of Stowmarket.
Dedication: St Mary.
Description: Lofty church with spacious nave, chancel and massive W tower.
Periods: c1320, apart from the tower which dates from c1392
Features: 14c octagonal font; double piscina, and windowsill sedilia - on the seat of which is a 13c sepulchral slab, in chancel; E window with fine tracery and W window with four panels of 14c stained glass; ; two ancient panelled benches bearing the arms of the Copinger and Herries families. The Copingers held the manor here from 1428-1948. Sir William Coppinger (born 1512), who became Lord Mayor of London, was noted for his wealth and hospitality, and 'to live like the Copingers' became a proverbial expression throughout the county.

CAMPSEA ASH

Location: 2 miles E of Wickham Market.
Dedication: St John the Baptist.
Description: Nave, aisle, chancel, vestry and slender W tower.
Periods: The embattled tower is 14c, but an almost complete rebuilding of the nave and chancel in 1792 has reduced its architectural interest.
Features: 14c octagonal font; Elizabethan cup, cover inscribed 1569, paten and flagon 1641; brass of Sir Alexandre Inghllysh, parish priest here in 1504; monuments to the Sheppard family.

CAPEL ST ANDREW

Location: 7 miles SE of Woodbridge.
Dedication: St Andrew.
Description: The church was in existence in 1529 but has entirely disappeared above foundations. It stood on the site of a farmhouse where many human bones have been unearthed.

CAPEL ST MARY

Location: 6 miles SW of Ipswich.
Dedication: St Mary.
Description: A fine structure with a nave, S aisle, chancel, S porch and W tower, formerly supporting a spire, taken down 1818.
Periods: The tower is late Perp. The chancel has good 14c windows, and the S aisle is 15c with large traceried windows. The S porch is also of this date.
Features: Hammerbeam roof to nave and fine chancel roof; priest's door on S side of chancel; lovely E window showing the four archangels; medieval bell in the tower with an inscription to 'Gregorie Pascal'; memorials to the Hingeston, Tweed and Maundrell families. The register dates from 1539.

CARLTON (nr. Saxmundham)

Location: 1 miles N of Saxmundham.
Dedication: St Peter.
Description: Formerly a separate parish but now united with Kelsale. The small church of flint and stone comprises a nave, chancel and brick W tower.
Periods: Principally Dec with a late tower.
Features: Plain sedilia; pulpit dated 1626; some 15c benches; brass in chancel with figure of man c1480.

CARLTON COLVILLE

Location: 3 miles SW of Lowestoft.
Dedication: St Peter.
Description: Over-restored nave and chancel, S porch and W tower with decorative flint battlements. The tower remained unrestored for 50 years after being damaged by lightning in 1812.
Periods: Mostly early Dec in origin but contains a Norman window in the N wall. The lower section of the tower is also early. The 14c nave and chancel were over-restored in 1883 when the porch was added.
Features: 15c octagonal font; Elizabethan cup, paten 1567; monument in vestry shows effigy of priest.

CAVENDISH

Location: 3 miles NE of Clare.
Dedication: St Mary.
Description: The church, standing back from the picturesque green, its tower rising majestically above a group of Suffolk pink-washed cottages, provides a scene epitomising the nationally held image of quintessential country life; subsequently it is constantly reproduced in paintings and photographs throughout the land. It consists of an aisled nave, clerestory, chancel, S porch and W tower, with a SE stair turret rising above the

parapet to support a frame for the bell - probable successor to the sanctus bell. Much of the church has fine flint panelling.

Periods: The tower was built c1340, and the porch is of a similar date. The chancel is a little later, c1381, and the remainder Dec and Perp, except for the chancel aisle added in 1865.

Features: The tower has a lower storey with a vaulted roof; fine roofs to nave and aisles; arcading inside S porch; 16c chancel door; 15c octagonal font; consecration cross in S aisle; orginal stained glass in several windows; 14c chest; early 16c two-sided reading desk with chained volumes of Bishop Jewel's Apology in Black Letter 1611 and a Book of Homilies; remarkable reredos in S aisle; sculptures - 16c Flemish relief of the Crucifixion and 15c altar statue to St Michael; 15c brass lectern - said to have been given by Queen Elizabeth I; the tower has five 18c bells each bearing a curious inscription; altar-tomb on N side of chancel to Sir George Colt 1570 and his wife Elizabeth; a stone slab in the floor of the tower basement bearing the arms of the Cavendish family on four brass shields, is thought to be the memorial to Sir John who is known to be buried in the church. The Register dates from 1594.

CAVENHAM

Location: 4 miles SE of Mildenhall.
Dedication: St Andrew.
Description: Small church of nave, chancel, S porch, and W tower with evidence below the belfry that there was once a two-storey building here.
Periods: The church was built c1200 but the windows are of various periods.
Features: Extrordinary font; Dec piscina in angle of SE window; curious handle on S door; painting of unknown subject discovered on the N wall in 1967; remains of rood-screen c1600; cup 1830; bell, dated 1676; brass to John Symunt 1588, and another of late 17c date.

CHARSFIELD

Location: 5 miles N of Woodbridge.
Dedication: St Peter.
Description: Nave and chancel in one, handsome brick S porch with flint decoration and fine, lofty brick W tower.
Periods: Nave and chancel are mainly Dec, but a Norman window remains in the N wall of the nave, and one 13c lancet in the chancel.
Features: Interesting octagonal font with carved figure of St Botolph(?) holding a church in his left hand; lower part of rood-screen; carved beam dated 1585 in ringers' gallery (from old rectory); Elizabethan cup, flagon 1576, paten 1679. The Register dates from 1727.

CHATTISHAM

Location: 5 miles E of Hadleigh.
Dedication: All Saints and St Margaret.
Description: Delightfully situated in tree-shaded churchyard with nave, chancel and short W tower. The tower has been much repaired and received battlements in 1772.
Periods: Early 14c, but over-restored in 1869 by which time the chancel arch had already been removed and the screen destroyed.

Features: 15c font; sedilia and canopied piscina in S wall of chancel; circular poor-box cut from solid piece of wood; Royal Arms of George II; various brasses including, part of one to John Revers and his wife Mary 1592 (John is missing), John Bennett 1608 and Daniel Meadowe 1651; crude memorials to the Flacke and Stockton families. The Register dates from 1556.

CHEDBURGH

Location: 7 miles SW of Bury St Edmunds.
Dedication: All Saints.
Description: Tiny church with septaria and flint nave and chancel, and grey brick N tower with spire.
Periods: Nave of c1300 but chancel and tower rebuilt in 1842.
Features: Sedilia, discovered in nave 1873; some fragments of old glass in the E window plus some good glass of 1923.

CHEDISTON

Location: 2 miles W of Halesworth.
Dedication: St Mary.
Description: Nave, chancel, S porch and W tower. Apart from the battlements of the tower which are flint panelled, the body of the church is all Victorian plaster. A brick projection on the N side of the nave is said to have been built as a burial chapel for the Fleetwood family.
Periods: Church is of c1300 period as seen in lower part of the W tower, S and N doorways and S porch. The rest is mainly Dec with Perp nave windows.
Features: Fine arch-braced nave roof; Perp font; 14c piscina and window-sill sedilia in chancel; ; fragments of 16c glass in three windows; traces of a wall painting of St Christopher on the N wall of the lofty nave is mutilated by the insertion of two windows; old benches; Jacobean pulpit of 1637 from Cookley Church; curious 14c chest; 17c communion rail; cup 1724, paten 1725.

CHELMONDISTON

Location: 6 miles SE of Ipswich.
Dedication: St Andrew.
Description: Totally destroyed by a bomb in World War II, and rebuilt.
Periods: Much enlarged in 1868, rebuilt in 1891, and rebuilt 'unimaginatively' again in 1957 as befits the period.

CHELSWORTH

Location: 5 miles NW of Hadleigh.
Dedication: All Saints.
Description: The church is hardly the vision you would expect in such a beautiful village. Stumpy and wide in appearance, 19c restorers saw fit to render over and paint the exterior. It comprises nave, aisles, clerestory, N and S porches and W tower. There was a chapel or vestry on the N side of the chancel, of which only the roof corbels and door remain.
Periods: Early 14c W tower, rest mainly Dec, with a Perp S porch.
Features: The S doorway has a rich canopy and the door itself is beautifully panelled; two original statues in niches over N porch; 14c font; small piscina in N wall; rood-loft stair with both entrances complete, on S side of

chancel arch; remains of a 'Doom' over chancel arch, discovered and then badly restored in 1849; 14c iron-bound chest; cup and cover 1663, paten and almsdish 1735; fine tomb recess with canopy in N aisle which once contained the monument of the Lord of the Manor, Sir John de St. Philiberto, Knight 1359, and a memorial to Sir Robert Pocklington 1840 in S aisle who in 1794 'rescued the Emperor of Germany, Francis II, from the French cavalry', for which act he received the insignia of the military order of Maria Theresa. The Register dates from 1559.

CHEVINGTON

Location: 6 miles SW of Bury St Edmunds.
Dedication: All Saints.
Description: Beautiful flint and septaria church consists of a nave, chancel, wooden porch and W tower.
Periods: The church is ancient, dating from the latter part of the 12c., and the N and S doorways and a window in the nave remain from this period. The chancel is 13c (shortened in 1697), the porch 14c and the tower c1444 - its ornamental pinnacles added c1800.
Features: Tall, narrow chancel arch with low pointed openings on either side; nave roof with beams dated 1590 and 1638 respectively; 15c octagonal font; Late 17c E window; fine carved chair in chancel; magnificent 14c church chest; carved bench-ends; Royal Arms of George I, dated 1726; cup 1595. The Register dates from 1560.

CHILLESFORD

Location: 9 miles NE of Woodbridge.
Dedication: St Peter.
Description: Flint nave and chancel, aisle, and a W tower built entirely of coralline crag.
Periods: Whilst the window tracery is early 14c, the church, which has been much restored after being struck by lightning in 1874, has a nave and chancel divided by a curious arch, altered in the 15c, but probably Norman.
Features: Late 12c or early 13c Purbeck marble octagonal font; Royal Arms of Queen Victoria in plaster; inscription tablet to Agnes Claxton 1624 and her daughter 1633.

CHILTON

Location: 1 mile NE of Sudbury.
Dedication: St Mary.
Description: Remotely situated on no road and near no village, the flint church has a Tudor brick tower, embattled with flint and pinnacled with stone. The Crane Chapel at the NE end is also of brick.
Periods: Well restored in 1972. Apart from the 16c tower and chapel, the church is mainly 15c.
Features: 15c octagonal font; base of screen; rood-loft and pews willed by Robert Crane 1500; two alabaster table-tombs, much mutilated, to George Crane 1491 and Robert Crane and his wife 1500, stand between the pillars dividing chancel from N chapel, and another tomb in the chapel itself is of Sir Robert Crane 1624 and his two wives. The Register dates from 1623.

CLARE

Dedication: St Peter and St Paul.

Description: One of the largest in the county and standing in its own sanctuary just off the town centre. The interior is very lofty with nave pillars which are remarkably 14c, re-used, and given new bases and battlemented capitals during 15c rebuilding. E of the S porch is a 14c chapel now containing a 17c galleried manorial pew which projects into the aisle. Fine clerestory and a sundial over S porch which says appropriately ' Go about your business'. The tower has an open wooden structure supporting the clock-bell.

Periods: Principally of 15c and 16c date, though some remains of earlier work can be seen in the lower stages of the tower, which has an excellent 13c W doorway, and in the porches, which are 14c. The chancel was extensively repaired in 1617.

Features: Dowsing smashed over 1,000 'superstitious pictures' here, but plenty remains of interest including: beautiful chancel arches; rood-loft staircases on either side of chancel arch; doors of N and S aisles, the vestry door and the priest's door, all 15c; early 15c octagonal font; Heraldic glass of 1617 in the E window and large windows in the aisle with some very modern glass; curious 17c choir stalls with return seats and altar rails; part of 15c rood-screen in W arch of S chancel chapel with remains of a chantry parclose screen close by; early 16c eagle lectern with slots in beak to receive coins which were extracted from a hole in the tail; the ringers' pitcher in S aisle dated 1729; 17c communion rail; cup and paten 1680, flagon 1713; a memorial to Robert de Godewyck c1300 which came from the priory, and it is said that Lionel, Duke of Clarence, who died at Piedmont in 1368 is interred in the chancel, though there is no monument evident to his memory.

CLAYDON

Location: 3 miles NW of Ipswich.

Dedication: St Peter.

Description: A church with ancient origins comprising nave, chancel with transepts, N porch and W tower with angels and beasts surmounting the parapet.

Periods: Chancel and transepts were built in lavish style 1882 by the then rector, George Drury, but there is Saxon long and short work at the W end, and inside the S wall, is the outline of a Norman doorway. The N porch is 15c.

Features: Octagonal Perp font with domed cover; modern carved statue of the Virgin and Child in the S transept, 1945 and 1949 by Henry Moore; original stained glass of 1862 at the E end; early 16c painting of the Pentecost; pulpit and bench-ends carved by Drury himself; paten 1676; brass inscription to Samuel Aylemar 1635.

CLOPTON

Location: 4 miles NW of Woodbridge.

Dedication: St Mary.

Description: The church is beautifully sited on side of valley. It comprises a wide nave, chancel and strong S tower, the lower stage forming a porch.

Periods: S doorway of nave is c1300 but the church is mostly 14c. except

for the chancel, which was rebuilt in 1883 when the church was restored.
Features: Fine hammerbeam roof to the nave and a plain hammerbeam roof over the restored chancel; simple octagonal Perp font; piscina in S wall, discovered during the restoration; cup 1639.

COCKFIELD

Dedication: 6 miles SE of Bury St Edmunds.
Dedication: St Peter.
Description: Large, well proportioned church with nave, aisles, clerestory, chancel, S porch and W tower.
Periods: The earliest part is the early 14c chancel. The W tower and N aisle are Dec and the S aisle and clerestory both Perp.
Features: Some good oak carving in S aisle roof; piscina, and remains of a triple canopied sedilia in chancel; fragments of old glass in windows and E window erected to memory of Rev Churchill Babington, author of *The Birds of Suffolk*; 17c communion rail and plain pulpit on a 15c base; two flagons 1743, almsdish 1759; fine restored tomb of 14c knight with a triple canopy in N wall and marble monument to James Hervey 1723. The Register dates from 1561.

CODDENHAM

Location: 3 miles SE of Needham Market.
Dedication: St Mary.
Description: The church lies between three 200' hills which have dictated its unusual layout. It comprises a nave with N and S aisles, clerestory, unusually long chancel, N porch and NW tower.
Periods: From traces of Roman tile in its flint and stone walls to the 19c restored chancel, the church covers all periods of development. Although the chancel was restored c1830 it retains a Norman window and another with later 13c plate tracery. Of Dec period are the NW tower, nave and S aisle; the fine panelled clerestory and N porch are Perp.
Features: Sanctus bell-turret over E gable of nave; inscription on N parapet of clerestory to John Frenche and his wife Margaret; double hammerbeam roof to nave; 17c pulpit and remains of old pews now fixed round aisle walls; 17c communion rail; painted panels from rood-screen; 14c iron-bound chest; 15c alabaster panel of the Crucifixion now incorporated in modern reredos; machinery of old church clock in S aisle; many fine hatchments; set of 1790 plate; monuments to Rev. Baltazar Gardeman 1739, and to Philip Bacon 1666.

COMBS

Location: 1 mile S of Stowmarket.
Dedication: St Mary.
Description: Quite a large church once accompanied by the Hall but now stands alone by Combs Wood. Nave, aisles, chancel, clerestory and big W tower with processional arches in its N and S walls.
Periods: The church is mainly 14c Dec.
Features: Stoup beside W doorway to nave, within tower; late 14c font; interesting 15c stained glass in aisle windows, particularly that depicting St Margaret; remains of rood-screen, and parclose screens in aisles; 17c pulpit;

some old bench-ends; two tankard-shaped Danzig flagons 1731; brass inscription to Thomas Dandy 1607 and his wife Martha, and another to Katherine Sotherbie 1624.

CONEY WESTON

Dedication: 6 miles NE of Ixworth.
Dedication: St Mary.
Description: Situated outside the village with a thatched nave, and a chancel and S porch; the W tower fell a long time ago, and a two-bay N chancel chapel has been removed.
Periods: Despite restoration 1869-76, it remains a good example from 14c.
Features: Octagonal 13c font (from an earlier church); beautiful canopied angle piscina in chancel; niches on either side of chancel arch; encaustic tiles at NW corner of nave; plate tracery in chancel windows; Elizabethan cup, paten 1678.

COOKLEY

Location: 2 miles SW of Halesworth.
Dedication: St Michael.
Description: Nave, chancel and slender, unbuttressed W tower.
Periods: The tower is Norman as is the blocked N doorway; the nave Perp and chancel Dec. The church suffered from very bad restoration in 1894 when the pulpit, dated 1637 was rescued and taken to Chedington Church.
Features: Hammerbeam roof to nave; fragments of rood-screen - retrieved and replaced; re-used brass to William and Margery Browne and their eight children, 1587.

COPDOCK

Location: 3 miles SW of Ipswich.
Dedication: St Peter.
Description: Fine church with aisleless nave, chancel, N transept, S porch and lofty W tower.
Periods: The chancel is Dec and the nave and tower 15c.
Features: Panelling on N door; stoup in S porch; 15c font with small canopied cover, and piscina; five carved panels fronting the W gallery, one showing Edward VI on horseback; Royal Arms of George III.

CORTON

Location: 3 miles N of Lowestoft.
Dedication: St Bartholomew.
Description: Big church on cliffs above the sea with 15c W tower, 92' tall, S porch and much of the nave roofless and in ruins. Only the tall, wide chancel and part of the nave are now in use following restoration and reroofing in 1870.
Periods: Thought to have been erected c1375 but much detail has perished from the time the church became ruinous in the late 17c.
Features: Lofty tower arch; 15c octagonal font; 14c piscina and triple sedilia in chancel; rood-loft stairs in thickness of S wall; reredos with (ancient?) statues; Elizabethan cup, flagon 1719, paten 1732.

COTTON

Location: 6 miles NW of Stowmarket.
Dedication: St Andrew.
Description: Large building has W tower, with tall open arch which forms a spectacular W porch, aisled nave, clerestory, chancel and decorative S porch.
Periods: The church is a handsome example of the 14c style to which a late 15c clerestory has been added. The tower arch is 16c.
Features: 14c S door with richly moulded arch; 15c double hammer-beam roof to nave, the eastern panels forming a Canopy of Honour to the rood; font (bowl not original); double piscina and sedilia; some ancient glass in aisle and clerestory windows; 17c communion rail and pulpit; some good benches; cup c1600, paten c1675, flagon 1727.

COVEHITHE

Location: 4 miles NE of Southwold.
Dedication: St Andrew.
Description: Once a medieval port, now even the village has virtually disappeared. Standing in melancholy splendour on the edge of the cliffs, the ruins of this great church still convey the extent of its former importance. Yet the sea has only hastened a destruction that was initially caused by the townspeople themselves during the Civil War in 1643. Imposing W tower and tall, majestic walls frame the void within, save only for a small thatched brick building consisting of nave, chancel and a S porch erected in 1672 and within which services have continued.
Periods: The W tower and arcades are 14c but the nave, aisles and chancel, which had a vaulted crypt, are later.
Features: The magnificent 15c octagonal font was taken from the ruined church and is still in use; cup and cover 1567, paten 1805.

COWLINGE

Location: 8 miles NW of Clare.
Dedication: St Margaret.
Description: The church is built of septaria and brick with a striking late brick W tower. There is also an aisled nave, chancel, clerestory. and N porch.
Periods: Walls incorporate fragments from 12c, but main church is early 14c with a Perp N porch and clerestory. The tower was built in 1733.
Features: Crown-post roof of nave; traces of a two-storeyed chapel or vestry on exterior of N wall of chancel; early graffiti on pillars of both aisles; Perp font; old glass in window lights; traces of painting of St Michael over chancel arch; 18c pulpit and western gallery; 14c rood-screen; parclose screen in S aisle; children's seat in W end of S aisle - earlier used for prisoners from the local House of Correction; Royal Arms of George II, dated 1736; Elizabethan cup; rather pompous marble monument on N wall of chancel to barrister Francis Dickins (who rebuilt the tower) and wife 1747.

CRANSFORD

Location: 3 miles NE of Framlingham.
Dedication: St Peter.
Description: Small church with nave, chancel, porch and W tower.

Periods: 'Drastically and dreadfully restored' (Pevsner) leaving virtually nothing of interest. What remains is all Perp.
Features: The tower contains an inscribed 15c bell; Elizabethan cup, paten 1568, almsdish 1697, flagon 1718.

CRATFIELD
Location: 6 miles SW of Halesworth.
Dedication: St Mary.
Description: Aisled nave, clerestory, chancel, N chantry chapel now used as a vestry, and fine tall W tower with pinnacles and stone carving decoration.
Periods: 14c origin - as seen in the nave arcades - but largely rebuilt c1470; the tower was embelished c1547. The church was restored in 1879.
Features: Fine roofs to nave and chancel; 15c Seven-Sacraments' font, 'probably the most beautiful in the kingdom' (Cautley); old glass in tracery of chancel windows; 17c pulpit, two desk lecterns and some benches; fragment of screen under tower arch; 15c inscribed chest in vestry; the clock bell in a turret on the tower - in the lower part of the tower is the ancient clock machinery which operates the striking gear; there is also a bell of 1585 in belfry; Elizabethan cup and paten, cup 1712. The Register dates from 1539 and is very well preserved.

CREETING ST MARY
Location: 2 miles NE of Needham Market.
Dedication: St Mary.
Description: There were formerly three parishes known as Creeting St Mary, Creeting All Saints and Creeting St Olave. These were consolidated under Creeting St Mary in 1884. The little church of St Mary which remains stands on an elevated site with extensive views over the Gipping Valley. It consists of an aisled nave, chancel, S porch and W tower. Immediately S of the porch is an old priest's chamber.
Periods: It is mainly 13c to 15c with earlier, much restored, Norman S door, and a W tower and N aisle restored between 1884-7.
Features: 15c octagonal font; modern Kempe windows; 17c communion rail; Elizabethan cup, cup with cover 1593, patens 1690 and 1730.

Dedication: All Saints.
Description: The church, which shared the same churchyard as St Mary, 'being much decayed' was taken down in 1813, when it was found to have no foundations, the building being merely erected on level ground.

Dedication: St Olaves.
Description: The church, which stood with its priory 1 mile NW of St Mary on the E side of the lane leading to Woolney Hall, was in use in 1532 when a John Pinkney was buried in the chancel, but disused as far back as 1660. Nothing of it now remains.

CREETING ST PETER
Location: 2 miles NE of Needham Market.
Dedication: St Peter.
Description: Set somewhat apart from the village and approached by a

green lane, the church comprises nave, chancel, S porch and W tower.
Periods: Crude Norman N doorway illustrates the church's ancient origins. Most of what now remains is unrestored Dec and Perp.
Features: 15c octagonal font; magnificent painting of St Christopher on the N wall of nave with an inscribed scroll in Latin, the translation of which reads 'Whosoever looks at the picture of St Christopher shall assuredly on that day be burdened with no weariness'; hectagonal 15c pulpit; some remains of a rood-screen; Eliabethan cup and paten - engraved with the Ferneley arms, paten 1779; copy of *The Degrees of Marriage* (1747).

CRETINGHAM

Location: 4 miles SW of Framlingham.
Dedication: St Peter.
Description: Plastered nave and chancel, flint porch and W tower.
Periods: Nave and chancel are partly c1300, the tower 14c and the remainder 15c.
Features: Good 15c hammerbeam roof to nave; 15c octagonal font; fine 17c two-decker pulpit with canopy and communion rail; box-pews; old bench-ends; Royal Arms of Charles II; monuments to Sir Richard Cornewaleys, and to Lady Cornwallis 1603, who still retained her long plaited hair, perfectly preserved, when the vault was opened in 1826. The Register dates from 1558.

CROWFIELD

Location: 2 miles NE of Needham Market.
Dedication: All Saints.
Description: Situated well outside the village is this unique church, the only one in Suffolk with a timber-framed chancel; the S porch is also of wood. An octagonal bell-turret is placed near the middle of the nave roof.
Periods: 14c, with a 15c chancel and S porch. The church was completely restored in 1862.
Features: The nave is covered by a hammerbeam roof and the chancel by a barn-like roof with massive tie-beams; 18c communion rail; cup and paten 1790; brass to William Middleton 1775; 17c memorial in chancel floor bearing arms of Winfield family, and near it an 18c memorial to the Harwoods.

CULFORD

Location: 4 miles NW of Bury St Edmunds.
Dedication: St Mary.
Description: Church stands in the grounds of Culford Hall and comprises a nave with N aisle, chancel, vaulted chapel, porch and W tower.
Periods: Completely rebuilt in 1856 in Early English style, and the brick tower heightened, pinnacled and refaced. The N aisle was added in 1908. The Tower still retains much of its original 14c work.
Features: Fine roof to chancel; monuments to Nathaniel Bacon, the painter and botanist, 1627 and his wife, one to Jane Bacon 1654, pathetic 17c memorials to four of the children of Charles Cornwallis who all died before they reached their fifth birthday, two of them in the same year, 1655, and in the vaulted chapel at E end of aisle, a magnificent marble tomb to Beatrix Craven, Countess Cadogan 1907. The Register dates from 1538.

CULPHO

Location: 5 miles W of Woodbridge.
Dedication: St Botolph.
Description: Tiny church mainly rubble built and comprising a bare, unrestored nave - the walls of which shape outwards, a chancel and truncated SW tower, the upper parts missing and the base forming a porch.
Periods: Nave and S porch tower are of c1280 with 14c alterations; the chancel was rebuilt in 1884 when the strange chancel arch was erected.
Features: 14c S doorway; stoup in jamb of tower arch; 15c octagonal font; 15c bench-ends; Royal Arms of George III; Elizabethan cup, paten 1710.

DALHAM

Location: 6 miles SE of Newmarket.
Dedication: St Mary.
Description: Stands delightfully with the hall and its grounds overlooking the charming village built in the valley of the river Kennet. The church comprises nave with a clerestory and N and S aisles, chancel, ruined N chapel, and a W tower on which a huge inscription on the S side reminds the villagers as they approach to 'Keep my sabbaths'.
Periods: The church dates from the 14c, with 15c additions, but most of the present tower is a rebuild of 1625 by Sir Martin Stuteville, which he topped with a spire, blown down 33 years later in the storm which signalled the death of Oliver Cromwell.
Features: Two 14c flint consecration crosses on S porch; remains of medieval wall-paintings on nave wall, one representing the Seven Deadly Sins and another over chancel arch; a painted board commemorates rebuilding of the 'steepl', and over this the Royal Arms of George III; lower part of the coloured rood-screen; set of plate 1691, flagon 1712; 17c funeral bier; belfry contains two bells dated 1627; inscription to Colonel Francis Rhodes, whose brother Cecil Rhodes, founder of Rhodesia, purchased the Hall just before his death; tombs to Thomas Stutevyle 1571 and to Sir Martin Stuteville 1631, 'who saw the new world with Francis Drake', and his two wives on N side of chancel. There is an obelisk in the churchyard to General Sir James Affleck 1833.

DALLINGHOO

Location: 4 miles N of Woodbridge.
Dedication: St Mary.
Description: The church had a central tower with herringbone masonry which has become an E tower with the demolition of the former chancel. There is also a vestry and S porch.
Periods: The masonry style identifies the tower as early Norman with the W arch and blocked E arch of c1300 or a little earlier. The eastern diagonal buttresses, N stair turret and belfry are early 15c and indicate the period when the chancel was destroyed.
Features: Oriel window in vestry removed from tower; fine 17c oak pulpit with back and sounding-board - one panel contains the arms of Catherine of Aragon, and a reading-desk of the same date made from very elabotate woodwork; 18c communion rail; reredos from Jacobean panelling; paten, flagon 1771.

DARMSDEN

Location: 1 mile SE of Needham Market.
Dedication: St Andrew.
Description: A most delightful tiny Victorian church, sited in a lofty position with breathtaking views over the Gipping Valley. It comprises a nave and chancel under one roof, S porch and bell-turret, all in Dec fashion.
Periods: Built in 1880.
Features: Re-used piscina; Elizabethan cup, almsdish dated 1650.

DARSHAM

Location: 5 miles NE of Saxmundham.
Dedication: All Saints.
Description: Slender W tower with flushwork panelling, nave and chancel.
Periods: Ancient church with poorly maintained Norman N and S doorways and a small 13c lancet window on the N side of the narrow chancel. The rest, including the tower, was rebuilt in 15c.
Features: Early 15c octagonal font, inscribed with name of donor, Geoffrey Symond, rector in 1404; Jacobean pulpit; bench-ends; Royal Arms of George IV; Elizabethan cup and cover, almsdish 1673, cup and paten 1683; defaced brass to Anne Bedingfield 1641 and a brass inscription to Marion Reeve c1500 and William Garrard c1530; monument to Sir Thomas Bedingfield 1662, Judge of Common Pleas under Charles I.

DEBACH

Location: 4 miles NW of Woodbridge.
Dedication: All Saints.
Description: Simple towerless church with nave and chancel combined, and a lean-to S vestry. The churchyard contains a log-steeple for one bell.
Periods: All was rebuilt in 1851 by Phipson.
Features: Octagonal font c1851; fine modern oak eagle lectern; cup 1586.

DEBENHAM

Location: 8 miles W of Framlingham.
Dedication: St Mary.
Description: Chancel and lofty nave with beautiful arcading, clerestory and aisles, and a W tower with both 'long and short' work and herringbone flintwork; this was once surmounted by a spire taken down in 1667 after being struck by lightning. An unusual feature is the two-storeyed W porch, the upper part appears to have once been used as a guild chapel.
Periods: The tower is the earliest part of the church, the lower half Saxon and the upper, Norman. The restored chancel dates from c1260, the nave from 1420, and the clerestory, aisles and porch also 15c.
Features: Nave roof has hammerbeams and tie-beams alternating; 14c font; piscina in chancel made up of various stone-carved fragments including a bishop's head of c1300; 17c pulpit and gate to the galilee; 14c chest; Elizabethan cup, paten 1760; brass of Sir John Framlingham c1425, who bought nearby Crow's Hall in 1397, and his wife Margaret, and a brass coffin-plate to Sir Charles Gawdy, Knight 1650; tomb of Sir Charles Framlingham 1595 with helmet above, and another tomb to Rev John Simson 1697.

DENHAM nr. Bury

Location: 7 miles SW of Bury St Edmunds.
Dedication: St Mary.
Description: Small church with nave, chancel, N chapel, S porch and W tower.
Periods: Although it has a plain Norman N doorway, the church is mostly of modern date. The brick Lewknor chapel was added in the early 17c.
Features: Modern stone high altar is in the chancel; paten 1728; monuments to the Lewknor family in the chapel include a large tomb to Sir Edward Lewknor and his wife Susan of 1605, and a beautiful marble monument to Edward Lewknor, his grandson of 1634 - all died of smallpox.

DENHAM nr. Eye

Location: 3 miles E of Eye.
Dedication: St John the Baptist.
Description: The church has lost its W tower and the N chapel dedicated to the Bedingfields family (see blocked arch on N side of nave); the nave, chancel and S porch remain with much brick repair.
Periods: The chancel is early Dec, the nave Perp and the S porch 18c.
Features: Stained glass in the W window; mutilated misericords in chancel - possibly connected with the college set up by Sir Edmund Bedingfield c1495; Royal Arms of Charles I, dated 1637; brass on floor beneath altar to Anthony Bedingfield 1574, engraved on the back of part of a Flemish brass to Jacobus Wegheeschede c1500; effigy of a late 13c lady - believed to be another Bedingfield; stone panelled inscription below the E window is to William de Kirksby, Prior of Norwich 1280-90.

DENNINGTON

Location: 2 miles N of Framlingham.
Dedication: St Mary.
Description: One of the most interesting churches in Suffolk especially for the quantity and quality of its wood furnishings. The large chancel contains a number of fine traceried windows and the W tower has a higher stair turret. The screens at the end of the aisles enclose two small chapels and retain their lofts. N of the sanctuary is a two-storeyed vestry.
Periods: Dec chancel and Perp nave, aisles, N porch and W tower.
Features: The furnishings are exceptionally rich and varied. Simple octagonal 15c font with 16c cover; 14c piscina and sedilia; early 14c stained glass in N and S chancel windows; pulpit of 1625, converted to three-decker; splendid benches with intricate tracery on the ends; box-pews in N chapel dated 1630, others late 18c or early 19c; traceried doors to rood-loft stairs in the N and S aisles; beautifully preserved parclose screens to S and N chapels; lower part of rood-screen; rare pyx canopy, suspended above altar and made from one piece of wood c1500; an old iron-bound chest has seven locks made thief-proof in as much as when one unlocks another is locked; late 17c communion rail; Royal Arms of George II, 1785; Elizabethan cup, paten 1756, cup 1763, flagon 1813; brasses to John Hersant 1568 and his wife Elizabeth 1585, Elizabeth Barker 1613, and Henry Edgar 1619; St Margaret's Chapel contains an alabaster tomb chest to William Philipp (Lord Bardolph) 1441, who fought at Agincourt, and his wife Joan 1447, and a monument to Sir Thomas Rous 1603 and his wife.

DENSTON

Location: 6 miles N of Clare.
Dedication: St Nicholas.
Description: Collegiate church, which although not large, and with a short W tower, it has an impressive interior comprising a nave and chancel, extending for seven bays in an unbroken line, with an excellent clerestory. Screens form chapels in the narrow, lofty aisles.
Periods: Apart from late 14c tower, church dates from shortly before 1475.
Features: Fine nave roof; S porch with fan-vaulting and external stoup; S door with 15c tracery; Seven-Sacraments font; whole E window consists of fragments of stained glass gathered and assembled from throughout the church; beautiful modern window by Martin Travers 1932; 17c pulpit; parclose screens forming chapels; unique rood beam over remains of rood-screen; decorated stalls and benches; four misericords remain from stalls of the collegiate priests; 18c box pews in S aisle; 18c communion rail; Elizabethan cup, paten 1640; Royal Arms of Queen Anne over tower arch; the Robinson tabard comprising helmet, crest and sword hanging in the S chapel; brasses to Henry Everard 1524 and his wife Margaret in chancel floor, and to Felice Drury c1530 in nave floor; early Tudor monument to unknown couple.

DEPDEN

Location: 7 miles SW of Bury St Edmunds.
Dedication: St Mary.
Description: Only approached via a footpath, the church of septaria and flint comprises a W tower, nave, chancel and two porches, that on the S being used as a vestry. The E wall of the chancel is supported by two heavy diagonal buttresses carried above the eaves and ending in curious pinnacles.
Periods: Norman S doorway, 14c chancel and Perp tower, 17c timber N porch. The church was thoroughly restored in the 19c.
Features: Early 18c painted octagonal font; beautiful late 13c piscina in chancel; stained glass in the E window; some carved bench-ends; Royal Arms of William IV; interesting plate - communion cup, two patens, flagon and almedish, all silver gilt, were presented by Dr. Anthony Sparrow, successively Bishop of Exeter 1667-76 and Norwich 1676-85, a native of the village; brass in NE corner of nave to Lady Anne Jermyn 1572 with each of her two husbands (the second being Sir Thomas Jermyn) and their children.

DRINKSTONE

Location: 7 miles SE of Bury St Edmunds.
Dedication: All Saints.
Description: Chancel, aisled nave, brick tower and modern S porch.
Periods: Chancel is Dec, aisled nave Perp and the tower of 1694. The S porch was rebuilt in 1874.
Features: Unusual eastern buttresses of chancel; 14c stoup in porch; 13c octagonal font of Purbeck marble; sedilia with parts of a traceried bench front re-set in the back; fragments of stained glass in chancel and aisles; pulpit standing on an altar stone which has been lowered; remains of beautiful 15c rood-screen with traces of original colour; old benches; 17c panelling in the sanctuary; paten 1564, cup 1567; brass inscription to William Twaytis 1499 and his wife Elizabeth.

DUNWICH

Location: 8 miles NE of Saxmundham.

The once great medieval city of Dunwich, now beneath the unrelenting North Sea, had but one church at the time of Edward the Confessor - possibly that of the missionary St Felix - but already by Domesday, three that had stood in a manor belonging to Robert Malet had been swallowed by the sea. The town again suffered considerable damage on New Year's Day 1286 when, in a violent storm, the sea overthrew 'several more churches', including St **Michael** and St **Bartholomew**. In 1327 the old port became so silted up that it was rendered useless and by 1350 a further 400 houses had been lost. After this the churches of St **Leonard** - standing eastwards of St Johns, St **Martin** - on the E side of town, and St **Nicholas**, a cruciform structure SE of Black Friars, were also submerged. 1540 saw the loss of St **John the Baptist**. This large impressive church stood near the market place in the centre of town. In a Will dated 1499 there is a legacy of ten marks for some ornaments for this church with the following clause:'If it fortune the church to decay by adventure of the sea, the ten marks to be disposed of by my executors where they think best.' By 1510 two legacies were given towards the building of a pier against the church, but by 1540 this church too was being dismantled to save it from the waves. In 1702 the sea reached St **Peter**, which stood NE of All Saints, which was dismantled; the building and its churchyard were gone by 1729. The last remains of St Nicholas's churchyard finally succumbed in 1740.The only remaining church, All **Saints**, had part of its building demolished in 1725 as the edge of the cliff approached. Services continued in the reduced church, but by 1754 they were down to once a fortnight from Ladyday to Michaelmas and monthly throughout the rest of the year. Services were discontinued permanently by 1774 and the church fallen into ruin, though interments in the churchyard continued. The last fragment of All Saints, its W tower, finally dropped from the cliff in 1919, and its churchyard is gradually following it into history. For nearly sixty years Dunwich remained without an active church.

Dedication: St James.

Description: The present church dates from 1830 and was built by Robert Appleton in the classical style.

Periods: Chancel added in 1881 when the church was restored and some of the windows were renewed.

Features: Monument to Michael Barne 1837. In the churchyard to the SE is the Norman apse of the Leper Hospital Chapel of St James, and within, the Barne mausoleum. Also in the churchyard is a tower buttress from All Saints church, salvaged from the beach.

EARL SOHAM

Location: 3 miles W of Framlingham.

Dedication: St Mary.

Description: Beautifully situated in the heart of this pretty village, forming a group with the old rectory and several fine old houses. It has an early chancel, a nave, S Porch, and W tower with fine flintwork.

Periods: The chancel dates back to c1320 and the tower to c1475. The nave and S porch are also of the latter period.

Features: Fine hammer-beam roof to nave; three canopied niches over W doorway; two tablets on tower buttresses, to the builder Thomas Edward and his assistant Ranulph Colnett; 15c font with inscription to the donor Robert Kinge; 17c pulpit; finely restored carved bench-ends; mid-17c communion rail; Royal Arms of Charles II; cup 1814, two patens 1808; monuments to the Hindes family. The Register dates from 1558.

EARL STONHAM

Location: 2 miles NE of Needham Market.
Dedication: St Mary.
Description: This early cruciform building has a W rather than central tower, nave, clerestory and S chancel.
Periods: Portions of the nave are probably Norman but no detail survives; the chancel and transepts are 13c and 14c, with a lancet remaining in the N wall of the chancel. The S porch, N door and nave windows are Dec and the clerestory and tower, 15c.
Features: Magnificent single hammer-beam roof to nave, ten bays long and one of the most elaborate in the county; similar but less ornate chancel roof; W door with tracery; 15c octagonal font; fine gabled 15c piscina and sedilia forming a window seat in chancel; several remains of wall paintings including a 'Doom' over chancel arch, and one depicting St George and the Dragon on W wall of transept; 17c pulpit with four hour glasses for dividing sermons into quarter hour segments; some old bench ends, one carved with a bagpipe player; chest of c1300; 17c communion rail; cup 1789, paten 1732; tablet memorial to Thomas Goodall 1614-87 records his loyalty to 'martyred sovereign King Charles I'.

EAST BERGHOLT

Location: 6 miles SE of Hadleigh.
Dedication: St Mary.
Description: The great church, 120' long and lit by forty windows, partly flint and partly brick is 'eminently picturesque' (Pevsner). It may owe the quirkiness of an incomplete W tower - the five bells of which now hang in a curious wooden bell-cage in the churchyard - to the fate of one of its benefactors, Cardinal Wolsey. Using his endowments, the new W tower was begun in 1525, but his demise also meant the same for his great plans. To compensate the E end brick gable is crowned by an 18c cupola and the church, still an impressive building by any standards, now comprises a chancel with flanking chapels, an aisled and clerestoried nave, and a S porch with upper chamber. The S porch has a lofty stair turret and on the N of the nave is a rood-loft stair turret of similar design. The N and S sides of the unfinished tower are pierced by large processional archways, and the room within was intended to be vaulted.
Periods: Mainly 15c and 16c.
Features: Piscinas in chancel and side chapels; recess in N wall of chancel for Easter Sepulchre; consecration cross on S wall of N aisle of chancel; memorial stained glass window to John Constable; 15c wall painting of the Resurrection; rood-screen, reredos and stalls by Sir T. G. Jackson; iron-bound chest c1450; a set of plate 1767, almsdish 1771. brass in nave to Robert Alfounder 1639; monument to Edward Lambe 1617 and members of the Cardinal, Parker and Hankey families.

EASTON

Location: 3 miles S of Framlingham.
Dedication: All Saints.
Description: The unelaborate church stands on an eminence in Easton Park with a W tower and nave with no separate chancel. The tower is square at the base and octagonal above.
Periods: 14c with Dec and Perp windows.
Features: Octagonal font; piscina and triple sedilia of c1300; 14c glass in window tracery; memorial window to the eleventh Duke of Hamilton; two very pompous late 17c carved family pews with canopies and arms of the Wingfield family; box pews of 1816; 17c communion rail; cup and paten 1678, credence 1726; 15c bell in tower; several brasses including one to John Brook 1426, John Wingfield 1584 and Radcliff, wife of Thomas Wingfield 1601; monuments to Dame Mary Wingfield 1675 and William Henry, fifth Earl of Rochford. The Register dates from 1561.

EASTON BAVENTS

Location: 1 mile NE of Southwold.
Dedication: St Nicholas.
Description: The church, situated on high cliffs above the North Sea, had a chapel dedicated to St Margaret. Burials were carried out here until 1568 and the last rector instituted in 1666, but by 1754, it had fallen into 'irreparable decay' and was soon after lost to the sea along with the village.

EDWARDSTONE

Location: 5 miles E of Sudbury.
Dedication: St Mary.
Description: In the grounds of Edwardstone Hall with nave, N aisle, chancel, S porch and W tower.
Periods: Nave and chancel 14c, chancel windows c1300. The N aisle is of 1460 and tower of the same period.
Features: Interesting king-post roof over nave; 13c font on modern base with 17c cover; good modern glass in nave and chancel windows; wall painting on W wall of N aisle; well preserved pews and wall-panelling; excellent modern reredos; magnificent carved Jacobean pulpit; 19c candelabra hanging in nave and chancel; Father Smith organ, with painted case in N chapel, rebuilt 1879; brass to John Brand 1642 and his wife Susan, and another of Benjamin Brand c1636 and his wife Elizabeth, with an inscription 'Whom when Providence after 35 years conjunction divided, Death after 12 dayes Divorcem't, reunited'; their six boys and six girls were 'all nursed with her unborrowed milk'. The Register dates from 1600.

ELLOUGH

Location: 3 miles SE of Beccles.
Dedication: All Saints.
Description: A rather bland church with lofty W tower, nave and chancel.
Periods: The tower is c1300; the nave and chancel 14c with Perp windows and a modern porch.
Features: The nave has a good 15c roof, restored c1880; 15c font; piscina

and windowsill sedilia in chancel; brasses to a Lady of c1520 and to
Margaret Chewt 1607 aged eighty-five, and wearing a massive headdress,
plus an inscription to Anne Gostling 1612.

ELMSETT

Location: 4 miles NE of Hadleigh.
Dedication: St Peter.
Description: Well maintained with nave, chancel, S porch and early W tower.
Periods: 13c tower, 14c nave and chancel, with inserted Perp windows.
Features: Norman font of Purbeck marble; niche in N side of chancel arch;
good 14c tracery in E window; Jacobean pulpit from St Mary-at-Quay in
Ipswich; Jacobean panelling made from former box-pews; late 17c communion
rail; Royal Arms of Queen Anne; Elizabethan cup, 17c paten, almsdish 1803;
alabaster monument to Edward Sherland 1609 on N side of chancel.

ELMSWELL

Location: 5 miles NW of Stowmarket.
Dedication: St John the Baptist.
Description: A fine church said to have been built by the monks of Bury -
the abbots had a country seat here on the site of the Hall. The prominent W
tower of 1476 has 'probably the finest flint and stone devices' in Suffolk
(Cautley). Also good flint panelling on the clerestoried nave and S porch.
Periods: Much has been renewed including the N aisle in 1872, and the
chancel in 1864, but clerestoried nave, tower and S porch are early Perp.
Features: 15c font; piscina and squint in the S aisle chapel formed by part
of screen; parclose screen; old bench-ends; large canopied tomb to Sir
Robert Gardner 1619, Chief Justice of Ireland, with life-size coloured effigy -
it was he who founded the pretty almshouses beside the church in 1614.
Churchyard cross with old base and good carvings.

ELVEDEN

Location: 5 miles S of Brandon.
Dedication: St Andrew and St Patrick.
Description: The old thatched Norman church N of Elveden Hall which had
been enlarged and reroofed by Maharaja Duleep Singh in 1869, was
completely rebuilt by Lord Iveagh between 1904-6 when he added a new N
nave and chancel and, in 1922, a new S bell-tower connected to the old
church by a long cloister-walk in memory of Lady Iveagh, all in Gothic style.
Periods: Of the old church only the 14c chancel arch, W tower of c1300,
fragments of the nave with its Norman window, and the S porch remain.
Features: 14c piscina and windowsill sedilia in former chancel; stained
glass in E window in old church by Kempe 1894 and in W window of new
church by Sir Frank Brangwyn 1937; Elizabethan cup, paten 1724, set of
1863-5; monument to Admiral Keppel.

ERISWELL

Location: 3 miles N of Mildenhall.
Dedication: St Lawrence.
Description: A simple church which took its dedication from the ruined

Chapel of St Lawrence close by. It consists of a nave with S aisle, chancel with lady chapel, S porch and W tower.

Periods: Late 13c S aisle, and S chapel with three lancets in S wall; the remainder is 14c. The church was completely restored in 1874 when the old thatched roof was replaced with slate.

Features: Early 14c octagonal font; piscina and triple sedilia in chancel; old 15c stained glass in chancel N windows; much restored 14c screen divides nave and chancel; old bench-ends in nave; Elizabethan cup. Outside the church and partly under the S wall is a sepulchral recess containing a tomb (of the church's founder?).

Dedication: St Peter.

Description: What remains is now incorporated into a dove-house in a farm building of Eriswell Hall Farm. It comprises part of the flint N and S walls, with a Perp window and the outlines of two 13c lancets in the N wall.

ERWARTON

Location: 9 miles SE of Ipswich.

Dedication: St Mary.

Description: Set away from the village and secluded by trees with fine views of the river Orwell from its massive tower, the spacious church, is a 15c rebuild, mostly in septaria, of an older structure. The church, which also has an aisled and clerestoried nave and a chancel, features a number of early monuments, some possibly not in situ, and intriguing links with Anne Boleyn. She is thought to have visited her aunt at Erwarton Hall on a number of occasions and legend has it that after her execution her heart was kept in a casket hidden in the walls here. Amazingly, one such casket, heart-shaped, was indeed discovered containing a handful of dust, during 19c restoration work. Was it the Queen of England's heart? We shall probably never know.

Periods: Chancel still mostly of 14c, though it was shortened in the 18c and rebuilt in 1839. The clerestory, aisles and W tower are all Perp.

Features: Rare Tudor font bearing the roses of the rival houses of York and Lancaster; old benches; cup and paten 1825; monuments to Sir Bartholomew Davillers on re-used tomb-chest 13c, to Sir Bartholomew Bacon and his wife Joan c1400 in a canopied altar-tomb, another to Isabel Davilers c1300 at the E end of the S aisle, the remains of a monument to Sir Philip Calthorpe 1549 who had married Anne Boleyn's aunt, and, in the N aisle, a standing monument to Sir Philip Parker 1736.

EUSTON

Location: 4 miles SE of Thetford.

Dedication: St Genevieve.

Description: The medieval church with its unusual dedication was remodelled in 1676 by an unrecorded architect but to a design typical of Wren's work in this period. Its position, outside both the park of Euston Hall and the present village strongly suggesting that the old village was forced to relocate when the hall was built. The design is cruciform with aisles, transepts and tall W tower with unusual pierced parapet; the clerestory has circular windows.

Periods: Its medieval origins have been entirely erased by the 17c rebuild.

Features: Good plasterwork ceilings; stained glass in E window, a memorial to the fifth Duke of Grafton; exquisitely carved pulpit of c1680 and carved reredos, both in the style of Grinling Gibbons; screen with openwork carving; fine carving on pews and panelling; set of late 17c plate in copper-gilt and a set of 1820-32; several brasses from the previous church include Civilian and Lady c1480, Lady c1520, disfigured Civilian and Lady c1520 and similar of c1530; memorials to the Fitzroy family and a monument to Lord Arlington 1685.

Dedication: St Andrew.
Description: The village of Little Fakenham was enclosed in Euston Park at the beginning of the 19c and abandoned along with its church. Nothing of the church, or indeed the village, now remain.

EXNING

Location: 2 miles NW of Newmarket.
Dedication: St Martin.
Description: An early church much restored. Cruciform in design with chancel, transepts, aisled nave and tall W tower surmounted by bell-cote.
Periods: Chancel and long transepts 13c, rest of the church of Dec period.
Features: Octaonal 14c font; double 13c piscina in chancel; on floor, a 13c slab with carved cross; 15c table-tomb on N side of chancel, possibly used as Easter Sepulchre; remains of fine niche in N wall of N aisle; old bench-ends and choir stall with traceried front; 18c pulpit with sounding board; 18c communion rail; Elizabethan cup, paten 1637, paten 1825, flagon 1830; early hatchment with unusual epitaph to Francis Robartson. In 1845, a pyx or casket in which the consecrated wafer was kept, and several altar candle-sticks, bells, etc. were found near the church where they had probably been hastily buried at the Reformation.

EYE

Dedication: St Peter and St Paul.
Description: The W tower, 101' high, battlemented, pinnacled, and panelled in flushwork from top to toe ie, 'one of the wonders of Suffolk' (Pevsner) and forms a unique grouping with the old timber-framed Guildhall. It bears the arms of its benefactor John de la Pole. The church is large with clerestoried nave with N and S aisles, chancel with N and S chapels and a two-storeyed S porch. It was given to the Benedictine Priory of Eye and the S chancel chapel, known as the Abbey Chapel, dedicated to Our Lady of the Abbey.
Periods: Earliest part is the nave S doorway which is 13c. The S chancel chapel was built c1410 and the aisles and N chapel belong to a similar period, with arcades and tower arch possibly a little later; the rest is 15c. The church was fully restored in 1868.
Features: Inside the tower is a fan-vaulted stone gallery; 16c nave roof, the eastern bay comprising a Canopy of Honour over the rood; fine coloured rood-screen of 1480 with panels, magnificently restored by Sir Ninian Comper in 1929, having paintings of St Paul, St Helen, St Edmund of Bury, St Ursula, Henry VI, St Dorothy, St Barbara, St Agnes, St Edward the Confessor, St John the Evangelist, St Catherine, St William of Norwich, St Lucy, St Blaise, St Celilia, and St Paul(?); modern(?) canopy over high altar; interesting 17c dole table in S porch is a monument to Henry Cutler who died

in 1601 and left money for the poor; Purbeck marble tomb-chest monument in the N aisle to Nicholas Cutler 1568, another in the Abbey Chapel to William Honying 1569, a monument to John Brown 1732 at the foot of a relief of the Good Samaritan, and a beautiful 14c recess minus its tomb.

EYKE

Location: 3 miles SE of Wickham Market.
Dedication: All Saints.
Description: The Norman church originally had a central tower with nave and chancel. Later the transepts were added, making it cruciform. Today only the nave, chancel, and lower storey of the tower remain with the two Norman arches which originally supported it. The N transept has disappeared and when the nave was widened in the 14c to include the S transept, the roof was carried over remains of the tower as far as the chancel arch. There was a 15c chapel against N wall of chancel.
Periods: Norman origins, though nave and chancel are now Dec.
Features: Octagonal 15c font; two piscinas in S aisle of chancel; piscina from chapel in N wall of chancel; 18c communion rail; Elizabethan cup; two brasses, one comprising two headless figures representing John de Staverton, Baron of the Exchequer, and his wife c1430, and the other, to Henry Mason, M.A. 1619.

FAKENHAM MAGNA

Location: 5 miles SE of Thetford.
Dedication: St Peter.
Description: Situated at the southern end of Euston Park, the church, which still bears traces of its Saxon origins, comprises nave, chancel, vestry and W tower.
Periods: Saxon 'long and short' work at the eastern corners of the nave, one N and one S blocked Norman windows, and the chancel features two 13c lancet windows. W Tower and the remainder of nave and chancel are 14c. The church was restored in 1859 when a new vestry was added.
Features: 14c gabled buttresses at western angles of nave; four 13c sepulchral slabs with crosses in tower basement; stoup in S porch; piscina and triple sedilia in chancel; much restored screen; cup 1629, paten 1703; monument on N wall of chancel to Reynold Taylor 1692. The Register dates from 1559.

FALKENHAM

Location: 9 miles SE of Ipswich.
Dedication: St Ethelbert.
Description: A rare dedication, one of only three to this saint in Suffolk. It consists of a combined nave (faced in 19c brick) and apsed chancel built in 19c brick, and a massive, lofty flint W tower with brick belfry.
Periods: 15c tower, chancel and vestry built 1806.
Features: Finely decorated W doorway bearing the arms of England, Warwick and Mowbray, Duke of Norfolk; good hammerbeam roof on nave; 15c octagonal font; reredos incorporating some fine tracery panels from a 14c Flemish chest; cup 1756; memorial tablets to the Everitt and Rodham families.

FARNHAM

Location: 3 miles SW of Saxmundham.
Dedication: St Mary.
Description: Situated on an eminence looking across the Alde, this flint church with a nave, chancel and brick W tower retains Norman traces.
Periods: The nave N and S walls each contain a Norman window, but the 14c chancel appears much restored and the tower is later.
Features: Font; piscina in chancel; remains of rood-screen on N side of nave with traces of colour; Georgian box-pews; cup and paten 1567, flagon 1636.

FELIXSTOWE

Dedication: St John the Baptist.
Description: The church of modern Felixstowe situated in Orwell Road. Large, spacious and built of red brick, it has fine windows and handsome woodwork. There is a clerestoried nave, chancel and tall S tower crowned by a stone spire.
Periods: Built 1894 from designs of Sir Arthur Blomfield, A.R.A. with the chancel, chapel and vestry added in 1899.
Features: Fine roofs to nave and chancel; interesting lancet windows, with those in the clerestory, in the shape of spherical triangles (Pevsner).

Dedication: St Peter and St Paul.
Description: The church of Old Felixstowe lies inland to the NW, and stands on part of the site of the old Benedictine Priory of St Felix. It has transepts and an apsed chancel but has been much rebuilt. The W tower of septaria is now only a stump. Septaria too in the S porch and N side of nave.
Periods: The nave bears traces of 13c and 14c work, the N doorway early 14c, but the transepts and chancel were built c1873.
Features: Octagonal font (17c?); pulpit, supported by part of a column from the priory; 15c bench-ends; 16c iron-bound poor-box; cup 1728; tower contains bell of 1665.

FELSHAM

Location: 8 miles SE of Bury St Edmunds.
Dedication: St Peter.
Description: Wide nave, modern chancel, fine flint N porch and impressive W tower with much flintwork panelling.
Periods: Nave and tower 14c, the N porch c1470, and chancel rebuilt 1873.
Features: 15c octagonal font on base of mutilated bowl of another; 15c glass in window tracery; Royal Arms of George III, dated 1820; Eliabethan cup, 17c paten, flagon 1717; memorials to the Risby and Goodrich families. The Register dates from 1656.

FINNINGHAM

Location: 8 miles N of Stowmarket.
Dedication: St Bartholomew.
Description: The quintessential scene of church romantically situated on the edge of the pretty village green. There was a church here at the time of the Conquest, and that of today comprises nave chancel, W tower and N

and S porches, the former simple and of brick, the latter with ornate flintwork panelling.

Periods: Tower and the S doorways of both nave and chancel are early 14c. The S porch is c1463 and retains its medieval door, and the remainder of the church is also mainly 15c, though much restored in the 1880s.

Features: Single hammerbeam roof to nave; late 15c font with beautifully carved pinnacled cover; 15c stained glass in E window; interesting carved bench-ends; brass inscription to John Dobyn, 'clarke' 1620; monuments to John Williamson 1781, to Sir John Fenn, Knight, the editor of *The Paston Letters*, 1794, and his wife Ellenor Frere 1813. There are a number of memorials to the Frere family who were living in the county as early as the 13c, John Frere settling in Finningham in 1598.

FLEMPTON

Location: 5 miles NW of Bury St Edmunds.
Dedication: St Catherine.
Description: The church, which consists of a nave, chancel and W tower, was long in a ruinous condition until repaired and partly rebuilt in 1839.
Periods: Earliest parts late 13c and early 14c. The tower was rebuilt 1839.
Features: Good door tracery; 14c font; fine double piscina in chancel; 17c pulpit and communion rail; Royal Arms of George III, dated 1763; paten 1760. The Register dates from 1561.

FLIXTON nr. Lowestoft

Location: 3 miles NW of Lowestoft.
Dedication: St Andrew.
Description: The church, already in decay, was destroyed by a hurricane on November 27th 1703 and never rebuilt. Only fragments of the wall survive to about 10' high beside Old Hall farmhouse.

FLIXTON nr. Bungay

Location: 2 miles SW of Bungay.
Dedication: St Mary.
Description: The W tower, rebuilt in 1861, complete with an unusual helm-like spire, is said to be an accurate copy of the Norman one which fell in 1835. However, Dickinson states that a drawing of 1818 does not support this statement. The nave was also rebuilt at the same time, and the chancel, which had long been in ruins, in 1893, also in Norman style. There is a lovely memorial chapel with a fan-vaulted roof in memory of the builder, Lady Adair.
Periods: Earliest parts of the church are the Early English nave pillars.
Features: 14c Italian paintings, presented by Sir Shafto Adair of Flixton Hall; Jacobean pulpit; old benches; brass inscription to Elizabeth Tasburgh 1583; memorial chapel at W end of aisle contains kneeling figure of Theodosia Lady Waveney 1871, and a monument to William Adair 1783.

FLOWTON

Location: 6 miles NW of Ipswich.
Dedication: St Mary.
Description: An attractive early Dec church which has been altered several

times. It consists of a nave, chancel and a W tower in knapped flint which may never have been totally completed. There is a large Tudor brick rood-loft stair turret with brick parapet.

Periods: Mostly of c1300 origin except for a large early 16c window with brick tracery. It was completely restored in 1878.

Features: Fine king-post roof to nave and a western gallery; 13c octagonal font of Purbeck marble; plain piscina with credence in chancel; good three-light E window; paten 1697, cup 1809.

FORNHAM ALL SAINTS

Location: 2 miles NW of Bury St Edmunds.
Dedication: All Saints.
Description: An early church consisting of a nave with N aisle and S chapel, lofty chancel with Mannock Chapel on the N. The low, pinnacled W tower has lively battlements with initials and shields in stone and flushwork.
Periods: The S doorway is Norman as is the lower part of the tower. The nave is a little later, c1300, the chancel Dec, and the S porch and S chapel probably added early in the 16c.
Features: Large font; piscina and sedilia in chancel; Mannock Chapel has squint pointing to the high altar; statue niche in E wall, N of high altar; carved bench-ends; cup 1566, paten 1660, flagon 1762; a number of brasses, one to Thomas Barwick 1599 and others to the Mannock family. The Register dates from 1560.

FORNHAM ST GENEVIEVE

Location: 2 miles NE of Bury St Edmunds.
Dedication: St Genevieve.
Description: The church was destroyed by fire on 24th June 1782 as a result of a man shooting jackdaws on the thatched roof. Nothing remains but the ruined, unbuttressed W tower in Fornham Park. Gone too the hall which stood beside it.
Periods: Lancet window in the tower suggests early origins and a Will of 1452 left money for the tower's repair.

FORNHAM ST MARTIN

Location: 10 miles from Thetford.
Dedication: St Martin.
Description: Nave, S aisle, chancel, N porch in Tudor brickwork and stepped gable, and a decorated W tower with tall bell-openings.
Periods: The church is mainly 15c, with the S aisle added in 1846 and rebuilt in 1870.
Features: Octagonal 15c font; Norman chevron carving on a stone built into N wall of chancel; two fine misericords representing St Martin and the Martyrdom of St Thomas Becket re-used to form part of modern lectern and reader's desk; mid-17c communion rail; cup c1566; brass to an ecclesiastic in academic dress c1460, and a brass inscription to John Chapman 1609; several memorials to the Ord family and one to Sir William Gilstrap, Bart 1896.

FOXHALL

Location: 4 miles SE of Ipswich.
Dedication: All Saints.
Description: The church was much decayed by 1530 and soon afterwards became unfit for services. All that now remains is one wall forming part of an outbuilding of Foxhall Farm.

FRAMLINGHAM

Dedication: St Michael.
Description: A large and regal church as befits a town with such a noble history. It comprises an impressively strong W tower, 28' square and nearly 100' high, decorated in flintwork, with panelled diagonal buttresses - the western ones have shields bearing the arms of the Mowbrays - and topped with battlements with lions in place of pinnacles. Within is a clerestoried nave with arcaded aisles, 64' long and 50' wide, a chancel with four-bay chapels 61' long and 68' wide, the chapels housing the tombs of the Dukes of Norfolk. There is also a S porch.
Periods: The church is mostly Perp, but piers and capitals of the chancel arch (12c), the pillars of the nave arcade, and a niche near the W end of the N aisle (Dec), remain from an earlier building. The chancel was completed c1549, and the S porch dates from c1770.
Features: Beautiful hammerbeam roof in nave; 15c octagonal font with fine carved cover; painting of the Trinity on N nave wall; framing of the old box-pews lining the aisles; early 18c reredos at the back of the high altar; Royal Arms of Charles II, dated 1661, in the tower; interesting organ case, dated 1674, brought from Pembroke College and given to the church in 1708; brass chandelier of 1742 in the chancel; cup and cover 1568, almsdish 1704, flagon 1742; key to Framlingham Castle in S porch. The chief treasures of the church are the series of six magnificent tombs in the N and S chapels, 'one of the best series of mid-16c Early Renaissance monuments in England, and among them one, of a quality almost to match leading works in France' (Pevsner). All but one are to the Howard family; the exception being one, in the SE corner of the S chapel, to Sir Robert Hitcham 1636, the Queen's Attorney, who bought the castle and the manor of Framlingham. The Howard tombs are: S of the high altar - Thomas Howard, third Duke of Norfolk 1554 and his second wife Elizabeth; on the N side of the high altar - Henry Fitzroy, Duke of Richmond and natural son of Henry VIII, 1536 and his wife Mary Howard, daughter of Thomas, third Duke of Norfolk, who were originally buried at Thetford Priory and removed here after the Dissolution; on NE corner of N chapel - Mary 1537 and Margaret 1562, two of the three wives of Thomas, fourth Duke of Norfolk who was beheaded in 1572, and adjacent - a small tomb with beautiful arched canopy in memory of Elizabeth, daughter of the fourth Duke by Margaret; to the W of this - the painted alabaster tomb of Henry Howard, Earl of Surrey, and his wife Francis de Vere, daughter of the fifteenth Earl of Oxford; at one end of the tomb kneel their sons, Thomas the fourth Duke, and Henry, Earl of Northampton, and at the other are the three daughters, Jane, Katherine and Mary. To the Earl's misfortune he was executed only nine days before the death of his judge and jury, Henry VIII, and to signify his being beheaded, his coronet lies beside him on the tomb. It is an extrordinary fact that the third Duke of Norfolk had been saved from a similar fate when Henry's death

came one day prior to that of his execution for high treason - he went on to reach the age of 80. With the fourth Duke also ending his days headless, they were indeed a family that sailed close to the wind! The helmet, with lion crest, hanging above the arch nearest the tomb of the third Duke is known as the Flodden Helm, said to be the very one worn by the second Duke at the Battle of Flodden Field in 1513. The Register dates from 1560.

FRAMSDEN

Location: 3 miles SE of Debenham.
Dedication: St Mary.
Description: Nave with S aisle and clerestory, chancel, and richly decorated S porch and tall W tower.
Periods: Main church is of two Dec periods, the chancel, with fine traceried windows, being the earlier. The fine W tower is Perp as is the E window of the chancel and the brick windows of the clerestory and N side of the nave.
Features: Small Saxon(?) figure of man re-used in wall by the chancel NW window; Double hammer-beam roof in nave and a good 17c roof over S aisle with beams dated 1620 and 1676; octagonal font; piscinas in chancel and S aisle; fine traceried windows; six 14c choir stalls with well-carved misericords and some old bench-ends; Elizabethan cup and cover.

FRECKENHAM

Location: 4 miles SW of Mildenhall.
Dedication: St Andrew.
Description: The church, which was thatched until the 19c restoration, comprising a nave, N aisle, chancel and W tower shows much sign of Victorian rebuilding.
Periods: Although considerable rebuilding took place in 1867 and the W tower had to be rebuilt in 1884, a year after it was partly blown down, there is evidence of c1300 Early English work in the lancet window in the chancel and in the arcade; the nave is late Dec.
Features: Good roofs of nave, chancel and N aisle with carved bosses; double pisina in chancel and a single in the N aisle; sedilia of three graduated seats in sill of chancel window; some fine windows in chancel; old carved bench-ends; 15c alabaster relief of a scene from the Life of St Eligius, patron saint of goldsmiths, from a former altar, in wall of N aisle; Elizabethan cup, paten 1723.

FRESSINGFIELD

Location: 4 miles NE of Stradbroke.
Dedication: St Peter and St Paul.
Description: W tower, aisled and clerestoried nave, chancel, with N chapel dedicated to St Margaret (a former a guild chapel), and porches, the S being vaulted and particularly ornate. There is a fine sanctus bell-turret over the apex of the E gable of the nave - 'probably the best in the county' (Dickinson).
Periods: Largely 14c with 15c clerestory, S porch and roofs.
Features: Finely carved hammer-beam roof over nave and a good roof in chancel; canopied sedilia and piscina in chancel and another piscina in N

chapel; traceried Dec and Perp chancel windows; some old glass in the windows; lower part of rood-screen; the nave is full of a magnificent series of carved oak benches - 'one of the best sets in the county' (Pevsner) and 'the country' (Cautley), one of which bears the initials of Alice de la Pole, grand-daughter of Geoffrey Chaucer; large iron-bound chest; brass of William Brewes 1489 and his wife Elizabeth. Tomb in churchyard, E of the porch, of Archbishop Sancroft 1693.

FRESTON

Location: 3 miles S of Ipswich.
Dedication: St Peter.
Description: Standing alone by the banks of the river Orwell with a nave, chancel, S porch and short W tower.
Periods: Over-restored 1875. What remains of original work is 14c and 15c.
Features: Perp octagonal font; piscina and windowsill sedilia in chancel; no chancel arch but instead massive beam, possibly for rood; cup 1656. The Register dates from 1537.

FRISTON

Location: 2 miles SE of Saxmundham.
Dedication: St Mary.
Description: Small church with odd W tower, with the buttresses carried above the parapet to end in strange-looking gabled pinnacles, and showing several periods of rebuilding. The nave and chancel are in one.
Periods: Late Norman S door, 14c? motifs on tower.
Features: Good nave roof; consecration crosses in jambs of S door; Jacobean pulpit; magificent Royal Arms of James I carved in wood. The Register dates from 1541.

FRITTON

Location: 8 miles NE of Beccles. (Taken into Norfolk in 1974).
Dedication: St.Edmund.
Description: Said to have begun as a Saxon wayside chapel dedicated to King Edmund the Martyr, this is surely one of Suffolk's most interesting churches, and another disgracefully torn from the county and given to Norfolk in 1974; but a Suffolk church it remains, providing a unique insight into what a Norman church originally looked and felt like. Norman round W tower, thatched nave and low Norman apsed chancel, with a S porch. As Pevsner stated 'As one enters, one is struck by the oddest lack of symmetry. The tower is not in axis with the wide nave but stands against its N half. The chancel is also attached to the N half of the nave E wall'. When they extended what was probably originally a Saxon structure, the Normans made a nave on 11' wide, and the 14c builders added 10' to its breadth, leaving untouched the Norman chancel arch. This mean the arch is no longer central and instead of ascending to the chancel we go down steps to it. The old Norman chancel still remains and is both interesting and impressive in its lowness and darkness. It is tunnel-vaulted 'a great rarity in England, and is followed by a vaulted apse..... the tunnel-vauting indicates that a tower was built or intended above the chancel bay' (Pevsner).

Periods: All of Norman date except the 14c nave extension. The porch and vestry were added in 1855.
Features: Modern 'Norman style' font; 13c pillar piscina in sanctuary; 15c painting of St Christopher on N wall, and possibly earlier painting of St Thomas of Canterbury in the E jamb of the SE nave window; part of 14c screen; 16c choir stalls; 17c three-decker pulpit; Georgian organ case; Royal Arms of George II; cup and paten 1627.

FROSTENDEN

Location: 5 miles NW of Southwold.
Dedication: All Saints.
Description: Frostenden is now three miles from the sea, and its church a relic from the Norman period when the village was a busy port. Tall round tower with lancet windows in the belfry. The church was enlarged in the 14c when a S aisle, continuing to a S porch with vaulted roof was added.
Periods: Late 12c tower, the chancel 13c and the remainder 14c, with 15c tracery on E window.
Features: Rims of two querns built into base of tower; octagonal 15c font with carved cover; piscina and the remains of a sedilia in chancel; some good bench-ends; 18c sun-dial over porch; Elizabethan cup, cover 1567, paten 1685, flagon 1703.

GAZELEY

Location: 5 miles SE of Newmarket.
Dedication: All Saints.
Description: W tower and mostly unrestored interior of nave, with arcaded aisles, clerestory, and chancel.
Periods: Early 14c chancel, 14c nave and arcades and Perp clerestory and aisles. The tower was rebuilt in 1884.
Features: 16c roofs of nave and chancel; 15c vestry door with massive iron studs; 14c font with 17c cover; piscina and windowsill sedilia in chancel; canopied Easter Sepulchre in N wall; fine chancel E window with unusual tracery; some old glass in clerestory windows; some 15c benches in the nave; 16c pulpit and part of contemporary rood-screen made up with new work; Royal Arms of George III, 1815; chalice-brass c1530 in floor of sanctuary; brass inscription to Robert Tailour 1586, and one to Mary Heigham 1618; Purbeck marble canopied altar-tomb at E end of S aisle having lost its brasses.

GEDDING

Location: 8 miles SE of Bury St Edmunds.
Dedication: St Mary.
Description: The church, which is surrounded by an ancient moat-like boundary ditch consists of a flint and stone W tower, which appears to have been reduced in height before being topped with brick in 1469(?), nave, and a chancel divided by a rare triple arch, the centre plain and the outers attractively ornamented.
Periods: Two Norman windows in nave, the rest, 14c.
Features: Stoup bowl; octagonal Perp font; three simple 15c benches; two bells in tower dated 1572.

GIPPING

Location: 4 miles NE of Stowmarket.
Dedication: Chapel of St Nicholas.
Description: In this tiny parish, providing the source of the river Gipping, stands the unique private chapel of Sir James Tyrell who died in 1502. It was he who, as Shakespeare said, carried out 'The most arch act of piteous massacre that ever yet this land was guilty of' - the murder of the Princes in the Tower. The chapel adjoins the site of his hall, now marked by a well. All in one piece with nave, chancel and a curious N annexe which may have formed the chaplain's house, Pevsner feels the plastered 19c W tower spoils what would otherwise be a singularly perfect piece of late medieval Suffolk architecture. However, the quantity and quality of the decorative flintwork which adorn the buttresses and walls and which are probably not exceeded on any building in the county, tend, in any case, to make the tower insignificant. The initials of the founder's wife, Anne Morley Lanherne Arundel are repeated six times in the stonework, and the Tyrell knot incorporated everywhere. A somewhat pathetic plea in the splay of the vestry door is inscribed 'Pray for Sir Jamys Tirell and Dame Anne his wyf', but on the NE buttress, a more defiant motto in French which translates to 'Let him complain who will'. Through history the Tyrelles appear to have been a rather tainted family, for it was one of Sir James's predecessors who, while out hunting, 'accidently' fired the fateful arrow which ended the reign of the Conqueror's son, William Rufus in 1100.
Periods: Built c1483.
Features: Early font; unusual 'double' windows on either side of nave; 17c communion rail; one original kneeling bench; two patens 1704, cup 1712.

GISLEHAM

Location: 5 miles SW of Lowestoft.
Dedication: Holy Trinity.
Description: Tall W tower, the lower part round, and the upper part formed by an octagonal belfry.
Periods: The round tower is Norman as is the arch to the nave and the chancel. The nave itself is 14c, and the belfry and S porch 15c.
Features: Blocked Norman door to the nave; well-carved 15c font; windowsill sedilia in chancel, the seat now being formed by a 13c coffin slab still marked with a cross; stained glass in E window by Kempe 1896; wall panting of St Dorothy on eastern jamb of NE window of nave; rood beam with plastered tympanum; banner staff locker in SE corner of tower; Elizabethan cup, paten 1702; brass to Adam Bland 1593.

GISLINGHAM

Location: 5 miles SW of Eye.
Dedication: St Mary.
Description: Well restored church with wide W tower of red brick, and a spacious and unspoilt interior comprising nave, chancel and a N porch.
Periods: The church is principally 15c, the only early work being the 14c E window, but the W tower is a 1639 replacement for the one which fell in 1598. The late 15c N porch, dedicated to its founders Robert and Rose Chapman, was reroofed in 1661.

Features: Double hammerbeam roof to nave; 15c font with 17c cover; 15c stained glass in nave windows; some 15c bench-ends; four panels of the rood-screen; 17c communion rails; 18c three-decker pulpit and high box-pews; 15c iron-bound chest; Royal Arms of George III; Elizabethan cup, almsdish 1639; large monument to Anthony Bedingfield 1652.

GLEMSFORD

Location: 5 miles NE of Clare.
Dedication: St Mary.
Description: The large church stands on an eminence overlooking the Glem valley. It comprises a W tower, aisled nave with clerestory, chancel, chapels, N porch and beautiful S porch with fine flint panelling.
Periods: The tower (which is built upon an earlier base) and nave arcades are 14c, while the aisles, chancel chapels, clerestory and porches are later Perp.
Features: Good N aisle roof with carved beams; the S chancel aisle has an inscription to its founders John and Joan Golding; S door with tracery; lovely 15c octagonal font; 17c pulpit; enormous iron-bound chest; 18c reredos in S chapel. The Register dates from 1550.

GOSBECK

Location: 5 miles E of Needham Market.
Dedication: St Mary.
Description: A large building with a nave, chancel, vestry and pinnacled SW tower, the basement of which forms a porch.
Periods: Traces of Saxon long and short work can be found in the corners of the E end of the nave, and possibly the small N door and deep, narrow window are also of this period. The chancel, though restored in 1883, may be c1300, and the rest of the church 14c.
Features: Hammerbeam roof to the nave and a fine roof to the chancel; font; iron-banded belfry door; pulpit, dated 1620; some remains of the painted rood-screen; Elizabethan cup with its original leather case, paten 1728.

GREAT ASHFIELD

Location: 8 miles NW of Stowmarket.
Dedication: All Saints.
Description: The church comprises nave with N aisle and chapel, chancel, brick S porch with fine flint panelling, and knapped flint W tower with a short spire.
Periods: The finely moulded S doorway, and lancet window in the much restored chancel, are 13c. The nave and N aisle are Perp as is the tower, and the S porch is 16c.
Features: There are good roofs over nave and chancel; internal staircase to rood-loft on N side of nave; 15c font; fine pulpit of 1619 and matching reredos; massive iron-bound chest in vestry; clerk's bench with carved symbols of the blacksmith's tools; good hatchments in chancel; a memorial chapel in the N aisle to the men of the 8th U.S. Air Force, who were stationed at the aerodrome here during the Second World War. The Register dates from 1698.

GREAT BARTON

Location: 3 miles NE of Bury St Edmunds.
Dedication: Holy Innocents.
Description: Of this unusual dedication little is known. The tall W tower with panelled battlements and flint and stone decoration, provides a prominent landmark for miles around. Church also features a nave with clerestory and N and S aisles, chancel and porch.
Periods: Chancel is late 13c, and although the S aisle has a window of early 14c, the rest of building is 15c Perp. The tower 'made new' in a Will of 1440.
Features: Single hammerbeam roof to nave; hexagonal buttresses at E end of chancel with canopies and pinnacles; 13c font; piscina; fragments of old glass in window-heads of N aisle; old carved benches; an altar tomb to Sir Henry Bunbury, given the task of conveying the delicate news to Napoleon of his exile to the island of St Helena, rather than imprisonment in England where his notoriety could be nurtured in public, and monuments to other members of the Bunbury family. Outside, on the S side of the chancel, is an arched tombed recess.

GREAT BEALINGS

Location: 2 miles W of Woodbridge.
Dedication: St Mary.
Description: Fine, well-situated church of W tower with flintwork decoration, nave and chancel, with a brick and flint N porch with an inscription to Thomas and Margaret Seckford whose family arms are above the arch.
Periods: Principally Dec and Perp with much loving restoration in 1842-51 by Canon Moor. The N porch is of c1520 and the W tower c1450.
Features: Good roofs to nave and chancel; rare tracery on N door; octagonal 13c font of Purbeck marble; late 13c shafted piscina in S wall; a stone reredos erected 1882 and dedicated to a Lord Chancellor, Lord Hatherley, who lies in the churchyard; 19c stained glass in W window, one chancel S window and one chancel N window; Jacobean pulpit and tester; fine selection of bench-ends, possibly carved by Moor and not in the 15c as supposed (Scarfe); Elizabethan cup, flagon and two patens 1799; monument to Sir Thomas Seckford 1575 and his wife, and one to John Clenche 1628 in the chancel. The Register dates from 1539.

GREAT BLAKENHAM

Location: 5 miles NW of Ipswich.
Dedication: St Mary.
Description: The church consists of a nave, chancel, timber S porch and unbuttressed W tower.
Periods: Lower section of tower is Norman as is the nave as shown by its two simple S and N (blocked) doorways, whilst the chancel has Early English lancet windows; there are also lancet windows in the nave S wall. Upper part of tower is 14c and the lovely timber S porch, 15c.
Features: Large sundial on S wall with early Mass-dial on SE corner of chancel and three later ones on S wall of nave; 13c roofs to nave and chancel; panelled 15c font; a rare late 12c piscina in chancel; 17c pulpit with tester; two inscribed 15c bells in tower; monument to Richard Swift 1645 with an interesting rhymed inscription.

GREAT BRADLEY

Location: 6 miles N of Haverhill.
Dedication: St Mary.
Description: Imposing W tower with higher SE stair-turret, nave, chancel and picturesque early Tudor S porch, using, it is said, bricks made by 'Henry VIII's own brickmakers' and the 'best brick porch in Suffolk' (Scarfe).
Periods: The nave has an ornate late Norman S doorway within the porch, and simpler N doorway. The chancel arch is also late Norman (mutilated by the insertion of a rood-screen, now removed), and the chancel itself mostly from c1300. It was shortened and over-restored in 18c. W tower early 14c.
Features: Open wagon roof of nave with king-posts and tie-beams; octagonal font; piscina in chancel; two recesses in E wall of nave for chapels beneath the rood-screen, each with a piscina; two-decker 18c pulpit; paten 1684, cup 1743 and another of 1809; tower contains early 14c bell made by Richard of Wimbish (Essex).

GREAT BRICETT

Location: 5 miles SW of Needham Market.
Dedication: St Mary and St Lawrence.
Description: The remains of a chuch of Augustinian Canons comprises one oblong building without aisles or tower, but excavations have shown that in the 12c the church also had apsed transepts.
Periods: The only remains from the priory church founded in 1115 by Ralph Fitz-Brian and his wife Emma and dedicated to St Leonard, is a Norman N doorway, one blocked Norman slit window in the N wall and one tall arched window in the S wall. There is also a window of c1300. The E window is probably an 1868 copy of the Dec window it replaced.
Features: Mass-dial on S wall of nave, possibly pre-Conquest and earliest example in the county; fine S door; remains of blocked arches to transeptal chapels; rood-loft turret on N of nave; very fine late 12c font; old glass in a S nave window and early 14c stained glass in E window; unusual Victorian pulpit; 16c bench-ends; 17c chest; Elizabethan cup; marble monument in the chancel to John Bright 1670 and his wife 1679 of Tollemache Hall.

GREAT CORNARD

Location: 1 mile SE of Sudbury.
Dedication: St Andrew.
Description: Nave, chancel, N aisle, S porch and flint W tower with circular belfry windows, slated, wooden spire and brick stair turret.
Periods: Tower and chancel 14c, stair turret 16c and the S aisle of 1887.
Features: Niches in W wall of tower; octagonal 15c font; traces of Elizabethan wall-paintings on aisle walls uncovered in 1934; paten 1710.

GREAT FINBOROUGH

Location: 2 miles SW of Stowmarket.
Dedication: St Andrew.
Description: Situated in the grounds of the Hall, with tall W tower with flying buttresses, an octagonal upper section, and massive disproportionate needle spire which can be seen for miles. The church is large but aisleless.

Periods: Formerly 14c but completely rebuilt, except for the 15c S porch, in 1876 by the Pettiwards.
Features: Paten c1680, cup 1733; monuments include one to the Rev William Wollaston, M.A., author of *The Religion of Nature Delineated*, who died in 1724, another to Charlton Wollaston 1729, and one to Roger Pettiward 1833.

GREAT GLEMHAM

Location: 4 miles SW of Saxmundham.
Dedication: All Saints.
Description: Imposing W tower with flintwork panelling on buttresses and battlements, nave with S aisle, chancel and knapped flint N porch.
Periods: Chancel c1300 with lancets in N and S wall and a 15c E window; W tower 15c Perp and the S aisle may be 19c addition. The church was partly restored in 1856 and completed in 1879.
Features: Very fine roof to nave; priest's doorway in early 16c brick; stoup in N porch; magnificent late 15c Seven Sacraments font; 13c piscina and windowsill sedilia; fragments of stained glass in chancel window; three 15c inscribed bells in tower; Elizabethan cup; monuments to the Wayth and Kilderbee families.

GREAT LIVERMERE

Location: 5 miles NE of Bury St Edmunds.
Dedication: St Peter.
Description: An old church with a tower only to roof height and capped by an unusual wooden belfry. The nave is thatched.
Periods: The church dates back to the 12c when the nave was built - the simple N doorway being c1200; the chancel is Dec but has blocked lancet windows of 13c date, and the main tower 14c.
Features: Low windows N and S of chancel, blocked externally and the latter retaining its original wooden shutter; unusual chancel roof; 14c canopied niches either side of E window; elaborate niche still retaining colouring in N wall, possibly for Easter Sepulchre; consecration crosses in nave and chancel; octagonal 15c font; wall-paintings in nave, one of St Christopher; three-sided 18c altar rails; three-decker pulpit of c1700; some crude benches in chancel, one dated 1601; massive 15c rood-screen; paten 1690, cup 1809, almsdish 1823. In the churchyard near the porch is a headstone memorial to William Sakings 1689 inscribed: 'Here lyeth ye body of William Sakings, forkner(falconer) to King Charles ye 1st, King Charles ye 2nd and King James ye 2nd'.

GREAT SAXHAM

Location: 5 miles SW of Bury St Edmunds.
Dedication: St Andrew.
Description: The church has a nave, chancel, S porch and W tower.
Periods: The N and S doorways are all that remains of the Norman church which was rebuilt in 1798 by Thomas Mills. The tower and porch are 15c. The church was fully restored in 1869.
Features: 15c octagonal font; W window contains good early 16c stained glass brought here in the late 18c from a dissolved German monastery, and

there is some of Flemish and Swiss origin in the E window; Jacobean pulpit; carved benches; wrought-iron chancel screen; squire's pew on N side of nave, facing pulpit; Royal Arms of Queen Anne 1702; marble monument and brass in chancel to the merchant traveller John Eldred who died in 1632, aged 80, he arrived home after five years of travelling the world with "the richest ship of merchant goods that ever came into this realm". There are other monuments to the Eldred family.

GREAT THURLOW

Location: 4 miles NE of Haverhill.
Dedication: All Saints.
Description: Aisled and clerestoried nave, chancel, and west tower with higher stair-turret and small lead spire.
Periods: There is evidence of the church's 12c Norman origins in the chancel, but was mostly remodelled and enlarged in the 15c when the present nave, aisles, clerestory and west tower were built. The church was completely restored in 1879-80.
Features: Nave arcade - pillars have no capitals; font with Norman (or imitation Norman) bowl; 17c pulpit and sanctuary chair; panels of rood-screen now placed against E wall; top beams of chapel parclose at E end of S aisle, dated 1610; cup 1567 and paten 1632; brasses, including one to knight in armour with lady in veiled head-dress c1460, and another to Thomas and Anne Underhill 1530.

GREAT WALDINGFIELD

Location: 3 miles NE of Sudbury.
Dedication: St. Lawrence.
Description: Aisled nave with single-windowed clerestory, chancel, W tower with large external stair-turret and N and S porches.
Periods: Most of the church was erected by John Appleton towards the end of the 14c and completed in the 15c, but the chancel was rebuilt in Dec style between 1866-69 and the N porch is of similar date. Restoration and 'beautification' continued on the church throughout the 1870s.
Features: The extrordinary internal chancel walls and reredos are panelled with coloured marbles collected from numerous temple ruins in Rome, and there is granite from Mount Sinai and pieces of syenite from Egypt which once formed part of a colossal statue to Rameses; octagonal Perp font; 17c carved woodwork in the chancel came from Wren's fine church of St. Michael, Cornhill, in the City of London, and may be the work of Grinling Gibbons; carved bench ends; good 19c stained glass and old glass in E window of S aisle; Royal Arms of George III over tower arch; interesting keyed bugle in glass case in nave; Communion rail, also from St. Michael Cornhill; Elizabethan communion cup, repaired 1618, almdish 1701; among the monuments are several belonging to the Kedingtons, formerly lords of the manor. The Register dates from 1550.

GREAT WELNETHAM

Location: 4 miles SE of Bury St Edmunds.
Dedication: St. Thomas A Beckett.
Description: The church has a small nave, N aisle and chancel, and a tiny

clerestory. At the W end is a wooden bell-turret for, although a Will of 1453 left money towards the building of one, the church remains towerless.
Periods: Of Early English origin (see the lancet windows) with a Dec nave. The bell-turret was erected in 1749 'at the cost of James Merest'.
Features: 15c font with 18c cover; double piscina in nave; 13c sedilia in chancel; fragments of old glass in chancel SE window; 17c pulpit incorporating some panels of c1500; cup 1658, almdish 1691, flagon 1717.

GREAT WENHAM

Location: 4 miles SE of Hadleigh.
Dedication: St. John.
Description: Plastered nave and chancel, as was the Victorian fashion, but tower has good modern flint-panelled parapet.
Periods: The church is of Early English 13c origin and the nave and chancel still show this and early 14c work. The tower is later Perp. The church was restored in 1842 and again in 1867.
Features: 13c S doorway; stoup by entrance; remains of rood-stair on N side of nave; squint in N wall; piscina and sedilia in chancel S wall; 15c tiles forming sanctuary pavement; Royal Arms of George II; East family crest, sword and helmet; memorial to Gilbert East 1768, and monuments to the Bailey, Whalley and King families. in chancel. The Register dates from 1648.

GREAT WRATTING

Location: 2 miles NE of Haverhill.
Dedication: St. Mary.
Description: Septaria and flint nave, chancel and W tower.
Periods: The earliest part of the church is the 13c Early English chancel, the wall pierced by a series of lancets. The rest, including the fine S doorway is mostly 15c, but was subjected to bad restoration in 1887.
Features: 13c sedilia and piscina; corbels under chancel arch originally supporting a rood beam; cup 1662, almdish 1676.

GROTON

Location: 7 miles E of Sudbury.
Dedication: St. Bartholomew.
Description: Fine flint church stands beside hall of the Winthrop family. Lofty, but narrow aisled and clerestoried nave, chancel, S porch and W Tower.
Periods: Whilst lower section of tower appears 13c, the church is chiefly 15c.
Features: Curious blocked squint in S porch which once looked into church; old heraldic glass and a beautiful traceried four-light E window dedicated to local worthy John Winthrop who sailed to America in 1629 and became the first governor of Massachusetts - married four times, he had 15 children; cup and cover 1726, almdish 1729; brass inscription to Adam Winthrop, 'lorde of Groton' 1562. The Register dates from 1562.

GRUNDISBURGH

Location: 3 miles NW of Woodbridge.
Dedication: St. Mary.
Description: Nave with S aisle and clerestory, chancel with S chapel and

brick S tower, the base of which forms a porch.

Periods: The church originally comprised a late 13c chancel and nave. In the 14c the nave was lengthened and the S aisle added, and a century later the nave windows were inserted and a clerestory added. In 1527 the beautiful little chapel was built with an inscription on the parapet to the founders, Thomas and Alicia Walle. The fine brick S tower, which replaced an old one which had fallen down, was added c1731.

Features: Excellent double hammerbeam roof to nave incorporating 58 carved angels arranged in three tiers - 'one of the most beautiful in Suffolk' (Pevsner); 15c font; 13c piscina in chancel; paintings on N wall of St. Christopher, and two 13c figures recently discovered 14c painted rood-screen; 15c screen in S aisle; old traceried bench ends; brass inscriptions to John and Margery Amall 1501, Anne Mannocke 1610, and Thomas Sulyard 1612; two communion cups, one Elizabethan, the other dated 1668, almsdish 1676; brass to John Awall 1501 in S aisle; monument to Sir Charles Blois 1738, and a wall-monument of Robert Brook, his wife and family 1657.

GUNTON

Location: 2 miles NW of Lowestoft.
Dedication: St. Peter.
Description: Nave and chancel under one roof, S porch and round W tower.
Periods: The tower is Norman with late 15c windows inserted in the belfry. Norman N and S doorways and a small Norman window in the nave. The chancel is 13c but much rebuilt in 14c. The church was restored and partly rebuilt in 1700.
Features: Piscina in chancel; stoup in S porch; remains of rood-loft stairs in N wall; cup 1660, paten 1670; brass memorial to General Charles William Wingfield 1872; monument to Charles Boyce, who restored the church.

HACHESTON

Location: 4 miles SE of Framlingham.
Dedication: All Saints.
Description: Situated on a bold eminence with nave with S aisle, chancel, S porch and W tower.
Periods: The N doorway and one N window in the chancel are of Norman date but most of the church is 14c and 15c. The S arcade and aisle are 16c.
Features: Hammerbeam roof to nave; 13c piscina in chancel; 15c font; early 20c stained glass in E window; rood-beam above chancel arch; lower part of painted rood-screen at W end of nave with possibly early 15c figures; 17c pulpit; fine carved 15c bench-ends; Elizabethan cup, almsdish 1808.

HADLEIGH

Dedication: St. Mary.
Description: The church, fifth largest in Suffolk, is 163 ft long and 73 ft wide, with aisled and clerestoried nave, a clerestoried chancel flanked by chapels, and a tower, crowned by a lead spire, 135 ft high. The S porch was once vaulted with a room above.
Periods: Externally mostly Perp except the 14c tower which is Early English in its lower stages. The church was restored in 1859 and again in 1871.

Features: Bell-cote on eastern side of spire contains the former 13c sanctus bell on which clock strikes - believed to be the most ancient bell in Suffolk; fine roofs of nave and chancel; late 14c octagonal font with remarkable 16 ft high cover of 1925 dedicated to John Overall; restored sedilia; three old chests, one 13c and another of 1659; elaborate 14c recess in S aisle; Easter Sepulchre recess N of sanctuary; Perp screens to N and S chapels; a bench-end in S chapel with carving depicting the finding of St Edmund's head by a wolf; organ, brought from Donyland Hall, Essex, c1738; cup and two flagons 1745, patens of 1685, 1730 and 1792; memorials include one to Thomas Spencer 1571 in N chapel, a much mutilated Purbeck marble tomb in N aisle said to contain Archdeacon Pykenham c1480, and a 14c tomb in the S aisle which is said to stand near the place where the Danish king Guthrum was buried in 889; among the brasses, one to Richard Glanville and his wife 1637 on floor of N aisle and to the Alabaster family dated 1593 and 1637.in the S aisle. On the chapel wall is a brass dedicated to Dr Rowland Taylor, the Protestant martyr burned on Aldham Common in 1555, and in the window opposite is a group of scenes illustrating his life - walking with a friend, preaching to his congregation, and standing bravely at the stake.

HALESWORTH

Dedication: St. Mary.
Description: Victorian additions have greatly increased the size of this church which now has double aisles on either side of the nave, a chancel with side chapels, N and S porch and a lofty W tower.
Periods: There is possible evidence of Saxon origins in long-and-short work on a corner of the chancel, and in the foundations of the round tower which preceeded the present tower, completed c1430. Evidence of the present church's immediate predecessor remains too in the 14c nave pillars and the two arches opening into chancel from the side chapels. What remains today is mostly of 15c date, with the outer N aisle and N chapel added in 1863, outer S aisle and S porch added in 1868, and the chancel arch rebuilt in 1889.
Features: Carved stones below the chancel piscina of c1050?, and fragments of an Anglo-Saxon frieze below chancel chapel; 15c octagonal font; piscinas in chancel chapels; vestry door with inscription above c1506; two cups, paten 1567, paten 1714, flagon and almsdishes 1822; brasses to John Everard 1476 and John Browne c1580 - both brasses found in river Waveney in 1825; Wedgwood medallion portrait of Sir William Hooker and his son Sir Joseph, the eminent botanists and first directors of Kew Gardens; fine painted wooden tablet of Richard Assheton 1622, and mural monument to Henry Bedingfield, Chief Justice of Common Pleas 1687.

HARGRAVE

Location: 6 miles SW of Bury St Edmunds.
Dedication: St. Edmund.
Description: Standing with the Hall away from the village. Nave, with simple N aisle, chancel and buttressed brick W tower. A bomb which exploded nearby, destroyed the 14c S porch during World War II.
Periods: The nave S door is Norman, the chancel windows early 13c and the

tower Tudor; the remainder is 19c including the N aisle of 1869.
Features: 15c font; 13c sedilia and piscina in chancel; 15c rood-screen with rood-beam above; cup 1663.

HARKSTEAD

Location: 7 miles SE of Ipswich.
Dedication: St. Mary.
Description: Built in flint and septaria and beautifully situated above the Stour estuary. Nave, S aisle, much restored chancel, and W tower.
Periods: Norman windows and blocked Norman doorway on N side of nave. Mid-14c S arcade and W tower. The chancel was restored in 1867 and the nave in 1875.
Features: 15c font; two piscinas, a sedilia and a credence shelf; fine 14c recess in N wall of chancel, probably for Easter Sepulchre; splendid tall three-light window in tower; wall painting of 13c figure in jamb of Norman window; reredos of tiles and mosaic by Powell's 1875; cup 1731.

Dedication: St Lawrence.
Description: There were apparently two churches in Harkstead at Domesday (1086), one of which may have been the chapel mentioned in 1540 and dedicated to St. Clement. Its site is still known, an enclosure known as Chapeldown some 800 metres from the bank of the river Orwell, though it has long been cultivated. Another field here is called 'Myrtle bones' perhaps a deviation of 'mortal bones' (Scarfe), possibly the site of a graveyard.

HARLESTON

Location: 3 miles NW of Stowmarket.
Dedication: St. Augustine.
Description: Little isolated single-celled building with nave and chancel under one thatched roof, and small Victorian bell turret. The chancel has been created by partitioning off the eastern part of the church with a screen which does not fit and appears to have come from elsewhere.
Periods: The dedication to Augustine is pre-Norman and there are Norman survivals in the plain S doorway, fragments of the N doorway, and in the nave itself. A 13C lancet window remains in the nave and there is another in the chancel. The modern W front and bell-turret are of 1860.
Features: Piscina and windowsill sedilia in chancel; 14c screen; cup 1754.

HARTEST

Location: 8 miles NW of Sudbury.
Dedication: All Saints.
Description: Picturesquely situated, the church comprises an aisled nave, chancel with chapels, N and S porch and W tower.
Periods: 13c chancel with two large lancets in E wall. The nave arcades are 14c, as is the tower which was restored in 1879, whilst the aisles are Perp; both porches have been rebuilt.
Features: Good roof to N porch which has three modern niches over the entrance and incorporates the original church door; attractive decoration to aisle roofs; 14c canopied piscina in E pillar of N nave arcade; Jacobean pulpit; part of rood-screen incorporated in front bench of nave; Elizabethan cup,

paten 1710; tablet memorial to Rev. William Butt 1707 and his wife 1711, whose son was Dr Robert Butts successively Bishop of Norwich and Ely, and a monument to Lt. Harrington, R.N., 1812 by Henry Westmacott. The Register dates from 1556.

HASKETON
Dedication: 1 mile NW of Woodbridge.
Dedication: St. Andrew.
Description: Nave, chancel, S porch and round tower with octagonal top.
Periods: The round tower is Norman, the octagonal top added c1300. The nave is also Norman, with remains of a S window which is thought to be of pre-Conquest date re-used by the Normans (holes drilled in the window and still retaining pieces of wood were possibly for a wooden framework used in the construction of the inner splay - a method employed in Saxon times). The nave, along with the chancel, was remodelled in the early 14c.
Features: Early 16c octagonal font; niche on N side of chancel with good ogee canopy, possibly Easter Sepulchre; fragments of 15c heraldic glass in chancel window, possibly the arms of Sir William Brewse and stained glass in S window of 1858; Elizabethan cup; paten 1578; 17c memorials include one to William Goodwyn.

HAUGHLEY
Location: 3 miles NW of Stowmarket.
Dedication: St. Mary.
Description: A large church, 110' long and 50' wide, comprising nave with clerestory, chancel, S aisle and S tower, the base of which forms a porch.
Periods: Present church is all of one period c1330-4; it was restored 1880.
Features: Beautiful nave roof; late 13c S doorway; simple sanctus bell-cote; 15c font; arms of Hailes Abbey in glass of W window (the church was given to the famous Gloucestershire abbey); excellent hatchments in nave; piscina and sedilia in S aisle; Elizabethan cup, set of 1758; 33 leather fire buckets of 1725 and 1757 hang in porch.

HAVERHILL
Dedication: St. Mary.
Description: Nave with aisles and clerestory, chancel with S chapel and W tower with stair-turret rising above tower.
Periods: The church suffered serious damage in the fire of 1665 when nearly every old house in the centre of town was burned. It has received major 19c restoration and remains a handsome building. It mostly dates from the 15c but the lower section of the tower is 14c and there is a blocked 13c lancet in the N wall of the chancel; the arcades were rebuilt in 1867.
Features: Two interesting hatchments on E wall of tower; 16c chest; cup and paten 1659; early 17c monument to John Ward on N wall of chancel.

HAWKEDON
Location: 6 miles NE of Clare.
Dedication: St. Mary.
Description: The church stands in an enclosure in the middle of the green.

It has a nave, chancel, S porch and W tower.
Periods: The church is mainly 15c.
Features: Fine roof of carved beams; canopied external stoup; old disfigured Norman font; old stained glass in E window above which is painting of the Transfiguration; lower part of rood-screen with traces of figure painting; 17c three-decker pulpit; modern singers' gallery at W end of nave; set of carved benches; Communion rail; the Royal Arms of George II dated 1750 but adapted from an earlier one to Charles II; cup and cover undated, silver-gilt flagon 1659; brass to a family of c1510; wall-monument to Richard 1670 and Dorothy Everard 1678.

HAWSTEAD

Location: 4 miles SW of Bury St Edmunds.
Dedication: All Saints.
Description: One of the most interesting in west Suffolk with nave, chancel, S porch and W tower with higher stair turret. The tower and porch have fine flintwork and the outside walls have a freestone 'skirt' projection for about 2' above the ground all the way round in the form of a buttress.
Periods: All four major periods of medieval architecture are represented here. The N and S doorways are Norman; the chancel has 13c windows (some blocked), the nave was rebuilt in the 15c, and the W tower in the 16c. In 1780 the thatched roof was replaced with tiles. The church was restored in 1858.
Features: Early 16c hammerbeam roof to nave, restored in 1858 and an attractive chancel roof; the sills of the nave windows form seats; 13c font; much old glass, some foreign, in a window on N side and memorial glass of 1856 in E window to Sir Gery Cullum; late 15c wooden lectern; early 16c pulpit; carved benches, stalls and family pew; late 15c rood-screen, on the top rail of which is fixed the sanctus bell - a very rare survival; communion rail in tower arch; one of the largest collections of monuments in any Suffolk church from 13c to 20c include: Eustace FitzEustace as a cross-legged Knight of c1270 lying on 14c tomb-chest, Sir William Drury, Knight, killed in a duel in France 1589, on N side of chancel a black and white marble monument to Sir Robert Drury 1615 and his beautiful 15 year old daughter Elizabeth 1610, with the moving epitaph 'Her pure and eloquent blood, Spoke in her cheeks and so distinctly wrought, That one might almost say her body thought', and on the S side a large coloured plaster monument to Sir Thomas Cullum 1664; in SE corner of the nave are brasses to Sir William Drury 1578, Lord Chief Justice of Ireland, in armour with his helmet, two wives and their thirteen daughters, in the chancel floor a brass to Ursula, fourth daughter of Sir Robert Drury c1525, another brass on the S wall of the nave shows effigies of a boy c1500 and a girl c1530, a group of late 18c to early 19c tablets include Lucy Metcalfe 1793, Viscountess Carleton 1810, Christopher Metcalfe 1794, C.B.Metcalfe 1801, Philip Metcalfe 1818 and Frances Jane Metcalfe 1830. The Register dates from 1558.

HAZELWOOD (nr. Aldeburgh)

Location: 2 miles NW of Aldeburgh
Description: The church became ruinous several centuries ago when the parish, now a hamlet, was eclesiastically united with Aldeburgh. It was said that the inhabitants used to marry and bury here as early as the reign of King John. Slight traces still remain.

HELMINGHAM

Location: 9 miles N of Ipswich.
Dedication: St. Mary.
Description: The church stands within the park of Helmingham Hall and comprises a nave, chancel, S porch, and a W tower with good flintwork decoration.
Periods: Late 13c-early 14c S doorway, 14c chancel and early 15c nave. The tower and S porch were built in 1543, and the nave roof dates from the turn of the 17c. The church was restored in 1954.
Features: S door with tracery; 15c octagonal font; carved benches; Elizabethan cup and cover, paten and flagon 1714; monuments of the Tollemache family, the largest against the S wall of the nave is of 1615 and moved here from Bentley, their original ancestral home. It records Lionel Tollemache, who died in 1552, his son and grandsons dated 1553, 1575 and 1605 with a long accompanying inscription; others are to Sir D Lionel Tollemache 1640 on N wall of nave, Lt. Gen Thomas Tollemache 1694, Sir Lionel Tollemache 1729, Countess of Dysart 1804, Lionel R. Tollemache 1810, Mrs Tollemache 1846, Vice-Admiral J.R.Delap Tollemache 1837 and Lord Tollemache 1890.

HEMINGSTONE

Location: 5 miles N of Ipswich.
Dedication: St. Gregory.
Description: Ancient church with nave and chancel in one, brick N porch and W tower. A detached building on the N, close to the chancel now used as a vestry, was known as 'Ralph's Hole'. Tradition suggests it was built by Ralph Cantrell, a Roman Catholic, who vowed he would never enter a reformed church, but whose property was liable to confiscation unless he attended the service. He was thus able to observe the strict letter of the law without violating his conscience.
Periods: There is evidence of Anglo-Saxon long and short work at the SW angle of the nave, the remainder being mostly 14c except for the early 16c porch.
Features: 14c iron-bound tower-door in NW corner of nave; magnificent 14c octagonal font with 15c cover; some old glass; lower part of 16c rood-screen with rood-beam above; vestry houses Royal Arms of William and Mary; set of plate 1759; monument to William Cantrell 1585 and other memorials of the Martin family.

HEMLEY

Location: 5 miles S of Woodbridge.
Dedication: All Saints.
Description: Remote and by the Deben, it has a rebuilt nave and chancel, and a red-brick W tower.
Periods: Although it retains its 15c brick tower, the bulk of the church was drastically restored and virtually rebuilt in 1889. The blocked N doorway appears to date from c1300.
Features: Fine square Norman font; reredos c1840-50 with Commandments, Lord's Prayer and Creed; Royal Arms of George III.

HENGRAVE

Location: 4 miles W of Bury St Edmunds.

Dedication: St John Lateran.

Description: A small church standing in the grounds of Hengrave Hall. It consists of a nave with N aisle and clerestory, chancel with N chapel, round tower and S porch. Ceased to be used for parochial purposes about the middle of the 16c and later appropriated as a private chapel for the hall. From 1589 to 1900 it was used as a mausoleum, afterwhich it was again used for services.

Periods: The tower is probably pre-Conquest and the chancel of c1300. The rest was largely re-built by Thomas Hengrave, who died in 1419, with a N chapel added in 1540.

Features: Very fine arcade to N aisle; stoup in S porch; traces of wall paintings. The chancel and chapel house contain a fine series of monuments to the Kytson family from Hengrave Hall. Sir Thomas Kytson lies with his two wives in the chancel, and his father, Sir Thomas, builder of the hall, lies in the N chapel, his magnificent tomb shows his wife, Margaret, Countess of Bath 1561, lying with her third husband John Bourchier, Earl of Bath, 1560; others show Sir Thomas Kytson the Younger (her second husband) 1552, John Bourchier, Lord Fitzwarren 1556, Sir Thomas Kytson 1608, Thomas Darcy 1614, Sir Edmund Gage 1707, and Sir Thomas Gage 1742.

HENLEY

Location: 4 miles N of Ipswich.

Dedication: St Peter.

Periods: Nave, chancel and W tower.

Description: Restored and mainly 14c and 15c. The earliest parts are the re-designed Norman S doorway and the chancel of c1300. The W tower was built by Thomas Seckford who died in 1505.

Features: Terra-cotta S nave window removed from old Shrubland Hall; piscina and sedilia in chancel; many interesting hatchments; two pre-Reformation bells c1480; lectern possibly 13c; Elizabethan cover, cup, plate and flagon 1728.

HENSTEAD

Location: 5 miles SE of Beccles.

Dedication: St Mary.

Description: The church has a nave and chancel in one under a decorative thatched roof. The S porch has ornate flintwork, and there is a brick W tower.

Periods: Norman with impressive S doorway of the period. The N wall shows interesting contemporary walling. A fire in 1641 severely damaged the chancel which was rebuilt and probably shortened (see the rood-loft stairs). The S porch and tower were built in c1470. The 1906 restoration removed the box pews and a three-decker pulpit.

Features: Stoup in S porch; banner-stave cupboard in SW corner of nave; cup and cover 1568, salver 1750; monuments to George Mitchell, and to a William Clarke who lost his life in a naval battle with Napoleon's ships a year before Trafalgar, both are dated 1806.

HEPWORTH

Location: 5 miles NE of Ixworth.
Dedication: St Peter.
Description: Rebuilt, after fire of 1898 completely destroyed the former thatched roof church. Nave, chancel, S porch and W tower.
Periods: The careful rebuild along former lines has retained some relics rescued from the previous church. The tower arch suggests that the lower part of the tower may be early 13c. Nave and chancel incorporate some 14c windows fragments from an earlier Norman church are in the porch.
Features: Small exposed bell-cote on W side of low tower spire; traceried low side-window in chancel; modern double hammerbeam roof over nave; rood-loft stairs; fine, unusual and unrestored late 14c font cover, 12'6" high; some bench-ends; Elizabethan cup, paten 1817.

HERRINGFLEET

Location: 6 miles NW of Lowestoft.
Dedication: St Margaret.
Description: Situated on the N bank of the river Waveney, the ancient thatched church comprises a nave, chancel, porch and retains its original round tower.
Periods: The tower, with its original windows reminiscent of Saxon work, is Norman as is the tower arch towards the nave, the S doorway and a window in the chancel on the N side. The chancel is 14c and 15c with a modern E window. Much window stonework was incorporated in the church after being removed from the ruined arches of nearby St Olave's Priory.
Features: 13c arched tomb-recess in N wall; piscina in chancel; stained glass incorporated in modern E window comprising 15c figures is said to have come from the Franciscan friary at Cologne at the time of the Revolution; upper part of rood-screen now forming front of W gallery; cup 1637, paten 1703; monument to J. Leathes 1787.

HERRINGSWELL

Location: 6 miles NE of Newmarket.
Dedication: St Ethelbert.
Description: The old church which only shares its rare dedication to St Ethelbert, King of East Anglia, with Falkenham and Hessett, was almost entirely destroyed by fire in 1869. It consisted of a nave, chancel, S transept, S porch, N vestry and W tower. The new church was built immmediately after the fire, the tower designed with ungainly buttressing.
Periods: The sparse remains of the former church which include the responds at the E end of the nave indicate a Norman date (Pevsner). The new church was built to the designs of Blomfield in Dec style.
Features: Nothing appears to have been saved from the old church and the only point of interest is the E window with 20c stained glass.

HESSETT

Location: 5 miles SE of Bury St Edmunds.
Dedication: St Ethelbert.
Description: Lovely ornate church with fine embattled and pinnacled tower,

nave with N and S aisles, clerestory, chancel, two-storey vestry, S porch and W tower. The S aisle originally had a chapel of Our Lady.
Periods: The church was originally built by the Bacons, who resided here from the reign of Henry II to that of Charles I, and is all Perp except for the 14c chancel. The N aisle was added, the vestry heightened and the whole attractively battlemented by John Hoo, who died in 1492; an inscription to him and Katherine, his wife, runs along the vestry and part of the N aisle.
Features: Font of c1500 with inscription to Robert and Agnes Hoo; small squint in chancel N wall piercing the back of a piscina in the vestry; wall paintings of St Barbara, on S wall E of SE window, St Christopher, over S door, and on the N wall, the Seven Deadly Sins and 'Christ of the Trades'; beautiful old stained glass in aisle windows; 15c repainted screen in chancel; complete set of carved benches in nave; old iron-bound chest; very rare c1400 'Sindon' or Pyx cloth of linen lace, and the Burse or Corporas case - the cloth on which the wafer lies during Mass; these are thought to be the only specimens of their particular types of church needlework in existence, they are now on permanent loan to the British Museum; monument to Lionel and Anna Bacon, 1633. The Register dates from 1538.

HEVENINGHAM

Location: 5 miles SW of Halesworth.
Dedication: St Margaret.
Description: Handsome church on high ground above river Blyth, comprising nave with S aisle and brick clerestory, chancel and W tower with brick battlements.
Periods: The nave and chancel are early 14c and the tower built c1400. The clerestory is early 16c and the church considerably restored 1857 and 1869.
Features: Early 16c double hammerbeam nave roof; 15c font; angle-piscina in chancel; niche in E respond of S arcade has remains of colour; modern stained glass in E and W windows; 17c manorial pew incorporates earlier screenwork; Royal Arms of George III; Elizabethan cup and cover; mutilated wooden effigy of a Knight, c1400, probably one of the Hevenigham family.

HIGHAM nr. East Bergholt

Location: 5 miles S of Hadleigh.
Dedication: St Mary.
Description: Attractively situated in the Dedham Vale near the confluence of the Brett and the Stour. The church comprises a nave with beautiful arcaded N aisle, chancel, porch and heavy, plain W tower.
Periods: The church has been much restored but the tower retains its small upper windows of c13 date and the tower arch may well be c1300. The rest is early Perp.
Features: Interesting ironwork on N door with escutcheons; damaged 15c octagonal font; curious tracery on W window; monument to Robert Hay who died in 1811. The Register dates from 1538.

HIGHAM nr. Bury

Location: 7 miles W of Bury St Edmunds.
Dedication: St Stephen.
Description: Higham was formed in 1861 from part of Gazeley, at which

time it was known as Higham Green. The hamlet became a parish in its own right in 1894. The church has a nave, chancel and round tower with an attractive arcaded belfry and conical spire, built in 13c Early English style to the designs of Sir Gilbert Scott, R.A.
Periods: The church dates from 1861.
Features: Cup 'bought in Florence, partly c15' (Pevsner).

HINDERCLAY

Location: 8 miles NE of Ixworth.
Dedication: St Mary.
Description: Nave with S aisle, chancel, porch and W tower with tall belfry. The church was thatched until 1842.
Periods: The earliest remains are the simple 12c N doorway and the early c13 S arcade. The chancel is 14c and the nave, S aisle and tower 15c.
Features: Unusually low 13c piers and arches separating nave from S aisle; piscina and window-sill sedilia in chancel; low side-window in chancel with remains of shutter hinges; 15c font; rood-beam; 17c bench-ends; box-pews in S aisle; Royal Arms of George III; cup c1680; bell-ringers' pitcher dated 1724; monument to George Thompson 1711. Local antiquary Edmund Farrer, who did much invaluable research on Suffolk houses, was rector here in the early part of the 20c. The Register dates from 1700.

HINTLESHAM

Location: 5 miles W of Ipswich.
Dedication: St Nicholas.
Description: Nave, S aisle, clerestory, chancel, W tower and timber porch.
Periods: The S aisle arcades are Early English, the aisle and chancel 14c and the tower, clerestory and porch 15c. The church was restored in 1849.
Features: Stone corbels either side of the junction of nave and chancel originally supported the rood-beam; three piscinas; fragment of a painting of St Christopher, in the nave opposite the S door; 15c panelling against the E wall may originally have been the rood-loft parapet (Cautley); 17c communion rail; tomb of blue marble of John Tympley and Margaret his wife, the former died in 1400, also a monument on the S wall of chancel to the builder of Hintlesham Hall, Thomas Tympley and his wife 1593, and one on the N wall to Capt. John Timperley 1629.

HITCHAM

Location: 7 miles NW of Hadleigh.
Dedication: All Saints.
Description: A fine large church situated at the S end of the village. It has a nave with clerestory and aisles, chancel with two-storeyed vestry, S porch with good flint panelling, and a W tower with stair turret.
Periods: Mostly 14c Dec although the chancel was virtually rebuilt in 1878. The S porch and W tower are 15c.
Features: W door with niches either side and finely carved S door of nave; fine double hammerbeam roof to nave; small canopied piscina in chancel; circular clerestory N windows; lower part of rood-screen c1500 with eight painted figures of the saints; two flagons 1637, cup and plate 1639, paten 1731; mural tablets to Sir George Waldergrave 1637 and to Prof. John

Stevens Henslow, the distinguished botanist, 1796-1861, one time companion and mentor to Charles Darwin. The Register dates from 1575.

HOLBROOK

Location: 6 miles S of Ipswich.
Dedication: All Saints.
Description: Aisled nave, chancel and S tower, the base of which forms a porch. The tower has a large battlemented stair-turret on the NW angle.
Periods: The tower is early to mid 14c, and the rest 14c and 15c, except the N aisle which was added in 1863 when the church was restored.
Features: Fine N door with shafted jambs and bold arch; 13c double piscina and double sedilia; a curious and macabre relic in the chancel is that of an embalmed head in a jar found during restoration work in 1863; brass to a Knight in armour c1480; table tomb to Judge John Clenche, first Recorder of Ipswich, Baron of the Exchequer and Justice of the Queen's Bench 1607, with Katherine his wife and fifteen children; consecration crosses in the form of stone disks built into the walls both inside and out.

HOLLESLEY

Location: 6 miles SW of Orford.
Dedication: All Saints.
Description: Nave, N aisle, chancel, S porch and lofty W tower decorated with flintwork on base, buttresses and battlements.
Periods: The 14c nave and chancel were restored in 1852 and again in 1886 when the N aisle was added, but the arcade which was left intact dates from early 13c. The tower was built c1450.
Features: Octagonal 15c font; Elizabethan pulpit; panels of rood-screen; old bench-ends with tracery and some modern carved bench-ends of traditional design considered to be the finest in Suffolk; Royal Arms of Charles II; paten 1718; 14c incised slab from the tomb of William de Geyton, prior of Butley Abbey.

HOLTON nr. Halesworth

Location: 1 mile E of Halesworth.
Dedication: St Peter.
Description: Small church comprises a nave, chancel, unusually tall round W tower (which despite being heightened still clearly shows the original bell-stage), and added N aisle and N chapel.
Periods: The round tower is Norman as is the S doorway. The N aisle and chapel were added in 1856, the former enlarged in 1870.
Features: Fine roofs of nave and chancel; octagonal 14c font; modern stained glass E window by Kempe, c1899; early 16c pulpit; Royal Arms of George III, dated 1815; paten 166, cup 1722.

HOLTON ST MARY nr. Hadleigh

Location: 4 miles SE of Hadleigh.
Dedication: St Mary.
Description: The flint and stone church has a massive yet incomplete W tower with brick parapet replacing its lost belfry, a nave and chancel.

Periods: Nave is 14c and the chancel a century older, though rebuilt c1863.
Features: Octagonal 15c font on 13c base; piscina in nave and another 13c piscina and aumbrey in chancel; recess in N wall of chancel possibly for Easter Sepulchre; some old stained glass in nave windows; Royal Arms of George II; two medieval bells in tower.

HOMERSFIELD

Location: 5 miles SW of Bungay.
Dedication: St Mary.
Description: Small flint church standing on a platform above the Waveney with nave, chancel and unbuttressed W tower with bell-openings.
Periods: The church was over-restored in 1866, but a window in the S wall of the nave shows its Norman origins.
Features: 12c font; 13c double piscina in chancel; 14c gable cross to nave; Elizabethan cup inscribed 'Humersfylde', paten 1567.

HONINGTON

Location: 3 miles NW of Ixworth.
Dedication: All Saints.
Description: Nave, chancel, S porch with flintwork panelling and W tower with brick stair turret.
Periods: The S doorway is Norman as is the chancel arch. The chancel and S side of the nave appear early 14c but the N side received some 15c remodelling when the S porch was added; the tower is also of this date with a Tudor stair turret on the S side. The church was restored in 1863.
Features: Fine 14c octagonal font; exquisite piscina; very faint wall paintings on the S wall of nave feature Martyrdom of St Thomas Becket and Legend of St Nicholas; carved bench-ends; Elizabethan cup, flagon 1735; brass of George Duke 1594, and another to Anne Curteis 1585; monument to Robert Rushbrooke who died in 1753 and an inscription in the nave remembers the famous local poet Robert Bloomfield.

HOO

Location: 4 miles SW of Framlingham.
Dedication: St Andrew & St Eustachius.
Description: On S bank of the Deben near Kettleburgh. Small rustic brick church with nave and chancel in one, and W tower.
Periods: The church with its rare dedication dates back to Domesday though nothing remains today from those ancient times. Some windows are 14c windows and the tower, Tudor.
Features: Early damaged octagonal font; old iron-bound chest; 17c Communion rail; cup early 17c, paten 1787. The Register dates from 1588.

HOPTON nr. Market Weston

Location: 7 miles NE of Ixworth.
Dedication: All Saints.
Description: Nave with N and S aisles and brick clerestory, chancel, S porch and a flint decorated W tower with attractive 18c top and arched bell-openings; the church previously had a spire which was blown down and its

remains built into the churchyard wall.

Periods: The chancel is c1300, the S aisle late 13c, the N aisle 15c and the clerestory Tudor. The lower part of the tower, including the arch to the nave, is Early English, but the belfry has been rebuilt. The S porch is 14c.

Features: Colourful hammerbeam roof to nave, the eastern bay formed a Canopy of Honour over the rood; iron-bound door to tower stair; niche in E respond of S arcade; interesting two-light window of c1300 in W wall of the S aisle, modern stained glass E window by Kempe 1905, plus old glass in other windows; rood-beam, cut off flush with the walls; massive iron-bound chest; Elizabethan cup; marble monument to Thomas Raymond 1680, "first sole keeper of the Papers of State to Charles II". The Register dates from 1634.

HOPTON nr. Lowestoft

Location: 5 miles N of Lowestoft.
Dedication: Old St Margaret.
Description: The old church which had a thatched roof was destroyed by fire in February 1865 and is now in ruins. The W tower and exterior walls remain, the gables of the nave and chancel retaining windows.
Periods: The body of the church is 14c and the tower 15c.

Dedication: St Margaret.
Description: The new church was built in flint and stone about a quarter of a mile from the old in an unusual cruciform style. It comprises an aisleless nave, chancel, S porch and massive low central crossing tower which has a low SE stair-turret with a conical roof. The tower is square in its lower stage with an octagonal belfry above.
Periods: 1866 by S. S Teulon.
Features: Beautiful stained glass in chancel of 1881 by William Morris and Sir Edward Burne-Jones; Gothic style organ case; set of plate 1864. The Register from the old church dates from 1675.

HORHAM

Location: 5 miles SE of Eye.
Dedication: St Mary.
Description: This small church has a nave, chancel and an impressive W tower featuring fine flintwork panelling on buttresses and battlements.
Periods: Norman N and S doorways and late 15c tower. The nave has 14c windows but those in the chancel were re-used when it was rebuilt in 1881.
Features: Consecration crosses on W wall of nave; 15c font; 14c piscina in chancel; old 13c and 14c glass on the S side of chancel includes arms of Edward III and the Black Prince; wall painting of Christ carrying the Cross; double-decker pulpit of 1631; set of old bench-ends; old iron-bound chest; Elizabethan cup and cover. The Register dates from 1594.

HORRINGER (formerly Horningsheath)

Location: 2 miles SW of Bury St Edmunds.
Dedication: St Leonard.
Description: Horringer church comprises a nave with N aisle, chancel, W tower with brick top, chapel and decorated S porch.

Periods: A window in the chancel is 14c but the main body of the church and its tower are Perp, with a belfry stage added in 1703. The porch was built in 1464 and the N aisle in 1845. A new chancel was built in 1867 and the interior of the church 'improved' in 1883.
Features: 14c font with modern painted shields; the N chapel has an unusual 15c window and there is striking stained glass in the four-light E window of 1946 by J. E. Nuttgens to commemorate the two world wars; cup 1567-8, flagon 1664, paten and almsdish 1699. The Register dates from 1558.

Horningsheath, or Horringer as it is now more commonly known, was formerly in two parishes. These were consolidated in 1548 after the church of Little Horningsheath had been demolished. It stood near Little Horningsheath Hall, but there are now no remains.

HOXNE

Location: 4 miles NE of Eye.
Dedication: St Peter and St Paul.
Description: A fine spacious church with nave, N aisle, clerestory, chancel, N chapel, S porch and a handsome, W tower 100' tall with pinnacles and a stair-turret,
Periods: Although the church is almost entirely Perp, it is thought that the nave arcade of six low arches rests on pillars which date to the 13c. The N chapel was added in 1740 and the chancel rebuilt in 1853 retaining its fine, original four-light E window. The tower was restored in 1847 and the church renovated 1869.
Features: Fine nave roof with remains of painting; 15c octagonal heraldic font; old altar-stone with consecration crosses; medieval wall paintings of St Christopher, the Seven Deadly Sins, the Seven Works of Mercy and the Last Judgement; some old carved bench-ends; 14c iron-bound chest; modern screen depicting the Martyrdom of St Edmund; set of plate 1790; three brasses to the Thurston family dated 1606, 1613, and 1640; monument to Thomas Maynard 1742, and some memorials to the Kerrison family.

HUNDON

Location: 3 miles NW of Clare.
Dedication: All Saints.
Description: A rebuilt church comprising a wide nave with soaring tower arch, S aisle, fine decorative clerestory of open lace stonework, chancel, W tower with higher SW stair-turret, S chapel and a S porch with flintwork panelling.
Periods: The original church was burned down in 1914 and rebuilt. The tower and clerestory survive from the original 14c building.
Features: Fine surviving pierced parapet of the S clerestory; Panelling in S chapel, preserved from the fire at the vicarage; copy of a Titian painting; Royal Arms of George III; cup and paten 1749; uninspiring monument by the S porch to Arethusa, wife of James Vernon and daughter of Lord Clifford, who died in 1728. In 1687, more than 200 Saxon coins were discovered by the sexton, while digging a grave in the churchyard.

HUNSTON

Location: 3 miles SE of Ixworth.
Dedication: St Michael.
Description: A small ancient church comprising a nave, chancel and W tower of knapped flint, plus a remarkable S transept.
Periods: Built into the base of the wall at the NE corner is the decorative head of a small Norman window - the earliest survival. The transept is of late 13c date as is the chancel with a number of Early English windows and doorways. The tower was built in 1472.
Features: Hammerbeam roof to nave; lovely elaborate niche in E wall; priest's door in chancel; Norman font; beautiful double piscina; half a circular window in S wall of chancel; some old carved bench-ends; 17c chest and pulpit canopy; Elizabethan cup and cover; cup, cover and flagon 1754; monuments to the Heigham family.

HUNTINGFIELD

Location: 4 miles SW of Halesworth.
Dedication: St Mary.
Description: Aisled nave with clerestory, chancel, S porch and W tower. There is much flintwork decoration on aisle parapets, tower and porch. At the E end of the N aisle is a mortuary chapel to the Huntingfield family, now used as a vestry.
Periods: A carved stone in the belfry wall has Saxon plaited decoration. The massive pillars of the N arcade of the nave represents the Norman N wall where an original window can be seen; the N aisle pierced through this wall in the late 12c. The S aisle was added in the 14c but has been largely rebuilt. The S porch and tower are Perp. The church was restored in 1860.
Features: Roofs of nave and chancel brightly painted by Mrs Holland, wife of a former rector, during the period 1859-66; 15c octagonal font with tall Gothic canopy made in memory of Mrs Holland who died in 1879; some old glass; 15c painting of Christ and the Angels; credence 1729, flagon 1753, cup and paten 1815; brass in N aisle to Elizabeth Coke 1586; forming part of an Easter Sepulchre on the N side of the sanctuary is a tomb-chest monument to John Paston 1575 with a brass inscription of twenty quaint verses, and at the E end of the N aisle is the Mortuary Chapel belonging to Lord Huntingfield, in the vault beneath which lie interred many members of this ancient noble family. The Register dates from 1565 but is incomplete.

ICKLINGHAM

Location: 4 miles SE of Mildenhall.
Dedication: All Saints.
Description: Icklingham comprises the two adjoining villages of All Saints and St James each with their church but now united under one parish. Although reduced to a minor role, All Saints is the more interesting of the two. It is a large unrestored thatched church with a SW tower, nave with wide S aisle, lofty chancel and porch.
Periods: The church is mainly late 13c and early 14c, although there are two blocked N windows in the nave wall of Norman date, and the porch is a 15c addition.
Features: 14c font; trefoiled piscina and low windowsill sedilia in chancel;

large stone coffin with carved cover; superb window tracery and some original stained glass; traces of wall painting 1730 on N aisle wall; lower part of 15c rood-screen; Jacobean pulpit; 17c family pew; old seating in nave and aisle; old reed hassocks; late 17c communion rail; early 14c chest with iron scrollwork - 'one of the most beautiful in England'; 14c tiles in chancel; Elizabethan cup, paten 1703.

Dedication: St James.
Description: The main parish church consisting of an aisled nave, chancel, N porch and rebuilt W tower.
Periods: The chancel is c1300 and the rest Perp with re-used Dec windows. The church was completely restored in 1866.
Features: Simple octagonal font; 13c piscina and windowsill sedilia in chancel; modern seats in chancel which incorporate parts of the former rood-screen; Elizabethan cup and paten; unusual memorial to Rev. Talbot dated 1689 and 1704.

ICKWORTH

Location: 4 miles SW of Bury St Edmunds.
Dedication: St Mary.
Description: Isolated in the Park of Ickworth Hall. Aisled nave and chancel under one roof with stuccoed W tower and porch.
Periods: There is the head of a Norman window in the porch. The knapped flint chancel is late 13c and the N aisle early 14c. The S aisle was added and the tower rebuilt in 1833.
Features: S aisle is raised above the nave to incorporate the burial vaults of the Hervey family; traces of chapel on N side of chancel of which a squint remains; double piscina in jamb of 14c window on N of nave; roundels of old Flemish stained glass; early 14c wall painting S of the E window probably the angel of the Annunciation; 18c Royal Arms embroidered in silk; flagon 1697, almsdish 1758, French paten c18, cup 1810; there are a number of sepulchral inscriptions to the Herveys including a stone to Mary Lepel, wife of Lord John Hervey bearing a charming epitaph written by Horace Walpole.

IKEN

Location: 3 miles W of Aldeburgh.
Dedication: St Botolph.
Description: The church stands in a lonely position overlooking the river Alde. It may well be the site where St Botolph established his monastery in the 7c. Fire destroyed the 13c thatched nave in 1968.
Periods: The knapped flint W tower is mid-15c and the chancel, which had been in ruins for a long time, rebuilt 1853. The S porch is before 1529.
Features: Tower contains four medieval bells; 14c octagonal font; niche on S side of chancel arch marking the site of a former altar; cup 1763.

ILKETSHALL ST ANDREW

Location: 4 miles SE of Bungay.
Dedication: St Andrew.
Description: Standing on a commanding, elevated situation, the ancient church comprises a long building with leaning walls. It has a nave, chancel,

brick S porch and round W tower with octagonal belfry and flintwork panelled battlements.
Periods: The tower is Norman (with a belfry added in the 15c), as are the N and S doorways; there is also one Norman window in N wall of the nave. The chancel is early 14c, and the remainder Perp except for the Tudor brick porch.
Features: Interesting nave roof; simple octagonal font; fragments of rood-screen in the chamber over the porch; richly carved late 16c bench with inscription to John Bonsey (married 1577); Royal Arms of Charles II in wood; Elizabethan Cup 1558, patens 1686 (or earlier) and 1825; brass to John Verdon 1624; fine tomb in S wall of chancel.

ILKETSHALL ST JOHN

Location: 2 miles SE of Bungay.
Dedication: St John the Baptist.
Description: Again standing on a bold elevated site, this small church has an unbuttressed W tower and a nave and chancel in one.
Periods: The church is 14c but has a 13c lancet in N wall of chancel. All other windows have been renewed.
Features: Remains of Canopy of Honour(?) over rood; banner stave cupboard in recess in S pier of the tower arch; Royal Arms of William IV; Elizabethan cup, paten c1680-90.

ILKETSHALL ST LAWRENCE

Location: 3 miles SE of Bungay.
Dedication: St Lawrence.
Description: This small church, which stands on a raised platform in an enclosure of uncertain age, comprises nave, chancel and W tower.
Periods: Chiefly 14c but the walling on the N side is probably Norman.
Features: 15c font; plain Easter Sepulchre on N wall of chancel; Royal Arms of George II, dated 1760; Elizabethan Cup and Cover, paten 1705; brass inscription to Richard Beetes 1613.

ILKETSHALL ST MARGARET

Location: 3 miles SE of Bungay.
Dedication: St Margaret.
Description: Another small church comprising nave and chancel with a round tower.
Periods: The round tower is Norman with a 15c belfry, and the remainder of the church 13c.
Features: 15c font; wall paintings on N wall, one probably of St Christopher; late 17c communion rail; Royal Arms of Queen Anne 1704; cup and paten 1568, another 17c paten.

INGHAM

Location: 4 miles N of Bury St Edmunds.
Dedication: St Bartholomew.
Description: This modern church of flint and stone comprises a fine tower with light and lofty nave and chancel.
Periods: The church was completely rebuilt in Perp style in 1861 using some

of the old material.
Features: Carved spandrel in chancel roof has the pomegranate of
Catherine of Aragon; 13c square font; 15c stained glass in S porch includes
Eagle of St John and Crowned Eagle and Sceptre of Anne Boleyn.

IPSWICH

There were fourteen churches standing in the town at the time of the
Domesday survey. These were Holy Trinity, St Austins, St Michael, two
dedicated to St Mary, St Lawrence, two to St Peter, two to St Julian, St
George, St Aldred, St Stephen and one unnamed. At a later period the
town claimed twenty-one but this no doubt included those attached to
monastic institutions.
The town's major churches are:

Location: Tower Street.
Dedication: St Mary-le-Tower
Description: The principal parish church of Ipswich, whose churchyard
provided the meeting place of the burgesses over several centuries. It was
here they assembled to receive the town's charter from King John. It
derives its distinctive name from a fortified tower, long demolished, in the
town's old defensive wall nearby in a street originally called Tower Ditches.
Its large impressive tower with prominent spire, reaches a height of 176' and
is decorated with much knapped and chequered flintwork; the eight
buttresses reach almost to the parapet. It also has an aisled nave, chancel
and S porch.
Periods: The foundation of this church is probably the oldest in Ipswich but
nothing of any original Saxon or Norman structure remains. The arches on
the S side of the chancel date from c1350 and the nave arcades are c1520,
but today's church is mostly from an 1860-70 rebuild in Gothic style.
Features: The tower contains twelve bells, said to be the only ring of this
number in the county; early 15c octagonal font; stalls with simple
misericords; canopied pulpit 1710, said to have been carved by Grinling
Gibbons, or one of his pupils; Royal Arms of Charles II carved in wood; two
18c sword-rests; pre-Reformation chalice remade 1867; cup 1631, credence
1665, two flagons 1679; almsdish 1728; spoon c1739; rare brasses in
chancel floor to two notaries, one of c1475, and the other c1490, and other
brasses to Alys Baldry 1506 and two husbands, Thomas Drayle c1525 with
two wives, and brass inscriptions to Robert Sparrow 1594 and Robert
Clarke 1697 and his wife; painted pictorial panel in the S aisle with
inscription to William Smart, portman of the borough, 1599, includes a view
of Ipswich; monument to John Robinson 1666 and his wife 1694.

Location: St Clements Church Lane, off Grimwade Street.
Dedication: St Clements.
Description: Comprising a nave with spacious aisles and very large
clerestory, chancel and simple slender W tower of brick and flint.
Periods: The church is mainly 15c but over-restored, the tower is partly 14c.
The chancel was rebuilt in 1860 in Dec style.
Features: West gallery with Corinthian columns; interesting but damaged
15c octagonal font; 17c carved oak screen enclosing the vestry; Royal Arms
of Charles II dated 1661 in wood; set of plate 1683-4; brass to John Tye,

merchant and portman, 1583 with his large family, and another to William Cocke 1607; Thomas Eldred, who sailed round the world with Thomas Cavendish in 1588, is buried here, as is Sir Thomas Slade who designed Nelson's Victory. The Register dates from 1563.

Location: St Helens Street, on the E side of town.
Dedication: St Helen.
Description: Much enlarged church with modern chancel, transepts, and tower with octagonal belfry and spire.
Periods: Erected in the 15c and rebuilt 1835, with new transepts added in 1837. The S porch with canopied niche is from the earlier period as is the adjoining S wall and some of the windows. The old tower was removed and a new one erected in 1875.
Features: 17c and 18c monuments; two ancient bells on floor of nave. The Register dates from 1672.

Location: Dial Lane.
Dedication: St Lawrence.
Description: Situated in the centre of town and 124' long, this is the finest of the medieval churches that remain in Ipswich. The beautiful W tower, rising to a height of 97', has lovely flint panelling and an openwork stone parapet.
Periods: The aisleless nave and tower were rebuilt by John Bottold in 1431 and the chancel by John Baldwyn in 1449. The tower was partly rebuilt in 1882 to its original design after it became unsafe.
Features: 15c W door with tracery; stone screen separating nave and tower; stained glass E window in Early English style by Charles Gibbs c1855; paten 1733, flagon 1745, cup and paten 1775, almedish 1820; five inscribed medieval bells in the tower; brass to John Moor 1580, and another to Margery Drury 1618; monument to Mrs Coleman c1700. The Register dates from 1539.

Location: St Margarets Green.
Dedication: St Margaret.
Description: Standing near Christchurch Mansion, and possibly the most picturesque of the medieval churches despite air-raid damage during the last war. It is a large church comprising a spacious aisled nave with a clerestory of lovely traceried windows, small chancel, transepts, S porch and fine W tower.
Periods: The church is mainly 15c Perp, although the nave has five arches a century older.
Features: A visit from Dowsing's commissioners in 1643 removed 'the twelve Apostles in stone' and ordered that 20 or 30 pictures which decorated the walls should be taken away and destroyed. There is a splendid late 15c double hammerbeam roof, painted in the 17c, over the nave; a damaged 15c font; 13c sepulchre slab built into wall of S aisle; a panel painted with the Prince of Wales feathers and dated 1660 in the vestry; framed set of Royal Arms of Charles II; two Elizabethan cups, paten 1632, flagon 1719, salver 1751; tower has a clock on its S side of 1737; tomb of Sir William Roskyn 1512 beneath the S window of the S chapel; memorial slab on N transept wall to Edmund Withipoll, the builder of Christchurch Mansion, who died in 1574 and some hatchments of the Fonnereau family. The Register dates from 1537.

Location: Elm Street.
Dedication: St Mary at the Elms.
Description: The small church, with a massive brick W tower, is centrally located yet peacefully situated within its own small intimate churchyard. It has an aisled nave - the third bay of which represents the Norman N transept; the remains of the former S transept can still be seen outside. The building was lengthened, a new chancel built beyond the old one (which was subsequently incorporated in the nave), and a N chapel added.
Periods: Norman S doorway and 15c nave and N aisle. The tower is built of early Tudor brick and the N chapel and present chancel were built in 1883.
Features: S door with ornamented ironwork possibly contemporary with doorway; Royal Arms of Charles II; set of plate 1758; monument to William Acton, 1616, a portman of the borough.

Location: Foundation Street.
Dedication: St Mary at the Quay.
Description: Damaged in air raids during the last war and now deconsecrated and closed. It has an aisled and clerestoried nave, chancel, S porch and W tower.
Periods: The church dates from the 13c, but in 1448, a Richard Gowty ordered his body to be buried in the churchyard, and gave Caen stone 'for the whole new church, which was to be erected.' He would be relieved to learn that his church has now been rescued by the Friends of Friendless Churches.
Features: Fine 15c hammerbeam roof in nave; 15c carved font; Elizabethan cup, amedish 1721. The pulpit has been removed to Elmsett and the font to Brantham. The brass memorial formerly in the N aisle to Henry Tooley 1551, local worthy and founder of the nearby almshouses, and the famous richly ornamented brass of Thomas Pownder 1525, which was formerly in the chancel, are now in Christchurch Museum. The Register which dates from 1559 has also been preserved.

Location: Belstead Road.
Dedication: St Mary at Stoke.
Description: Situated on the S side of the river near the point at Stoke Bridge where the Gipping becomes tidal and changes its name to Orwell. Enlargement and restoration has virtually disguised the old medieval church whose aisleless nave has now become the N aisle of a new church with nave, chancel, fine W tower and brick porch.
Periods: 15c N aisle (see above), new nave and chancel built 1872 by Butterfield.
Features: Good plain hammerbeam roof to old nave; disused 15c font; trefoil-headed piscina; stained glass E window by Clayton & Bell and N aisle E window of 1864; cup and paten 1797. The register dates from 1570.

Location: Portman Road.
Dedication: St Matthew.
Description: This large church has an aisled and clerestoried nave, chancel with modern S chapel, handsome S porch and embattled W tower.
Periods: Mainly 15c Perp with considerable 19c alterations; the upper part of the tower rebuilt 1884, S aisle widened 1843 and refaced 1884, S chapel widened 1859, N aisle widened and enlarged 1876, E wall rebuilt 1866 and altered again in 1890.

Features: Hammerbeam roof in chancel; very fine 15c ctagonal font with interesting carved panels; six fine painted panels of former rood-screen, probably representing members of the guild of St Erasmus, now used as a parclose screen in the N aisle, much modern stained glass in aisles from c1853-82; Elizabethan Cup; two hanging monuments to Richard Cock 1629, his wife and family and to Anthony Penning 1630 with wife and sixteen children. The Register dates from 1559.

Location: Friars Road.
Dedication: St Nicholas.
Description: Situated in the lower part of town near the river and thought to have been built upon the site of, and using materials from, the Domesday church of St Michael. It comprises an aisled nave, chancel, chapels, decorated W tower and S porch.
Periods: The aisles are early 14c, the chancel chapels 15c, as is the W tower which was rebuilt in 1886. The brick S porch is probably 18c.
Features: Three exciting stone carvings thought to be late 11c or early 12c in the N aisle, one showing priests or apostles, one St Michael fighting the Dragon and the third, the tympanum of a doorway, showing a wild bird, which must have come from the earliest building which stood on the site (see above); aisle windows carried down to form seats; dormer window in roof to light rood; 14c niche in N chapel; two fonts, one Perp, the other Georgian; painting of Christ at Emaus, 1807 on chancel N wall; mid-17c pulpit with tester; 18c communion rail; 17c panelling on aisle walls created from former box pews; Elizabethan cup, flagon 1703, paten and almsdish 1766; brasses to William Style 1475 and his wife Isabel 1490, to William Stiles c1500, and to a Civilian c1600. The Register dates from 1539.

Location: St Peters Street.
Dedication: St Peter.
Description: One of the oldest and best churches in town, situated close to the site of the Augustinian priory of St Peter and St Paul founded in the late 12c. Aisled and clerestoried nave, chancel, S porch and tower, 93' tall. The arms of Henry VIII on an external buttress of the chancel wall probably came from, and relate to, Wolsey's ill-fated College for which it served as a chapel. There are traces of a continuation E of the E end of the chancel which probably connected it or was planned to connect it to the College.
Periods: The aisles, windows and arcades are 14c Dec as is the N clerestory. The S clerestory and tower are from the second half of the 15c. The N aisle was lengthened in 1878 and the upper part of the tower restored in 1882.
Features: Good 15c aisle roofs; two blocked doorways at E end of chancel which probably connected with the adjacent priory; late Norman font of black Tournai marble - one of only seven in the country; two patens 1736, cup 1772, flagon 1792, two cups 1812; good brass to John Knappe, merchant and portman, 1604, and wife Martha. The Register dates from 1657.

Location: St Stephen's Lane.
Dedication: St Stephen.
Description: Situated in the heart of the town beside the new Buttermarket shopping centre, the redundant church now provides home to the Ipswich Tourist Office. With the churchyard now a public garden, what a delightful home it makes. It still retains its fine arches opening to the S

chancel chapel, and three similar ones to the S aisle of the nave.
Periods: 15c Perp, but much restored in 1866 and 1881.
Features: Hammerbeam chancel roof, the 16c nave roof has tie-beams and king and queen posts; blocked priest's door to S chapel; niche in wall of nave with vaulted canopy; handsome monument on N side of chancel to Sir Robert Leman, Lord Mayor of London, and his wife Mary who died on the same day in 1637. The Register dates from 1585.

Of the churches mentioned in Ipswich at Domesday but now lost, the site of All Saints is unknown, but stood within St Matthews parish; some remains of St George were seen in a barn in George Street in the 19c; St Mildred stood on the Cornhill and was converted into Ipswich's first Town Hall; and St Austin, which stood on marshland near the site of the lepers' hospital of St Leonards on the SE edge of town, was in use until the end of the 15c - the present church of St Augustines probably stands on or close to the site.

The modern town churches comprise:

Location: Chevallier Street.
Dedication: All Saints.
Description: Red brick, with SW porch tower, nave, chancel with chapels.
Periods: 1886-7 by S. Wright.

Location: Felixstowe Road.
Dedication: St Augustine
Description: The church is cruciform in design with massive central crossing tower.
Periods: 1927 by H. Munro Cautley.
Features: Perp octagonal font from Linstead Magna.

Location: Newton Road.
Dedication: St Bartholomew.
Description: The church has a conventional exterior in red brick. The planned NE tower was not built.
Periods: 1896-1900 by Charles Spooner.
Features: At E end above the altar is a beautiful rose window with flowing tracery and at the W end a window of seven stepped lights.

Location: Fore Hamlet
Dedication: Holy Trinity.
Description: Aisleless church with narrow W tower in Suffolk brick with large arched windows.
Periods: Built in 1836 by local architect Harvey. The chancel was added in 1895.

Location: Cauldwell Hall Road.
Dedication: St John the Baptist.
Description: The previous church of 1857 stands just S of its modern replacement, a large brick towerless church with bell-cote and polygonal W baptistery.
Periods: 1898-9 by Sir Arthur Blomfield.

IXWORTH

Location: 6 miles NE of Bury St Edmunds.
Dedication: St Mary.
Description: Nave, N and S aisles, clerestory, chancel with N chapel, and big W tower with flintwork on base and battlements.
Periods: The chancel was almost entirely rebuilt in the 14c and the W windows, doorway in the S aisle and S porch are of the same period; the rest of the church is Perp, the tall W tower being built c1470 by Robert Schot of Ixworth, Abbot of Bury 1469-74. In 1856 the church was completely restored and the N aisle extended the entire length of the chancel.
Features: Early 16c hammerbeam roof to nave and a similar roof over the chancel; 14c font; early 13c double piscina in chancel and a piscina with a squint above in N aisle; cinque-foiled niche in E end of chancel; priest's door with external stoup; lower part of rood-screen; 16c canopied tomb monument and brasses to Richard Codington 1567 and his wife 1571 - he was granted the manor of Ixworth in 1538 after the Dissolution of the Abbey in exchange for Codington in Surrey, then renamed Nonesuch.

IXWORTH THORPE

Location: 1 mile NW of Ixworth.
Dedication: All Saints.
Description: Rubble built, with a thatched roof, this small church has lost its red-brick base apart from the red-brick base and had it replaced with a picturesque wooden bell-turret.
Periods: Mainly 14c and 15c, except for Norman doorways and 13c lancet windows in the N wall. Well restored in 1972.
Features: Beautiful 16c S porch of red brick; Norman N and S doorways; 14c font with 17c cover; piscina in chancel; wooden tracery in E window; good carved bench; 17c pulpit and communion rail; cup 1676, paten and flagon 1678; Royal Arms of George III; 17c mural tablet to John Croft 1644.

KEDINGTON

Location: 3 miles NE of Haverhill.
Dedication: St Peter and St Paul.
Description: A large and fascinating church sitting on the remains of a Roman building and comprising an aisled nave, chancel, S porch and W tower.
Periods: One of the most interesting and surprising churches in Suffolk covering virtually every period of history. The earliest evidence for the church itself is the chancel arch which is early 13c with 12c jambs; the nave and chancel are early 13 (the E window a Perp insertion), and the N aisle and tower are Dec. The S porch is 18c.
Features: Beneath the floor of the nave and N aisle are some remains of a Roman building (seen by lifting trap doors in the floors of two pews); beneath the eastern part of the nave is a large burial vault of cruciform shape approached by a wide flight of steps in the central alley near the pulpit and now covered by a trap-door; the nave pillars were painted to represent fluted columns and the capitals veined to look like marble during the 18c when Gothic was out of favour and Classic in; false hammerbeam roof to nave; N jamb of chancel arch contains staircase which possibly led to rood-loft; over the western side of the chancel arch are remains of two

corbels which once carried the rood-beam; 15c octagonal font; strangely shaped piscina; the chancel contains much early 18c panelling; superb three-decker pulpit, made c1610, with tester and hour-glass stand, reputed to be the oldest of its type in England, and wig stand by the pulpit; rood-screen of 1619 is hinged and folds back; rare 18c communicants' stalls; canopied Barnardiston pew made up of parts from a 15c rood-screen; 18c and 19c box pews line the aisle walls, more in the nave; childrens' benches; early 19c semi-circular singers' gallery at W end of nave; simple 15c poor box hewn from a tree-trunk; communion rail 1707; Anglo-Saxon Crucifixion Cross, assigned to c900 discovered in the nave during 19c restoration and placed above the main altar; cup and paten 1663-4, flagon 1740; extensive range of monuments to the Barnardistons include: tomb-chest to Sir Thomas 1503 and Elizabeth his wife, another to Sir Thomas 1519 and wife 1520, a standing wall monument to a Sir Thomas who died 1610 with his two wives, a memorial to Grissel, a daughter, 1609; and in the N aisle, Sir Nathaniel 1653, and his wife Jane 1669, and another to Sir Thomas 1724.

KELSALE

Location: 1 mile N of Saxmundham.
Dedication: St Mary.
Description: A large church standing on a hill comprising an aisled nave, chancel with S chapel, S porch and SW tower with an openwork bell-turret.
Periods: The earliest part is the Norman N doorway with the old Norman S doorway re-set as priest's doorway in the chancel. The S aisle (restored 1880) and tower are 14c, and the nave and S porch 15c. The chancel and S chapel are Perp, rebuilt in 1877.
Features: 15c octagonal font; unusual pulpit of c1620; iron screen of 1890; reredos with nine painted panels; Royal Arms of Queen Victoria 1837; cup and paten 1706, flagon 1788; splendid marble table-tomb to Thomas Russell 1730 and a statue to Samuel Clouting 1852.

KENTFORD

Location: 4 miles E of Newmarket.
Dedication: St Mary.
Description: A simple church sited on hill with nave, chancel, porch and W tower.
Periods: All 14c Dec except for 15c porch and the brick top to the tower.
Features: Pleasant five-light rose window in tower; faint 14c wall paintings of St Christopher, the Seven Deadly Sins, the Seven Works of Mercy and the Legend of the Three Quick and the Three Dead; box pews; cup 1662.

KENTON

Location: 2 miles NE of Debenham.
Dedication: All Saints.
Description: Nave with brick S aisle, chancel, S porch and W tower.
Periods: The nave, with 15c alterations, dates back to Norman times, with a 12c S doorway. The Chancel, restored in 1872, and tower are originally 14c and the S aisle was built by the Garney family in the 16c.
Features: Steps to rood-loft; canopied niche behind old pulpit; 13c octagonal font of Purbeck marble; 14c chest; some old benches, one with

open balustrading and dated 1595; Elizabethan cup; brass to John Garneys 1524 and Elizabeth his wife on S aisle wall.

KERSEY

Location: 2 miles NW of Hadleigh.
Dedication: St Mary.
Description: Stands prominently on a hill above the village with a magnificent Perp W tower visible over the surrounding countryside. It also comprises an aisled and clerestoried nave, chancel and N and S porch.
Periods: The main fabric of the church is probably Norman, though nothing of this period now remains following drastic restorations in the 17c and again in 1888. The N aisle was added in 1335, and the tower rebuilt c1430 and battlemented 1445; the S porch is also of this period. The chancel was rebuilt in 1862.
Features: Tracery on west door; hammerbeam roof to nave, and there is a good roof to N aisle; 15c font; late 15c piscina and sedilia in the Sampson Chapel; damaged niches flanking E window of chapel; fragments of an alabaster altar; wall painting of St George and the Dragon on S wall; six painted panels of rood-screen now in S aisle; lectern with 15c stem; paten 1711, cup, paten and flagon 1791; monuments to the Thorrowgoods.

KESGRAVE

Location: 4 miles NE of Ipswich.
Dedication: All Saints.
Description: The village is now a virtual suburb of Ipswich, but the rubble-built church stands ringed and shaded by magnificent cedars. It comprises a nave, chancel, S porch and W tower. The nave and chancel have 13c lancet windows. The porch is 14c, as is the lower part of the tower - the brick upper stage is 16c.
Features: Fine nave roof; ball-flower ornament on hood-mould of S porch doorway; 14c piscina; small, narrow sedilia in chancel; unusual triple lancet E window under one arch; Royal Arms of George III; set of plate of 1799.

KESSINGLAND

Location: 5 miles SW of Lowestoft.
Dedication: St Edmund.
Description: Thatched nave, chancel and tall W tower, 96' high with flintwork panelled buttresses, plus a brick parapet. There was once a S aisle but this has now gone.
Periods: Built on a grand scale during the 14c and 15c when it was in the hands of the nuns of St Clare of London, probably on the site of a Norman predecessor of which no trace remains. However, deprived of this income after the Dissolution, it soon fell into decay. The chancel, S aisle and S chapel were pulled down towards the end of the 16c when the S arcade was built up, an E wall built on the site of the chancel arch, and the porch moved to its present position. In 1686 the roof fell in and services suspended. In 1694 rebuilding commenced with the wall being rebuilt of brick inside the position of the old one by John Campe and Thomas Godfrey. Only the tower, built c1439, remains complete from the original period, with its rebuilt late 17c brick top. Traces of the 14c arcades with octagonal pillars which once

opened into a S aisle - fragments of which remain in the churchyard - may also be seen in the reconstructed S wall. A new chancel was added in 1909.
Features: Fine W doorway; beautiful late 14c octagonal font - one of the best in the county- carved with eight figures of saints; stained glass in E window by Kempe & Tower 1912; Royal Arms of George II; cup, paten and flagon 1750, two almsdishes 1826.

KETTLEBASTON

Location: 7 miles NW of Hadleigh.
Dedication: St Mary.
Description: An ancient church of flint and stone, well restored. It has a nave, chancel, brick S porch and W tower.
Periods: The nave is Norman, with a blocked N window and S doorway of late 12c. The chancel and tower are mid-14c and the porch 18c.
Features: King-post roof; two side altars in the nave; traces of consecration crosses on the interior walls; large square Norman font; early 14c piscina and triple-canopied sedilia; tomb recess in N wall, probably for Easter Sepulchre; contemporary painting in the internal splays of the blocked Norman window; very fine modern reredos and screen; brass inscription to the wife of John Prick - she died in 1599; tablet memorial to Lady Jermy 1649. The Register dates from 1578.

KETTLEBURGH

Location: 2 miles SW of Framlingham.
Dedication: St Andrew.
Description: Nave, chancel, S porch, and W tower with brick battlements. There was once a N chapel which has now been demolished.
Periods: All 14c, except for the 15c clerestory windows inserted under the eaves of the nave, probably as a preliminary to the construction of aisles which was never carried out.
Features: Traces of N chapel to nave including a blocked arch and piscina; 15c octagonal font; pulpit incorporating Jacobean panels; 18c painted commandment boards; some old benches; Royal Arms of Queen Anne and contemporary set of Ten Commandments; mid-17c communion rail; cup and cover 1569; brass to Arthur Pennyng 1593 and his two wives. The Register dates from 1560.

KIRKLEY

Location: Merged with borough in 1907 and now part of South Lowestoft.
Dedication: St Peter.
Description: Nave, with N and S aisles, chancel and W tower 72' tall.
Periods: After long being in a dilapidated condition, the church was rebuilt in 1750 on a smaller scale, retaining the old W tower and using mostly materials from the old building. A complete rebuild in Perp style then took place in the 19c starting with the restoration of the tower in 1870, followed by a new chancel in 1876, S aisle in 1878 and in 1879, the new nave. The church was completed by a N aisle added in 1908.
Features: The tower has a medieval bell; iron screen 1896; reredos; Elizabethan cup inscribed 'for the towne of Kyrkley' dated 1567. The record of rectors and patrons is perfect from 1308.

KIRTON

Location: 6 miles S of Woodbridge.
Dedication: Unusual double dedication to St Mary and St Martin.
Description: The church consists of a nave with N aisle, chancel, and massive stone W tower.
Periods: With the exception of the N aisle, which was built in 1858, the church is mainly 15c, but the tower, built in 1520, may have been a new addition.
Features: 13c font; 14c piscina and windowsill sedilia; Elizabethan cup.

KNETTISHALL

Location: 8 miles NE of Ixworth.
Dedication: All Saints.
Description: Disused for many years and in a state of decay. Nave, chancel and W tower of knapped flint with panelled parapet.
Periods: Norman window still visible in S wall of nave. The tower is mid 15c.
Features: Most of the fittings have been removed and transferred to Riddlesworth just over the border in Norfolk.

KNODISHALL cum BUXLOW

Location: 4 miles SE of Saxmundham.
Dedication: St Lawrence.
Description: Nave, chancel and W tower.
Periods: The N side retains a simple Norman doorway built up to incorporate a window, and the chancel, though much renewed, is of c1320. The tower dates from the end of the 15c and the nave was largely rebuilt in brick in 1840.
Features: 13c octagonal font of Purbeck marble; painting, Jacob and Rachel 1851; 17c pulpit; part of early 16c screen re-used in the tower gallery; Elizabethan cup and paten; endearing brass to John Jenney 1460 and wife.

Buxlow, anciently a separate parish, was united with Knodishall in 1721. The sparse remains of Buxlow church, which was disused by the time of Queen Elizabeth, stand beside two cottages and can be viewed from a public footpath. They comprise the ruined base of a round Norman tower.

LACKFORD

Location: 6 miles NW of Bury St Edmunds.
Dedication: St Lawrence.
Description: Nave with N aisle, chancel with N chapel, S porch, and W tower with walls 3' thick, which replaced a former central tower.
Periods: All 14c Dec, except the N aisle which was later pulled down and rebuilt in the 19c. The tower battlements were added in brick in the 16c.
Features: Fine late 13c octagonal font; unusual chancel arcade forms canopies over the late 13c piscina and sedilia, and runs over the recess on N side of the chancel which forms an Easter Sepulchre; 13c stone coffin-lids; lofty lancet-shaped tower arch; late 13c eastern arch of the modern N arcade which once opened to a transept; stained glass E window by Powell 1871; 17c pulpit; old bench-ends. The Register dates from 1560.

LAKENHEATH

Location: 5 miles N of Mildenhall.
Dedication: St Mary.
Description: The church is among the most beautiful and interesting in Suffolk. It comprises an aisled and clerestoried nave, chancel, N and S porch and W tower. On W side of tower is two-storeyed 15c building, the basement of which forms a porch and the upper floor once a chantry or guild chapel.
Periods: Norman chancel arch. The present chancel with several lancet windows dates from 13c but is an extension of the Norman chancel, the length of which can be traced on the outside S wall. The tower is 14c but the lower part has some blocked late 13c lancets. The N aisle is 14c and the S aisle, clerestory and two porches are 15c Perp.
Features: Lovely nave roof with alternating tie-beams and hammerbeams; circular 13c font - best of its kind in the county; 14c wall painting on one of the nave piers shows a seated figure of St Edmund, and over the chancel arch, some traces of a Doom; 15c pulpit; delightful set of carved benches c1483; Jacobean family pew; splendid Royal Arms of Charles II dated 1678; Elizabethan cup, paten 1696; ladder in W tower may be the original; three medieval bells; brass of a Civilian and wife c1530; tomb chest monument of Purbeck marble in S aisle of Simon Styward 1568, a marble tablet in memory of Lord Kitchener, whose ancestors once resided in the parish, and a tablet to Joanna Bartney 1583.

LANGHAM

Location: 3 miles E of Ixworth.
Dedication: St Mary.
Description: Standing peacefully in the park of Langham Hall, this small neatly preserved church comprises nave, chancel and Victorian bell-cote.
Periods: The nave was rebuilt in 1887 and the chancel is late 14c with an E window of 1877.
Features: Late 14c octagonal font; canopied 14c piscina; some old glass in SE window of chancel; lovely 15c rood-screen; flagon 1712; brass inscription to John Jollye 1630. The Register dates from 1562.

LAVENHAM

Dedication: St Peter and St Paul.
Description: One of the most famous churches in Suffolk both architecturally and historically. It was built from the wealth of the local clothiers, notably the Spring family, and the Lord of the Manor John de Vere, thirteenth Earl of Oxford, whose arms appear on the S porch. It is dominated by a mighty tower 137' high of knapped flint, disproportionate to the body of the church which is long at 156', but not long or high enough relatively. This being said, the building proves a worthy monument to the wealth generated in this part of Suffolk at the time. It comprises a long chancel with an eastern vestry, side chapels, an aisled and clerestoried nave, the great W tower and a S porch. The tower should have been topped with corner pinnacles but these were never completed.
Periods: Apart from the 14c chancel, sadly spoiled by 19c restoration work, the church is one of the best examples of Perp work in the country, being

built principally of the period 1468-1525. The tower was built c1486-95, the Branch N chapel c1500 and the S porch c1508, while Thomas Spring left money for the completion of the tower and to build the beautiful S chapel to contain a monument to himself and his wife in 1523. Recent restoration work on the tower was carried out between 1861-7.

Features: Exterior walling almost entirely faced with cut stone, an unusual feature for Suffolk; W door with tracery and S door with linenfold panelling; fine arch-braced roof to nave, the eastern bay of which formed a Canopy of Honour over the rood; octagonal Perp font; old stained glass in N aisle windows; E and W windows by Lavers & Barraud; rare rood-screen of c1330-40, contemporary with the chancel; Spring Chapel at E end of N aisle, with superb parclose screen; stalls with traceried fronts; misericorde; Hanoverian Royal Arms; brasses in E vestry to Thomas Spring I, 1486, near N door of nave to Allayne Dister 1534 and his wife and children, and, in front of the altar, to little Clopton d'Ewes, only ten days old when he died in 1631; tomb-chest monument in the Oxford Chantry at E end of S aisle to the thirteenth Earl who died in 1513, and in the chancel a monument to Thomas Spring III, and another to Dr. Henry Copinger 1622. Also in the chancel is an old gravestone which formerly bore a Saxon inscription, now defaced.

LAWSHALL

Location: 6 miles S of Bury St Edmunds..
Dedication: All Saints.
Description: Aisled and clerestoried nave, chancel, S porch and tall W tower with fine flintwork decoration.
Periods: Mostly mid-15c. The church was totally restored at great expense in 1857.
Features: Richly moulded nave arcade and fine clerestory; 15c font with modern colouring; two chests, one 17c, the other 18c. The Register dates from 1558.

LAXFIELD

Location: 6 miles NE of Framlingham.
Dedication: All Saints.
Description: Laxfield was home to the notorious Dr William Dowsing, appointed by the Earl of Manchester in 1643 to demolish superstitious pictures, images, ornaments, inscriptions, etc., in the churches of Suffolk. Despite failing to spare even his own church, he lies buried in the churchyard. Large impressive church, despite being aisleless, with a nave, white-brick chancel, vestry, S porch and stone-faced W tower with pinnacles and flint panelling.
Periods: 15c Perp except for the Dec nave, and the chancel rebuilt in 1841.
Features: Eastern bay of nave roof retains coloured traces of a Canopy of Honour; late 15c Seven Sacraments' font; fragments of old stained glass in N window; 17c pulpit and reader's desk; remains of painted rood-screen; carved 15c benches; box pews; poor box, dated 1664; massive iron-bound chest; banner-stave cupboard in SW corner of nave; Royal Arms of Queen Anne; Elizabethan cup and cover 1567, paten late 17c, flagon 1724; brass inscriptions to John Smyth 1597, John Jenner 1606, William Dowsing 1634 (a relative of Dr. Dowsing), and Elizabeth Jenner 1634.

LAYHAM

Location: 1 mile S of Hadleigh.
Dedication: St Andrew.
Description: Nave, chancel, brick W tower and modern S porch and vestry.
Periods: The windows are all styled c1300 but renewed. The original tower of c1300 was replaced in 1742. The church was restored in 1861.
Features: 13c hexagonal font of Purbeck marble; double piscina in chancel; small squint piercing S respond of chancel arch; fragments of 16c rood-screen in NE corner of nave; interesting painted panel in chancel, dated 1626, commemorating Ann Roane; elaborate mosaic reredos; Elizabethan cup and cover, flagon 1774, paten 1796.

LEAVENHEATH

Location: 5 miles NE of Bures.
Dedication: St Matthew.
Description: Built as a chapel-of-ease to nearby Stoke by Nayland. When this area of onetime heathland became the new parish of Leavenheath in 1868 - formed from parts of Stoke-by-Nayland, Assington, Nayland, Polstead and Wissington - it became the parish church.
Periods: Built in Early English style in 1835, it was unsympathetically enlarged in 1883 by Satchell & Edwards to include a chancel, curious S tower and S aisle.

LEISTON

Dedication: St Margaret.
Description: The old medieval thatched church suffered an 'exotic' enlargement in the 19c when it was made cruciform by E. B. Lamb mostly by the contributions of Lady Rendlesham. It has a spacious nave, chancel and transept, and retains its original 15c tower.
Periods: Rebuilt in Dec style in 1854 and reroofed in 1871.
Features: Late 13c circular font; 19c painting on jambs of sanctuary arch; stained glass E window by Kempe 1898, N transept N window by M. E. A. Rope c1928; reredos; interior filled with wildly imaginative 19c carpentry; spoon 1763, cup and paten 1765, flagon 1766, paten 1772; monument to Richard Garrett 1866, in the N transept, founder of the world-famous local engineering firm.

LETHERINGHAM

Location: 3 miles SW of Framlingham.
Dedication: St Mary.
Description: The parish church consists of the two W bays of the ruined Augustinian Priory church's aisleless Norman nave, plus a modern brick S porch and a W tower with flint panelled parapets and buttresses. The chancel and part of the nave were decayed in 1750, and the church subsequently fell into ruin. It was rescued, the chancel demolished, and the remainder restored in 1797. The lower courses of the N wall of the former chancel now form part of the churchyard wall.
Periods: The Augustinian Priory was founded in c1200 and the nave dates from this period - the tower arch being of c1180.

Features: Interesting sundial, dated 1608; font, said to have been constructed from part of a monument; good three-light E window, reused from former chancel; late Georgian pulpit; some box pews; three-sided communion rail; Hanoverian Royal Arms; Elizabethan cup; very early brass to Sir John de Wyngefeld 1389, and a stone sculpture to another Sir John Wingfield 1481, unfortunately, many others to the Boville, Wingfield and Naughton families have been destroyed. The Register dates from 1558.

LEVINGTON

Location: 7 miles SE of Ipswich.
Dedication: St Peter.
Description: Stands on the N bank of the Orwell by Levington Creek. It comprises a nave, chancel and broad brick tower.
Periods: Nave and chancel in late Dec and Perp style have some brick windows of late 15c; the tower was built in 1636 by Sir Robert Hitcham. The church was sympathetically restored in 1949.
Features: Arch-braced nave roof; rood-beam in place of chancel arch; 15c octagonal font; 17c pulpit; chancel panelling from Brightwell Hall (built 1663); 17c communion rail.

LIDGATE

Location: 7 miles SE of Newmarket.
Dedication: St Mary.
Description: The ancient church, situated in the bailey of the castle, comprises an aisled nave, chancel, S porch and square W tower.
Periods: Pevsner suggests the nave is Norman, as in the S door with Perp mouldings, but most that remains, including aisles, W tower and S porch, is 14c. The chancel, which was restored in 1863, has 13c lancets on the N side.
Features: 15c font with 17c cover; piscina and double aumbry in chancel; 17c pulpit; fine early 15c rood-screen and contemporary parclose screen in the N aisle; modern parclose in S aisle; old benches with linen-fold panelling; candelabra suspended in the nave; 17c silver-gilt cups, said to be German; brass memorial, with new head, is thought to be to John Lydgate, the poet, born here 1375, and who died c1451.

LINDSEY

Location: 5 miles NW of Hadleigh.
Dedication: St Peter.
Description: The church was at an early period appropriated to Kersey Priory. Simple aisled nave and chancel. The W tower has been replaced with a weatherboarded belfry and the S porch is also of timber.
Periods: The body of the church is almost entirely of good 14c Dec work with fine traceried windows. Being in a poor condition, the W tower was taken down c1830.
Features: 14c nave roof with tie-beams and king-posts; font of c1300 with 17c cover; piscina with original wooden credence shelf; mutilated statue niches in jambs of NE nave window; especially attractive two-light window on N side of nave; remains of wall paintings on nave and S aisle walls; remains

of rood-screen below pulpit; 17c pulpit and three-sided communion rail; 19c box pews; Elizabethan cup and cover.

LINSTEAD MAGNA

Location: 5 miles SW of Halesworth.
Dedication: St Peter.
Description: The ruined church is at the end of a lane in a very isolated position. The nave was lost in the latter part of the 19c but the chancel only fell into disrepair in the middle part of this century. All that now survives is the brick W tower and a small section of the SE corner of the nave.
Features: The 15c font and medieval bell are now in the modern church of St Augustine, Ipswich, and the old bench-ends and plate at neighbouring Linstead Parva.

LINSTEAD PARVA

Location: 5 miles W of Halesworth.
Dedication: St Margaret.
Description: Small church comprising a nave, chancel, porch and wooden belfry.
Periods: The chancel is 13c, and the nave probably of the same period with Perp brick-mullioned windows added. The church was restored in 1891, and in 1894 a porch was built.
Features: 15c nave roof; 15c octagonal font; plastered tympanium over rood-beam; old bench-ends in nave (see Linsted Magna); almsdish 1812; paten 1509, Elizabethan cup, almsdish 1812 (see Linstead Magna).

LITTLE BEALINGS

Location: 3 miles SW of Woodbridge.
Dedication: All Saints.
Description: Nave with N aisle, archless chancel, and S tower with unusual parapet, and its basement forming a porch.
Periods: Chancel appears c1300, the nave 14c, its S side of early 16c brick; the N aisle as added in 1850.
Features: Mutilated 14c octagonal font; 17c pulpit; Elizabethan cup; a wooden cornice runs the whole length of the church.

LITTLE BLAKENHAM

Location: 4 miles NW of Ipswich.
Dedication: St Mary.
Description: Nave, chancel and unbuttressed W tower.
Periods: The chancel is c1300, the nave 14c, as is the tower, restored in 1868.
Features: Piscina in S wall; three lancets in E window; painting of two 13c figures in the jambs of the Early English lancet, repainted 1850, and others, repainted and remodelled either side of E window, of Christ carrying the Cross and St John the Baptist; Royal Arms of James II, dated 1685; Elizabethan cup, paten 1816.

LITTLE BRADLEY

Location: 5 miles NE of Haverhill.
Dedication: All Saints.
Description: In a remote hamlet and approached by a long tree-lined lane, the little church of All Saints, with nave, chancel, porch and round tower, is one of the oldest still standing in the county.
Periods: Anglo-Saxon long and short work at the NW and SW angles show a very early date, possibly c1040 for the nave and W part of the chancel. This building was no doubt added to the Anglo-Saxon round tower which still stands and may be as old as 950. It is beautifully built with the flints laid herringbone fashion and originally stood alone with no entrance at ground level. The three Norman windows, about 12' from the ground, are insertions. An octagonal belfry was added c1455. The E extension to the chancel was made by the Normans about 1080 as seen from the E and N windows and the simple S doorway. The S porch has been rebuilt incorporating some 14c woodwork. The church was restored in 1879.
Features: 14c font; early piscina in eastern splay of SE chancel window with windowsill sedilia to W; some old mismatched stained glass in chancel SW window and modern stained glass in S window of nave; pulpit with 18c tester; cup 1789; three brass memorials to Civilian and wife c1520 on the N chancel wall, headless Knight (probably Thomas Knighton 1530) on chancel S wall and, above the Civilian, John Daye, the famous printer, who died 1584, and his second wife Alys; monument to Richard le Hunte 1540 and his wife 1558 and, on S wall of chancel, to Thomas Soame 1606, and wife Elizabeth.

LITTLE BRICETT

Location: 4 miles SW of Needham Market.
Dedication: St Lawrence.
Description: Offton was stated to have had two churches at Domesday. One was the church of the old manor of Parva Bricett, now Talmage or Tollemache Hall. When the parish of Little Bricett was formed, this manorial church became the parish church. In 1503 Little Bricett was re-annexed to Offton. Nothing remains of the church which stood near Tollemache Hall, now a farmhouse.

LITTLE CORNARD

Location: 2 miles SE of Sudbury.
Dedication: All Saints.
Description: Nave, chancel, S porch, two-storeyed brick vestry and flint W tower with low spire and curious belfry.
Periods: Dec and Perp with early 14c tower and a 17c vestry. Restored 1848.
Features: Good octagonal 14c font bearing arms of Cornard, Ufford and de Vere families; piscina; modern stained glass E window by Clutterbuck, 1857; 14c iron-bound chest; Royal Arms of Queen Victoria; cup 1643, paten 1707.

LITTLE FINBOROUGH

Location: 2 miles SW of Stowmarket.
Dedication: St Mary.
Description: A small church with nave, chancel and bell-turret.

Periods: The chancel is 14c as is the bell-turret and, whilst the nave was rebuilt in 1856, it retains part of a 12c S door.
Features: Perp font; the Royal Arms of George III, dated 1767, hang on the plain wooden tympanum above the rood-beam.

LITTLE GLEMHAM

Location: 3 miles NE of Wickham Market.
Dedication: St Andrew.
Description: Nave, chancel, N chapel, S porch and tall W tower with panelled flintwork on base, buttresses and battlements.
Periods: The oldest part of the church is the Norman N doorway in the nave. The tower is 15c Perp and the brick chancel rebuilt in the 18c and 'Gothicised' in the 19c when the North's family chapel was added.
Features: Early 13c octagonal font of Purbeck marble; stained glass in a N window of c1929; fragment of a panel of the Trinity; interesting set of early 18c Commandments, Creed, and Lord's Prayer with figures of Moses and Aaron; cup 1566, paten 1567, flagon 1636, paten 1732; a number of brasses to the Glemham family, ardent Royalists, who suffered accordingly during the Cromwellian period, include Sir John Glemham, Knight 1535, Christopher Glemham 1549 and Thomas Glemham 1571; fine life-size monument of Dudley North, 1829, in the chapel with other memorials to the North family, Earls of Guildford.

LITTLE LIVERMERE

Location: 5 miles NE of Bury St Edmunds .
Dedication: St Peter and St Paul.
Description: The village has almost disappeared and the church, which stands in Livermere Park, close to the northern end of the lake, is in ruins. The gutted interior has a nave and chancel in one, a brick porch and a W tower, heightened so that it could be seen from the Hall (now-demolished).
Periods: Although the blocked N doorway of the nave has a decorated lintel of early Norman or even Saxon date, and the NE corner shows Saxon long-and-short work, the tower is medieval with a lofty belfry added in the 18c, and most of what now remains is of this later date.

LITTLE SAXHAM

Location: 4 miles W of Bury St Edmunds.
Dedication: St Nicholas.
Description: The church comprises an aisled nave, chancel with N chapel, S porch, and one of the best Norman round towers in East Anglia.
Periods: The tower, with its belfry of four round-headed windows, is mid 12c and the S doorway is also Norman. The S porch and N aisle were built in the 14c, the chancel in the 15c, and the chapel added early in the 16c by Thomas Lucas, Solicitor-General to Henry VII, who built himself a tomb in the arch between chancel and chapel. He died in 1531 but was buried in London. The estate was subsequently sold to Sir John Crofts and it is his family who occupy the chapel.
Features: Curious round-headed recess in W wall of nave, S of Norman tower arch; lower rood-loft doorway and staircase; 17c pulpit and bier; curved 18c communion rails (from disused church at Little Livermere, see above);

remains of rood-screen behind the high altar; choir stalls and old bench-ends; two patens 1799; monuments to Thomas Lucas (erected before his death), and others to Lord Crofts 1677 and his wife Elizabeth, Elizabeth Crofts 1642, William Crofts 1694, and to Ann Crofts 1727.

LITTLE THURLOW

Location: 4 miles NE of Haverhill.
Dedication: St Peter.
Description: Aisled and clerestoried nave, chancel and W tower. On the N of the chancel is the Soame Chapel.
Periods: The church was rebuilt in the 13c. The clerestory is partly 17c and partly modern. The W tower is 14c and the chapel 16c, much altered in the early 17c.
Features: Fine early 17c roof; square Norman font; 13c piscina in S aisle, and a double piscina in chancel; W window of tower has fine tracery and E window with excellent 19c heraldic glass; three-sided 17c communion rails; 17c squire's pew; lower part of coloured rood-screen; 17c-18c brass chandelier; brass in nave of a Knight and Lady c1520; magnificent coloured monument in the N chapel of Sir Stephen Soame, Knight, 1619, Lord Mayor of London in 1593, and his wife Dame Anne, 1622, and a memorial to another Stephen Soame who died 1771.

LITTLE WALDINGFIELD

Location: 4 miles NE of Sudbury.
Dedication: St Lawrence.
Description: Fine church with a tall battlemented tower with two large octagonal turrets containing staircases and capped with small crocketed spires. There is an aisled and clerestoried nave, chancel - which formerly had a N vestry, and N and S brick porches.
Periods: The building is 15c Perp with a fine 16c arcade to the nave. The porches were built c1466. The roof was repaired and the nave restored c1874.
Features: Traceried N and W door; Blocked door, piscina and aumbry of former N vestry; mutilated octagonal 14c font; 17c communion rail and pulpit; some 16c bench-ends; early 14c chest and a fine one of 15c date; brasses to John and Katherine Colman 1506, Roger and Mary Appleton 1526, John Wyncoll, clothier, 1544, and one of a Lady c1530. The Register dates from 1568.

LITTLE WELNETHAM

Location: 2 miles SE of Bury St Edmunds.
Dedication: St Mary Magdalen.
Description: The small church comprises a nave, chancel, brick S porch and W tower. In the churchyard are the remains of a circular flint building which may have been either the bi-apsidal chancel of the former Saxon-Norman church which stood on the site, or a Saxon watch tower (Alec Clifton-Taylor).
Periods: The tower is Early English with Dec windows, the chancel 14c, and the nave and porch late Perp.
Features: Unusual hammerbeam roof to nave, the hammers being carved figures; remains of former Norman pillar-piscina on S side of nave; original

altar stone with traces of consecration crosses; blocked squint or niche N side of chancel; sexfoil light over chancel arch; octagonal 15c font; lower part of rood-screen incorporated in tower-screen; old nave bench-ends. The Register dates from 1557.

LITTLE WENHAM

Location: 6 miles SW of Ipswich.
Dedication: All Saints.
Description: Nave, chancel, S porch, and W tower with brick top.
Periods: The church is c1300, with a 15c tower and S porch.
Features: The lower part remains of a stone screen which separated the nave and chancel in place of the usual chancel arch; large tomb recess in S wall of nave; piscina; complete rood-stairs in N side; 13c lancet provides a low side-window on N side of chancel; font c1300; good three-light E window; exceptionally fine wall paintings on the E wall depict Virgin and Child with four Angels, and St Margaret, St Catherine and St Mary Magdalene, and on the N wall a St Christopher - less good; simple 18c pulpit; panels forming reredos for the altars against the base of the rood-screen; communion rail of c1700; two benches with linenfold panelling; Royal Arms of Queen Anne; cup and paten 1791; fine brasses to Thomas Brewse and his wife Joan, 1514; good coloured monument to Sir John Brewse 1585 on chancel S wall (its construction led to the destruction of two of the three seats of the 13c sedilia), and a nameless tomb may have been that of Gilbert de Debenham who died in 1371.

LITTLE WORLINGHAM

Location: 2 miles SE of Beccles.
Dedication: St Peter.
Description: Formerly the parish of Little Worlingham, Worlingham Parva or Worlingham St Peter, it is now extinct, without even a single house in the 19c. The parish church dedicated to St Peter, last mentioned in 1492, has long since been destroyed.

LITTLE WRATTING

Location: 2 miles NE of Haverhill.
Dedication: Holy Trinity.
Description: The little church, built in septaria and flint, stands on an ancient platform site on a lonely hilltop. It comprises a nave, chancel and wooden belfry. There is evidence in part of a curved enclosure bank that the churchyard was once circular.
Period: The masonry and the shapes of the S and blocked N doorways suggest that the nave is probably Saxon. The E half of the chancel is 14c Dec but the 'Norman' chancel arch is a Victorian copy.
Features: Jamb of an arch which once opened into the Turnour Chapel - pulled down in 1710 - can still be seen in the NW corner of the chancel; S door with Norman ironwork and a stone lintel over the doorway with a crude Latin inscription recording the dedication of the building but so far not satisfactorily translated; fine 14c piscina; simple 15c benches and 18c squire's box-pew; cup 1684, paten 1711; part of a monument, comprising a kneeling 17c female figure in poor condition, which once stood in the former Chapel.

LONG MELFORD

Location: 3 miles NW of Sudbury.

Dedication: Holy Trinity.

Description: Pevsner describes Holy Trinity as 'one of the most moving parish churches of England; large, proud, and noble'. Indeed, it bears more relationship to a cathedral than a parish church. I will not go into too great a detail here as the literature available is vast and comprehensive; suffice to say it is one of the finest parish churches in England and a must to visit. The church is 268' long and has over a hundred windows. The plan consists of an aisled and clerestoried nave of seven bays, a chancel of three bays flanked by chapels of two bays; to the E of that on the N side is the Clopton Chantry, and on the S, the vestry. E of the chancel and connected by a narrow room is the Lady Chapel consisting of a three-bayed inner chapel surrounded by an ambulatory. The exterior of the church has elaborate flint and stone panelling. Running round under the cornices are inscriptions recording names of benefactors and dates of the erection of various parts.

Periods: It is almost entirely Perp, rebuilt between c1460 and c1495 to replace an earlier church of which no more survives than the 14c piers of the five W bays of the arcade. The tower was struck by lightning and rebuilt 1711. The church was thoroughly restored in 1869.

Features: Simple octagonal 15c font of Purbeck marble; sedilia in Clopton Chapel; late 15c stained glass in E window, W windows of N wall, E window of Clopton Chapel and in N aisle tracery; good carved screens separating nave, chancel and chapels; reredos 1877; seat of c1500 in S chapel given in 1948 from Granada Cathedral in Spain; late 14c(?) sculpture of Adoration of the Magi, the Virgin reclining on a couch; set of Plate 1775; monuments include: in the Clopton Chapel - the tomb of Sir William Clopton 1446 together with a brass of his second wife Margaret, and a tomb of John Clopton 1498; in the N aisle - monument to Sir William Clopton 1530 and a fine brass to Francis Clopton, his son, 1558; on the S side of the chancel - large monument to Sir William Cordell, Knight 1580, Speaker of the House of Commons; in the Martyn Chapel - altar tomb to Laurence Martyn 1460 and his two wives, a memorial to Roger Martyn 1542, and brasses to Roger Martyn 1615 and his two wives Ursula and Margaret, Richard Martyn 1624, and Sir Richard Martyn 1762. There are other memorials in the church to the Darcy, Middleton and Parker families.

LOUND

Location: 5 miles NW of Lowestoft.

Dedication: St John the Baptist.

Description: The church, thatched until 1846, has a nave, chancel, S porch and round tower.

Periods: The base of the tower is Norman and upper stages c1470, the rest of the church 14c Dec.

Features: The interior was richly decorated in 1914 by J. N. Comper and is a blaze of colour. Finely painted roof of chancel; inscribed octagonal 15c font; piscina in nave with another piscina and triple sedilia in chancel; squint in W wall; good late 14c E window and modern 19c stained glass in chancel N and S windows; modern 20c wall painting of St Christopher - with a car in the background!; richly regilded 14c rood-screen; 17c pulpit.

LOWETOFT

Location: Oulton Road.
Dedication: St Margaret.
Description: This large church, 183' long and 57' wide, stands high to the
NW of the town. This is the parish church of Lowestoft, erected some half
mile from the medieval town centre to protect it from being undermined by
the sea - which at that time approached much nearer the cliffs than it does
now. It consists of a nave with aisles and clerestory, chancel, W tower
surmounted by a spire, and a S porch with a room above known as the
'Maide' Chamber' from a tradition that it was occupied by two female
recluses at the time of the Reformation.
Periods: The tower is the oldest part of the church, built c1330, though the
crypt under the chancel, now used as a vestry, may be 13c. The nave, aisles
and porch were erected c1483, when the tower was heightened and the spire
added to make a total height of 120'. The nave and chancel are continuous -
a rood-screen and over it a rood-loft orginally repalcing a chancel arch - and
under one roof of short hammerbeams restored and redecorated by Bodley
in 1899. The S aisle was rebuilt in 1871.
Features: Mutilated 14c font; richly canopied piscina and windowsill sedilia
in chancel; lovely E window and other fine traceried windows in aisle and
chancel; high altar and a memorial screen; banner-stave locker; brass eagle-
lectern dated 1504; 17c chest; brasses including one of two skeletons in
shroude c1500, and another to a man and wife c1540, plus various
inscriptions from 1507 to 1651; in the middle of the chancel is a stone,
carved with an effigy of a bishop, all that remains of the monument of a
restless fanatical, Thomas Scroope, Bishop of Dromore in Ireland, and a
former rector who died here in 1491 - 'at first a Benedictine, and afterwards
a Carmelite monk; sometimes retiring to his convent for several years, and
at others wandering about the country, clothed in sackcloth, girt with an
iron chain, and crying out in the streets and lanes'. His sermons must have
been memorable!

Other Lowestoft churches:

Location: Gordon Road.
Dedication: Our Lady Star of the Sea.
Description: Large red-brick church with tall and broad W tower and an
apse.
Periods: Built 1900-2 in Early English style.

Location: Whapload Road.
Dedication: Christ Church.
Description: Built of white brick.
Periods: Built 1869 in Early English style and enlarged 1879.

Location: South Lowestoft.
Dedication: St John the Evangelist.
Description: Built in Kentish rag stone with Caen stone dresings and
comprising a nave with N and S aisles, transepts, chancel and SW tower. The
church has as many as 30 windows, all in differing styles.
Periods: Built in 1853-4, the W aisle added in 1881.

MARKET WESTON

Location: 7 miles NE of Ixworth.
Dedication: St Mary.
Description: Nave, chancel, S Porch and pinnacled tower with belfry.
Periods: The church has a Norman S door but has been much rebuilt. The older portions are mainly 14c Dec, and the 15c Perp S porch. It was fully restored and the chancel rebuilt by Cottingham in 1846.
Features: Modern double hammerbeam roof to nave; Hanoverian Royal Arms over chancel arch; 18c bier; Elizabethan cup, paten 1661, flagon 1699.

MARLESFORD

Location: 5 miles SE of Framlingham.
Dedication: St Andrew.
Description: Nave with S aisle, chancel, S porch and W tower. There is a stone sanctus bell-cote over the E nave gable.
Periods: The chancel and tower are 14c and the nave has re-used Norman pillars of c1200 forming the S arcade. The S aisle is Perp, as is the flint-panelled porch.
Features: Nave roof has traces of colour; octagonal 15c font; 17c pulpit; two inscribed 15c bells in tower; Elizabethan cup and cover, paten 1728; monument to William Alston 1641. The Register dates from 1660.

MARTLESHAM

Location: 2 miles SW of Woodbridge.
Dedication: St Mary.
Description: Stands on high ground overlooking a creek of the river Deben. It comprises a nave, chancel, S porch and W tower of knapped flint.
Periods: Dec nave and S porch, Perp tower, and modern chancel rebuilt in 1837 but retaining part of the original roof.
Features: Heptagonal wagon roof to nave and old hammerbeam roof to chancel; arms of the Noon family, lords of the manor 1412-1639 and probable builders of the tower, on the spandrels of W door; 14c font; three piscinas and sedilia in chancel; modern stained glass in nave 1903; painting of St Christopher on N wall; rood-screen panels used as a front to a pew recessed in S wall; 15c bench-ends; pulpit of 1614; Royal Arms of Charles II; Elizabethan cup.

MELLIS

Location: 4 miles W of Eye.
Dedication: St Mary.
Description: Towerless church with wide nave, chancel and two-storey S porch.
Periods: 13c nave and chancel, mostly rebuilt in the late 15c (see Perp windows) and the interior restored 1859. The tower fell in 1730 and was never rebuilt, but the fine tower arch at the W end of the nave remains.
Features: 15c font; Easter Sepulchre in N wall of sanctuary; stained glass in a S window with complete 15c figures; repaired 15c rood-screen; 17c communion rail; Royal Arms of Charles I, dated 1634; cup 1682, paten 1734, almsdish 1775; mutilated tomb chest monument to Richard Yaxley 1570.

MELTON

Location: 1 mile NE of Woodbridge.
Dedication: St Andrews.
Description: New church of nave with S aisle, chancel, vestry and S tower 'containing a clock and three bells and surmounted by a handsome spire'.
Periods: It was built in 1867-8 to replace the old church which still survives.
Features: Seven Sacraments' font (removed from old church); stained glass S window by Kempe c1903; finely carved Caen stone reredos.

Dedication: Old St Andrews.
Description: Stands about a mile from the new church and some distance NE of the village on the banks of the river Deben. Only its nave, with a 19c apse, and W tower now remain
Periods: The 14c tower has good flint panelling and fine belfry windows. The nave is also 14c.
Features: Brass with three effigies in the nave floor, a Priest, Civilian and a Lady with veiled headdress c1430.

MENDHAM

Location: 8 miles SW of Bungay.
Dedication: All Saints.
Description: The church has a fine exterior, much restored. It comprises an aisled nave with tall clerestory, chancel, tower and S porch.
Periods: The church is mainly 14c Dec, but the N arcade and clerestory are 15c, as is the S porch. Many of the windows are Perp insertions. The church was restored in 1868 and the chancel rebuilt a few years later.
Features: Wooden chancel arch; 14c font; painting Presentation in the Temple c1600; late 17c communion rail; Elizabethan cup, paten 1666, flagon 1710; brasses of Cecily Friston 1615, Richard Friston 1615, and Richard Friston 1634; monuments to James Rant 1743 and William Rant 1754.

MENDLESHAM

Location: 7 miles NE of Stowmarket.
Dedication: St Mary.
Description: This large impressive church emphasises Mendlesham's former market town status. It comprises an aisled and clerestoried nave, chancel, fine N and S panelled porches (the N has a chamber over), and a beautiful Perp W tower with two two-light belfry windows in each face and a fine panelled parapet. The six-bay arcade is broken by a little wall which Pevsner suggests may relate to former transepts.
Periods: The earliest part of the church is the nave, arcades and N and S doors, all 13c. The chancel, clerestory and most of the windows are a century later.
Features: From 1593, the N porch priest's chamber, with its iron-bound door fastened by an ancient lock, was used for the parish armour, a remarkable collection dating from 1470 to 1630, and the most complete of any English parish church; sanctus bell-cote incorporated with the parapet of the E nave gable; canopied niche in E wall of N aisle; beautiful font cover made in 1630 by local craftsman John Turner; Jacobean pulpit also made by Turner in the same year; benches with buttressed arm-rests; Elizabethan

cup 1588 and two flagons 1664, paten 1736; brass of John Knyvet 1417, and an inscription to Barnaby Parker 1617 and his son John 1629.

METFIELD

Location: 7 miles NW of Halesworth.
Dedication: St John the Baptist.
Description: Nave, chancel, fine flint-panelled two-storeyed S porch and tall W tower
Periods: The chancel walls and the lower part of the tower are 14c Dec. The rest of the church is Perp, the upper part of the tower being c1385.
Features: Eastern bay of nave roof is painted and forms a Canopy of Honour to the rood; 15c font; lower portion of the 15c rood-screen; 17c carved church chest; Royal Arms of George IV; inscribed 15c bell in tower; cup 166, paten 1593; brasses to John Jermy and his wife Isabel 1504, and to Anne Franklin 1636.

METTINGHAM

Location: 2 miles E of Bungay.
Dedication: All Saints.
Description: Aisled nave, chancel, S porch and round tower with flint panelled parapet.
Periods: The tower is Norman and there is a Norman N doorway. The rest of the building is of various dates with late Dec and Perp windows.
Features: Octagonal 15c font; two piscinas inchancel; some armorial glass in a N window; traces of wall painting on N wall; several old bench-ends; Royal Arms of George III; Elizabethan cup 1568, paten 1570; canopied tomb in recess in S aisle thought to be that of John de Norwich, builder of the nearby castle.

MICKFIELD

Location: 3 miles SW of Debenham.
Dedication: St Andrew.
Description: Rather plain with nave, chancel and an imposing S tower, the basement of which forms a porch.
Periods: William White is alone in considering the church to have Saxon origins and to be one of the oldest in the county. Most authorities consider the church to be mainly 14c work with most windows later Perp insertions.
Features: Splendid 14c chancel arch; stoup in S porch; massive painted font of undetermined date; piscina and windowsill sedilia in chancel; five excellent 15c bench-end; Elizabethan cup and paten, both dated 1599; brasses to Peter Preston 1616 and his wife Thomasine 1617, and inscriptions to Francis Dade 1615 and Peter Preston 1631. The Register dates from 1558.

MIDDLETON-cum-Fordley

Location: 4 miles NE of Saxmundham.
Dedication: Holy Trinity.
Description: Middleton church comprises a nave and chancel under one roof, porch and a tall W tower with flint-panelled battlements and lead

needle-spire. The church was seriously damaged by fire during restoration in 1955 when the thatched roofs were destroyed. They are now tiled.
Periods: That a Norman church preceeded the present one is evident in the SW corner of the nave, the fine S doorway, in mouldings over the E window and on another chancel window. The E window is c1300 and the tower 15c.
Features: Octagonal 15c font; piscina in chancel made up from small Norman shafts; modern stained glass in the chancel of c1877; wall painting of top half of St Christopher on N wall (affected by water damage during fire); two old 15c bench-ends; Royal Arms of George III in cast-iron; cup and paten 1808; brasses of Anthony Pettow 1610, and of a Civilian and wife c1500 in nave floor.

Description: The churchyard once contained two churches; the smaller, that which served **Fordley**, has long gone and no vestiges remain. In 1620 complaint was made to the Bishop of Norwich that when services did not begin and end at both churches exactly at the same time, the bells and steeple of one disturbed the congregation of the other. To remedy this problem, the bishop directed that in future the same minister should serve both and officiate in them alternately.

MILDEN

Location: 4 miles SE of Lavenham.
Dedication: St Peter.
Description: A small church with nave, chancel, and a bell-cote which replaced the 14c W tower which was taken down in 1860 as unsafe.
Periods: A nave S window and the S doorway are Norman. The chancel appears to have been rebuilt in the 14c.
Features: Good king-post roof to nave; square Norman font; 14c piscina in S wall of chancel; painted Commandments on E wall; 17c pulpit; benches dated 1685; cup c1600, paten 1696, paten 1783; fine alabaster tomb monument to James Allington 1626 on the N side of the chancel, and another monument on the S wall of the nave to John Canham 1772. The Register dates from 1558.

MILDENHALL

Dedication: St Mary and St Andrew.
Description: The magnificent parish church is 168' long, one of the largest and finest in Suffolk. It comprises a spacious aisled nave, chancel, N and S porches - the former, 30' long, and vaulted with the 2-bay Lady Chapel above - and a W tower 120' tall, in the lower stages of which is a fan-vaulted passage with a gallery above. It originally had a lead spire which was taken down about 1830.
Periods: The chancel dates back to c1240-1300 with early 14c windows and a late 13c chancel arch, the N chapel is also 13c, and the nave, aisles, porches and tower all of c1420.
Features: Beautiful roofs of nave and aisles - that of the nave with alternating hammerbeams and cambered tie-beams being one of the finest in the county, despite being pitted with Puritan's buckshot; N door with tracery; two rood-loft doors, one above the other; octagonal 15c font of Purbeck marble bearing the arms of Sir Henry Barton; 13c double piscina and sedilia in chancel; remarkable E window with unique tracery; Royal Arms of

George II, dated 1758; cup 1625, almsdish 1632, cup and paten 1642, two enamelled pewter dishes given 1648, flagon given 1720; brasses include those to Sir Henry Warner, Knight 1617, Edward Warner 1618, Mary Warner 1601 and an inscription to Master Richard Baggott 1424; memorials include: on S side of tower - large plain altar tomb to Sir Henry Barton, Lord Mayor of London in 1416 and again in 1428, in the S aisle - Sir Henry North 1620 and his wife, also his grandson Thomas Hanmer, 1746, an MP at 24 and Speaker at 37, in the chancel floor - to its builder Richard de Wicheforde, and one to Hugh Hovel 1690; On the S side of the church the remains of the charnel house with a chapel to St Michael over. The chapel was endowed in 1387.

MONEWDEN

Location: 5 miles SW of Framlingham.
Dedication: St Mary.
Description: Nave, chancel, brick S porch and fine W tower.
Periods: The church is mostly 14c Dec but there are some early Norman windows in the N and S walls with later heads added. The S porch is early 16c.
Features: Fine roofs over nave and chancel are modern copies; octagonal Perp font; 17c pulpit; old benches; Elizabethan cup and cover; brasses to Thomas Reeve 1595 and to William Reeve and his wife Rose 1587, who had 15 children!

MONKS ELEIGH

Location: 6 miles NW of Hadleigh.
Dedication: St Peter.
Description: The village green runs up to the large church comprising nave with aisles and clerestory, chancel, N and S porches, and fine W tower with large stair turret.
Periods: The building is mostly Perp in date but the chancel and its vestry were built in 1845. Earlier remains from the 14c include the pillars of the S arcade.
Features: Consecration crosses either side of entrance to the S porch; nave roof with a Canopy of Honour to the rood at its E end; S door with tracery; a squint to the high altar at N end of rood-loft; unusual 13c font; 15c pulpit with traceried panels; 14c inscribed bell in the tower; Royal Arms of Queen Anne; poor-box 1636.

MONK SOHAM

Location: 3 miles NE of Debenham.
Dedication: St Peter.
Description: Nave, chancel with large five-light E window, porch and W tower.
Periods: The chancel, tower and N window of the nave are c1300, while the nave windows and porch are 15c Perp.
Features: Hammerbeam roof over nave; mutilated Seven Sacraments' font; piscina and niche in S wall of nave; pulpit dated 1604; the rood beam remains in situ while parts of the screen are in the E door of the tower; old benches; 14c iron-bound chest; Elizabethan cup, two patens 1808.

MOULTON

Location: 4 miles E of Newmarket.
Dedication: St Peter.
Description: Imposing, if rather bulky, church stands on rising ground overlooking the river Kennett. Cruciform in plan with a battlemented chancel (raised six steps above the nave formerly to accommodate a crypt), transeptal chapels, lofty aisled and clerestoried nave and a low W tower.
Periods: The exterior E and W walls of the S aisle retain Norman work and the tower is late 13c, but the main church is of 15c and early 16c.
Features: Fine 16c nave arcades; modern font with 16c cover; damaged pillar piscina in N chapel.

MUTFORD

Location: 5 miles SE of Beccles.
Dedication: St Andrew.
Description: Nave, chancel and round tower. To the W is a galilee porch.
Periods: The round tower is Norman with a later Dec octagonal belfry. There is also Norman work in the N wall of the nave, but the church is mostly 14c. The chancel was fully restored and reroofed in 1881.
Features: Roofs to nave and aisle; interesting font given by Elizabeth de Hengrave c1380; fine 14c canopied piscina in S aisle; a round arched recess in N wall of the nave; remains of an amusing wall painting of St Christopher on N wall; lower part of rood-screen; some old benches; Royal Arms of William IV, dated 1831; inscribed Elizabethan cup 1568.

NACTON

Location: 4 miles SE of Ipswich.
Dedication: St Martin.
Description: The church has an aisled nave, chancel and short W tower.
Periods: Mostly of 14c and 15c date. It was newly roofed in 1858 and restored in 1870 when the S aisle was built; the N was added in 1907.
Features: 15c octagonal font; piscina in chancel; modern stained glass E and N windows by Kempe; Elizabethan cup; brass inscription to Richard Fastolf 1479; memorial inscriptions to three local naval heroes, Admiral Vernon, Sir Philip Broke and his brother Sir Charles Broke Vere.

Alnesbourn Priory and Purdis Farm, formerly ex-parochial, but now civil parishes and annexed to Nacton. They are said to have had three churches, Hallowtree, St Petronille and Bixley, but their sites are unknown.

NAUGHTON

Location: 5 miles N of Hadleigh.
Dedication: St Mary.
Description: Standing in a moated churchyard and comprising nave, chancel, S porch and W tower.
Periods: The chancel, which has been restored, is late 13c and the remainder mostly early 14c.
Features: 14c king-post roof to nave; mutilated Norman font; mutilated painting of St Christopher discovered in 1953 on N wall; 17c benches known locally as 'rockers'; organ by Robert Gray dated 1777; paten 1711, cup 1730.

NAYLAND with Wissington

Location: 9 miles SE of Sudbury
Dedication: St James.
Description: Spacious church with aisled nave, chancel, N and S porch and W tower. A fine clerestory runs the entire length of the church.
Periods: Dec chancel, Perp aisled nave, 15c N porch, and a fine SW porch rebuilt by William Abell in 1525 and restored 1884. The tower is 14c with modern brick top of 1834 and an even more recent spire replacing one taken down when the top was added.
Features: Linen-fold panelling on N door; stained glass E window illustrates the martyrdom of St Stephen (to whom the church was originally dedicated?), and modern stained glass in the N aisle W window by Kempe; a painting by William Constable 'Christ blessing the Elements' of 1809 forms a reredos to the high altar; 18c western gallery with early 16c screen beneath; eight painted panels of rood-screen c1500 along wall of S aisle; a number of 16c books in a case at W end of N aisle; cup 1562, paten and flagon 1825; several brasses: part of large double canopy in N aisle c1440, upper part of lady (Mrs Hacche) with parts of another double canopy c1485, effigy of Civilian and wife with double canopy c1500, and another of Civilian and wife - probably Richard and Joan Davy 1514; tomb of William Abell in S wall bearing the letter 'A' and the figure of a bell. The Register dates from 1558.

NEDGING

Location: 4 miles N of Hadleigh.
Dedication: St Mary.
Description: United with the parish of Naughton in 1934. The small church of Nedging consists of nave, chancel, S porch and tower.
Periods: Dec except for Late Norman N and S doorways and c1300 chancel.
Features: 14c king-post nave roof; 15c font; 14c piscina and window-sill sedilia in chancel; old benches; interesting inscribed 14c 'Dawe' bell; cup 1562. The Register dates from 1558.

NEEDHAM MARKET

Location: 3 miles SE of Stowmarket.
Dedication: St John the Baptist.
Description: Situated in the high street, the exterior of the church is towerless and unassuming. Within, however, is its crowning glory, the famous roof. Crossley enthusiastically calls it 'the climax of English roof construction', and Cautley claims it to be 'the culminating achievement of the English carpenter'. The design is such that, as Pevsner explains, it provides the impression of 'a whole church, nave, aisles and timbered clerestory suspended in mid-air'. Until its separation in 1907, Needham Market was only a hamlet of Barking for whom its church provided merely a chapel-of-ease; funeral biers were conveyed between the two along the Causeway which now provides a pleasant green-lane for walkers. The building was erected at the expense of William Grey, Bishop of Ely, between 1458 and 1478 and still looks what it clearly was, a chapel. It has no churchyard or tower and the odd-looking bell-turret and clock erected in the 1880s, when much of the church was restored, are perched on the roof of the S porch. Here, the remarkable roof is all; an experience not to be missed.

NETTLESTEAD

Location: 4 miles S of Needham Market.
Dedication: St Mary.
Description: The church, damaged by enemy action during the last war and closed until 1950, has a nave, chancel, W tower and charming brick S porch.
Periods: Although chiefly 14c in date, there remains a small Norman window from the previous church in the N wall. The porch is 16c.
Features: Interestingly decorated 15c font; good three-light 14c E window; Jacobean pulpit; Royal Arms of George IV; cup and cover 1601, paten 1713; brass effigy of Knight c1500; marble monument to Samuel Sayer 1625 and his wife Thomassine 1647 in chancel.

NEWBOURN

Location: 7 miles SE of Ipswich.
Dedication: St Mary.
Description: Nave, red-brick S aisle - extended to form a chapel to the Rowley family, chancel and a S tower, its basement forming a porch.
Periods: The early 13c shafts of the E window and the Dec tower are probably the oldest parts. The aisle has been encased in 16c brickwork and there is much alteration of this period.
Features: Hammerbeam nave roof; 15c carved font; piscina and sedilia in chancel, and 13c piscina in chapel; 15c choir stalls in chancel; lower part of 16c rood-screen; Elizabethan cup, paten 1570; late 15c graffiti - illustration of ship inside W jamb of arch; 13c stone coffin lid; memorial to Wolton family with carving of the Suffolk stallion 'Monarch'.

NEWMARKET

Location: Market Street.
Dedication: St Mary.
Description: The old parish church lies on the W side of High Street, close to the old quarter of town and comprises aisled and clerestoried nave, chancel and W tower with tall spire and little 17c bell-cote.
Periods: The S arcade is 14c but the remainder of the church, including the tower, is 15c though much restored and renewed. The chancel was completely rebuilt in 1856.
Features: Two piscinas, 13c and 14c?; modern stained glass in windows, some by Christopher Webb; 17c paintings; buried beneath the floor are the remains of Cardinal Wolsey's father.

Location: E side of High Street.
Dedication: All Saints.
Description: Good example of late 19c architecture. Aisled and clerestoried nave, apsidal chancel and SW tower.
Periods: Rebuilt 1876-7 by subscription as a memorial to Lord John Manners, and called the 'Manners Memorial Church'
Features: Much modern stained glass in windows.

Location: Bury Road.
Dedication: St Agnes.
Description: Small modern church built in red-brick with much interior

decoration in Spanish tile.
Periods: Built 1886 by Carpenter.
Features: Large reredos by Sir Edgar Boehm representing the Assumption of the Virgin; cup (Norwegian) 1707.

NEWTON nr. Sudbury

Location: 3 miles E of Sudbury.
Dedication: All Saints.
Description: Standing down a lane N of the green. It comprises nave, chancel, S porch and tower.
Periods: The church originates from Norman times, from which period the N doorway remains. The nave is c1300, and the remainder mostly Dec. It is suggested that the tower may have been built by the Boteler family who resided in Newton but went to Ireland at the time of the Reformation.
Features: Octagonal 15c font; early 14c piscina and sedilia in chancel and another, even earlier, W of the priest's door; 15c pulpit inscribed Richd Modi; 17c lectern; fine canopied altar-tomb to (Margaret Boteler c1310)?, on N side of chancel; effigy of lady c1320 (another Boteler)? in recess in S wall of nave, discovered during restoration. The Register dates from 1558.

NORTH COVE

Location: 3 miles E of Beccles.
Dedication: St Botolph.
Description: Long narrow building comprising a thatched nave and chancel all in one, S porch and W tower of flint and (Roman?) brick.
Periods: Norman S doorway, Early English nave, N doorway and one window, the remainder Dec.
Features: Early 15c octagonal font; 14c piscina and sedilia in S wall of chancel; early 14c wall paintings (repainted late 19c) depicting Scenes from the Passion (chancel, W of the N window), Deesis (W of S window), Resurrection and Harrowing of Hell (E of N window), Ascension (E of S window); Inscribed Elizabethan cup 1568; altar-stone in floor of nave with consecration cross visible and a small brass to Margaret Berney 1548 now affixed to it; brass inscription to Thomas Sengylton 1498, and another to William and Alice Manthorpe c1500.

NORTON

Location: 3 miles SE of Ixworth.
Dedication: St Andrew.
Description: A large building with nave, N and S aisles, chancel, S porch and W tower.
Periods: Except for the c1300 chancel and the early 14c N aisle, the church is of c1460.
Features: Unusual pillars of nave arcades; carved font - one of finest in the county; 15c glass including representations of St Christopher, St Ethelreda and St Andrew; eight beautifully carved late 14c misericords in the nave and chancel;, again some of the best examples in the county; interesting 15c benches; old chest; paten 1722, almsdish 1761; coloured tomb of 1624 with no inscription.

NOWTON

Location: 2 miles SE of Bury St Edmunds.
Dedication: St Peter.
Description: A small church consisting of a nave, chancel and W tower stands isolated near the hall.
Periods: There are traces of genuine Norman work beside neo-Norman. The N and S doorways are of this early period as is a window in the E wall of the N aisle. The chancel is c1300 and the tower 14c, but the aisle is 'Norman' circa 1843.
Features: Pictorial medallions contain about 75 pieces of 16-17c Flemish glass brought back from 'monasteries at Brussels' by Orbell Ray Oakes whose wife is commemorated in a monument of 1811 by John Bacon; mutilated remains of part of rood-screen; cup 1643, cup 1678.

OAKLEY

Location: 3 miles NE of Eye.
Dedication: St Nicholas.
Description: The church stands overlooking the Waveney valley on the Norfolk border and some distance from the village. It comprises a nave, chancel, 2-storeyed S porch with flintwork panelling which also adorn the battlements of the W tower.
Periods: The tower and nave doorway are Dec, but all the rest is 15c Perp, except for the modern vestry.
Features: Rood-loft staircase which ascends through a jamb of a window; stained glass in S porch; reredos with representation of 'The Last Supper' donated to the church in 1882; cup c1673, paten c1675; plain alabaster altar-tomb of Sir William Cornwallis 1611.

It is said that Oakley was anciently in two parishes. In what was called **Little Oakley** stood St Andrew's Church, but there are no remains and the site is not known.

OCCOLD

Location: 2 miles SE of Eye.
Dedication: St Michael.
Description: Nave and chancel (not on the same axis), with a 2-storeyed NE vestry and W tower.
Periods: One N window in the chancel is Norman, and the N and S doorways of the nave are Early English. The remainder is Dec except for the tower which was built in 1426.
Features: Old ironwork in S door; mutilated 15c font; old stained glass in first window on S side of chancel; some traceried panels of the rood-loft; pulpit of 1620; choir-stalls, one with its misericord; Royal Arms of Charles II; Elizabethan cup, paten c1675; painted memorial on N wall of nave dated 1598 to the Humfrey family; brass to William Corbald and wife c1490.

OFFTON

Location: 4 miles SW of Needham Market.
Dedication: St Mary.
Description: The church has a nave, chancel, timber S porch and W tower.

Periods: Simple Norman S doorway, 14c tower and late 14c porch.
Features: King-post roof to nave; 15c octagonal font; 15c glass added to SE window in 1871; 17c pulpit; remains of rood-screen, part of which is worked into a bench; Elizabethan cup.

OLD NEWTON

Location: 3 miles NE of Stowmarket.
Dedication: St Mary.
Description: Nave, chancel with vestry, S porch and W tower.
Periods: The church is mainly Dec with some exceptionally fine 14c windows. The vestry and E end of the chancel are modern.
Features: Painted octagonal 15c font; fine niches in E wall and sedilia, uncovered 1972; pieces of old glass in heads of the nave N windows; some 17c benches; Royal Arms of George III; cup c1680.

ONEHOUSE

Location: 1 mile NW of Stowmarket.
Dedication: St John the Baptist.
Description: Small, ancient church with nave, chancel, brick S porch and round tower.
Periods: The early Norman round tower was recently partially dismantled as unsafe and rebuilt. The nave was much restored in the 14c and the chancel rebuilt in the 19c.
Features: Much damaged square Norman font.

ORFORD

Location: 5 miles SW of Aldeburgh.
Dedication: St Bartholomew.
Description: At the time of Domesday, Orford was a mere hamlet of Sudbourne and its church merely considered a chapelry to the latter. However, the growing success of the medieval port and the erection of Henry II's great castle in 1165 brought great prosperity to the town as seen by the ruinous Late Norman chancel, begun in 1166 and planned to be 6-bays long with vaulted 5-bay aisles, transepts and chapels. The later Dec church with its impressive nave, aisles, small clerestory, W tower and S porch (added c1450) began from a period when this wealth was beginning to drain away with the silting up of the harbour. The building still remains large and impressive, though the top of the massive W tower, its showpiece, and containing the belfry, fell in 1829, and was not rebuilt until 1972.
Features: Font of c1400 with an inscription commemorating John Cokerel and his wife Katherine; three piscinas in nave; paintings of Holy family with St John and the donor above the high altar c1520, also the Nativity, above the S altar; fine modern rood-screen is carried right across the church and replaces a screen of 1712 bearing the Royal Arms of William and Mary, which is now in the W end of the nave; cup and flagon 1773; three bells, two 17c and one 18c placed on the floor at the W end of S aisle after loss of belfry; eight brasses of between c1480 and 1631, include those to John Coe, first mayor of the borough 1580, and to John Coggishall, 1631, a mayor here three times, and a fine brass to one of his family, Henry Coggeshall, who invented the sliding-rule known by his name; a memorial to Rev. Francis Mason 1621,

chaplain to James I, was removed from the old chancel, and resited in the nave. The church is notable as providing the venue for the first performances of Benjamin Britten's Noye's Fludd, 1958, and Curlew River, 1964. Britten lived and worked at nearby Aldeburgh.

OTLEY

Location: 6 miles NW of Woodbridge.
Dedication: St Mary.
Description: Nave with S aisle and clerestory, chancel, S porch and fine W tower with flintwork decoration on base and brick battlements.
Periods: Late 14c and 15c Perp throughout.
Features: Hammerbeam roof to nave and 17c chancel roof; W door with tracery; mutilated 15c octagonal font, and rare immersion font below the floor of the vestry; piscina in chancel; transomed windows of S aisle; 17c pulpit; bench-ends; the original 15c lower half of rood-screen; Elizabethan cup; monument to John Gosnold in chancel 1628. Samuel Rogers was rector here for 67 years, one of the longest on record in all England.

OULTON

Location: 2 mile W of Lowestoft.
Dedication: St Michael.
Description: The church stands on the crest of a hill commanding wide views over the marshlands of the Waveney valley. It is Norman in design with a nave, chancel, central tower, and a ruined chapel dedicated to the Holy Trinity on the S side. There were originally transepts, but these have gone.
Periods: The lower part of the tower is Norman, as is the S doorway and simple blocked N doorway, but the belfry is 13c and later. The chancel was rebuilt on a larger scale in the 14c and the nave much altered in the 15c.
Features: 15c octagonal font; 14c piscina and windowsill sedilia in chancel; three niches and stoup in porch; some old glass; Royal Arms of James II, said to have come from St Margaret's Westminster; Elizabethan cup; on the chancel floor is a large stone which once bore effigies in brass (now stolen) of Sir John Fastolf and Katherine his wife who died in 1445 and 1478 respectively. Sir John fought under three Henrys, gaining glory at Agincourt, had the distinction of being defeated by Joan of Arc, and appeared in the first part of Shakespeare's Henry the Sixth, though his character as with many of his actions has been described as vengeful and pitiless - perhaps an unfair analysis bearing in mind the traumatic times in which he lived.

OUSDEN

Location: 7 miles SE of Newmarket.
Dedication: St Peter.
Description: Another Norman church, of a rare design for Suffolk but similar to Oulton, above. Nave, chancel, small brick transept (or chapel), central tower and N porch.
Periods: The tower and nave are Norman but the chancel is a late 18c or early 19c rebuilding. The tower opens to the nave and chancel with plain Norman arches. The tower belfry has Norman windows but the battlements are 15c. The nave was lengthened 20' in 1860. The N porch doorway is unusual in having one 12c jamb and the other 13c. The blocked S door is

Norman. N of the nave, an 18c brick chapel has good imitation Norman work.
Features: Late 14c octagonal font; canopy of side altar on S side of western tower arch and Hanoverian Royal Arms over tower arch; late 17c communion rail; cup 1678 or 1736, paten 1710, flagon c1730, almsdish c1750; monument to Laeticia Mosley 1619.

PAKEFIELD

Location: 1 mile SW of Lowestoft.
Dedication: St Margaret & All Saints.
Description: After continuing attention to its well-being throughout the 19c with repairs and restorations, the church, badly damaged in 1941 during the Second World War when an incendiary set the thatched roof on fire and burnt out the interior, stood roofless for nine years. Now totally restored it is in fact two churches in one. There were originally two parishes and two rectors here servicing two churches divided by a single solid wall. In 1743 the parishes were united and the dividing wall pierced by seven arches. The building is two-naved rather than aisled and the W tower from the southern church now serves the whole. With the sea at the SE corner of the churchyard, Pakefield church again faces an uncertain future.
Periods: Most of the church appears 14c Dec.
Features: Late 14c octagonal font; cup inscribed 'Pakefield Sante Margaret, 1337' and paten 1769; brasses to John Bowf 1417 and his wife, and to Richard Ffolcard 1451. A set of stocks remains outside the N gate of the churchyard.

PAKENHAM

Location: 5 miles NE of Bury St Edmunds.
Dedication: St Mary.
Description: Another rare (for Suffolk) cruciform design, consisting of chancel, central square tower with an octagonal belfry, long transepts and an aisleless nave.
Periods: The church, which stands on a site yielding prehistoric finds, originally had only an Early English S transept, but when this was rebuilt during an 1849 restoration, a N transept was added. The chancel is also 13c altered c1500 when the large five-light E window was inserted. The upper part of the tower is 14c. There are remains still of the first Norman church in the S and W doorways and in the chancel arch.
Features: Exceptionally fine Perp font; interesting window in the S wall, and the one opposite show the transitional period of window tracery; simple choir stalls; restored 15c screen; old chest hollowed from a tree trunk; late 17c communion rail; cup 1566, cup and paten 1817; four old 13c coffin lids on exterior of S chancel wall. The Register dates from 1562.

PALGRAVE

Location: 5 miles NW of Eye.
Dedication: St Peter.
Description: Aisled nave, chancel, ornate S porch and W tower.
Periods: The earliest remaining structure is the chancel arch of c1300 - the chancel itself is early 18c and the N aisle is modern. The tower is Dec and the remainder Perp.

Features: Fine painted hammerbeam roof to nave; late Norman font; Royal Arms of Queen Anne; set of plate 1728; some parish armour above the S door; marble monument to 'Honest' Thomas Martin, the antiquarian 1697-1771. There are two interesting tombstones in the churchyard; one with an inscription to a blacksmith, the other, of 1787, to a wagoner showing his team of six horses drawing a wagon.

PARHAM

Location: 2 miles SE of Framlingham.
Dedication: St Mary.
Description: The church was built by William de Ufford, Earl of Suffolk and comprises a nave, chancel, porch and massive flint W tower still containing the original 14c bell frame.
Periods: Mainly of 14c date except for the 15c N porch and windows in the nave and chancel.
Features: Stone Willoughby armorial shields in N wall of chancel, probably brought from Campsea Abbey at the Dissolution, and the Arms of the Earls of Suffolk throughout the church; rood-loft stairway; early 15c font; two piscinas; niches either side of chancel arch; some old stained glass; mid-17c communion rail and Peter's Pence box; badly restored 15c screen; Royal Arms of Charles II; cup 1785, paten 1803; hat bracket, dated 1716, in chancel; huge padlock on N door; two medieval 14c? bells in tower; brass in memory of Alice Wingfield 1603; memorials to the Warner, Rous and Corrance families include a monument to Edmund Warner 1617 and his wife. The Register dates from 1538. In the churchyard, the parish stocks have been preserved in the roof of the lychgate.

PEASENHALL

Location: 5 miles NW of Saxmundham.
Dedication: St Michael.
Description: Nave, chancel, attractive N porch and pinnacled W tower with flintwork decoration.
Periods: Little remains of the earlier church. The tower is 15c but the nave and chancel were entirely rebuilt in 1860-1, after which the tower was heightened and restored.
Features: Transitional Norman font; modern stained glass in E window; communion cup inscribed 'The Towne of Pesnaulle'.

PETTAUGH

Location: 3 miles S of Debenham.
Dedication: St Catherine.
Description: Nave, chancel, S porch and unbuttressed W tower.
Periods: The base of the tower appears Early English with a later 15c parapet. Apart from the modern porch, the remainder of the church is of 14c Dec period.
Features: 15c octagonal font; two piscinas include the remains of Norman pillar-piscina; old priest's door; bench-ends, and reading desk dated 1615; Elizabethan cup and paten; brass of Civilian and wife c1530 (probably members of the Fastolfe family).

PETTISTREE

Location: 4 miles NE of Woodbridge.
Dedication: St Peter and St Paul.
Description: Nave, chancel and tall W tower with wide buttresses and flint-panelled and battlemented parapet.
Periods: The nave, which was evidently heightened in the early 18c, and the tower are late 15c. The chancel was restored in 1884.
Features: 14c angled piscina in chancel and two piscinas in nave; fragments of 13c and later stained glass; some old benches; old chest; Royal Arms of George III; cup and cover, paten 1704; three inscribed 15c bells in tower; brass to Francis Bacon 1580 and his two wives.

The parish of Pettistree included the manors of **Loundham** and Bing. The former had a well-endowed church which long stood as a picturesque ruin in the park in front of the Elizabethan Loudham Hall.

PLAYFORD

Location: 4 miles NE of Ipswich.
Dedication: St Mary.
Description: Nave, chancel, and SW tower, its basement forming a porch.
Periods: The church was rebuilt by Sir George Felbrigge sometime before his death in 1400, leaving the N doorway of the nave which appears of c1300. The chancel was rebuilt again in 1873, and the nave restored the next year.
Features: Font with Early English pedestal and modern bowl; standing cup 1619, paten 1774; two medieval bells in tower; brass of Sir George Felbrigg, Knight; memorial to Thomas Clarkson 1760-1846, co-worker with William Wilberforce in his campaign to abolish slavery.

POLSTEAD

Location: 4 miles SW of Hadleigh.
Dedication: St Mary.
Description: Aisled and clerestoried nave, chancel, porch and tower with the only original stone spire remaining in Suffolk.
Periods: One of the most architecturally interesting churches in the county. It would appear that the site was first occupied by an early Norman aisleless church. About 1150 it was considerably enlarged with aisles added, the nave extended westwards, and the chancel rebuilt. In the 14c, the aisles were rebuilt and in the 15c, the chancel was altered. The 12c building incorporated what Pevsner considers the earliest surviving English bricks.
Features: Norman doorway in belfry; king-post roof to nave and panelling of eastern bay of N aisle roof to form Canopy of Honour over the altar; octagonal 13c font; arched recess in N aisle, W of N doorway; 15c and later stained glass in chancel; traces of wall-paintings on N wall of nave; 18c three-sided communion rail; Royal Arms of Queen Anne adapted for one of the Georges; set of plate 1816; brasses of priest c1440, and of Civilian, wife and children, c1490; curious coloured monument, dated 1630, over pulpit and memorials to the Brand, Cooke and Vincent families. The grave of Maria Marten, victim of the universally famous Murder in the Red Barn in 1827, lies in the churchyard, just beyond the W door, her stone whittled away by souvenir hunters until virtually nothing now remains.

POSLINGFORD

Location: 2 miles NE of Clare.
Dedication: St Mary.
Description: Nave, chancel, brick S porch and W tower.
Periods: Although much restored, the church retains its Norman doors and a small window in the nave. The tower is late 13c and there are windows of the same period in the chancel. The porch is early 16c. The church was restored 1882.
Features: Stoup in porch; Norman font; 14c piscina and sedilia in chancel; niche in jamb of NE nave window; 13c painted scrolls in a chancel window; with no chancel arch, the space above the fine 15c rood-screen was originally filled with a wooden tympanum featuring a Doom painting, unfortunately accidently destroyed in 1881; Royal Arms of James I; an old chest and a bell were brought here from the ruined Chipley Abbey a mile away.

PRESTON

Location: 2 miles NE of Lavenham.
Dedication: St Mary.
Description: Nave with aisles and clerestory, chancel, flint-panelled N porch (also used as a chapel), and fine W tower.
Period: Dec chancel, 15c nave, aisles, clerestory and porch. The church was thoroughly restored in 1868 when the tower was rebuilt.
Features: Early Norman font; 14c piscina and sedilia in chancel; tomb recess in N aisle; in the chancel a tablet to Rev Nicholas Colman 1673, who 'in bad times was ejected, in better was restored'; about 50 pieces of heraldic stained glass remain from the 167 pieces inserted into many of the windows by Robert Ryece; lower part of restored screen; Elizabethan Commandment board (exceptionally early example) and magnificent Royal Arms of Queen Elizabeth I, erected by Robert Ryece c1678; paten 1624; brasses to Mary Ryece 1629 and Robert Ryece 1638; in the porch, which was also used as a chapel, is a table tomb devoid of its brass but possibly to one of the de Veres, Earls of Oxford and once owners of Preston Hall, and, in the floor on the N side of the altar, a memorial slab bearing the arms of Robert Ryece of Preston Hall, a noted antiquarian and a student of Heraldry, who died in 1638.

RAMSHOLT

Location: 5 miles SE of Woodbridge.
Dedication: All Saints.
Description: Situated above the E bank of the Deben near its estuary, the ancient church has a nave, chancel, S porch and round septaria tower - its three tall butresses which run to the top making it appear oval rather than round.
Periods: The flint tower is Norman with its original archway into the nave. The latter is 14c as is the chancel, although the N nave and S chancel doorways are c1300. The porch is modern.
Features: Octagonal 15c font with early shaft; 14c piscina and window-sedilia; early 19c double-decker pulpit and box-pews; 18c carved chest; Elizabethan cup.

RATTLESDEN

Location: 5 miles W of Stowmarket.
Dedication: St Nicholas.
Description: Attractive church standing prominently above village with an aisled and clerestoried nave, chancel, S porch and W tower with unusual buttresses and surmounted by a late 15c belfry and spire.
Periods: The church has Early English origins (see S doorway of c1300) but was much enlarged by 14c and 15c additions. The tower is early 14c, and the vestry, which was formerly a chapel with a room over, was added in the early 16c, at which time the clerestory was built. The church was much restored in 1863 and again in 1878 when the N side of the clerestory was rebuilt.
Features: Fine early 16c double hammerbeam nave roof and interesting coved roof to chancel; 14c octagonal font; 14c aumbry on N side of chancel; remains of canopied niches at the E end of both aisles; some old stained glass in window tracery; 17c pulpit; some old benches; fine modern rood-screen and parclose screen, plus remains of the old screen preserved under tower arch; late 17c communion rail (formerly three-sided); Royal Arms of George I, dated 1714; Elizabethan cup, flagon 1729, paten 1731. The Register dates from 1558.

RAYDON

Location: 3 miles SE of Hadleigh.
Dedication: St Mary.
Description: A simple building comprising a nave and large chancel, but no tower. A single bell is housed in a small, low turret at the west end of the church. A notable feature of the exterior is the V-shaped buttresses.
Periods: The nave and chancel windows, with their beautiful Dec tracery, and the N and S doorways, point to a late 13c and early 14c date for the church.
Features: Stoup near door; 14c piscinas in chancel and nave; two leper's windows; two wooden brackets over chancel arch which originally supported a rood-beam; brasses of Elizabeth Reydon 1479 and of Thomas Reydon 1479; arched recess in N wall - probably a founder's tomb (Robert de Raydon had a grant of a market and fair here in 1310). The Register dates from 1562.

REDE

Location: 7 miles SW of Bury St Edmunds.
Dedication: All Saints.
Description: Small church comprising nave, chancel, S porch, and W tower with a sanctus-bell window filled with open-traceried woodwork.
Periods: The nave may be Norman, and the tower c1300. The porch is 15c and the chancel was completely rebuilt in 1874.
Features: Modern stained glass in E window; late 17c pulpit; some old 17c benches; Elizabethan cup, paten c1662; three bells in the tower of 1578, 1586 and 1602.

REDGRAVE

Location: 5 miles SW of Diss.
Dedication: St Mary the Virgin.
Description: The church has an aisled and clerestoried nave, large chancel

and W tower of Suffolk brick.

Periods: Dec period, except the 15c S aisle windows, the fine clerestory and the tower of c1800.

Features: Hammerbeam roof to nave; 14c octagonal font; piscina and handsome triple sedilia in S wall of chancel and another piscina in S aisle; seven-light E window in chancel with flowing tracery of an uncommon type; 15c iron-bound chest; fine 18c altar rails; top of former early 18c reredos featuring Commandments and paintings of Moses and Aaron in N aisle; cup and cover 1623, cup 1668 and paten 1696; in the chancel is what Pevsner calls 'one of the best post-Reformation brasses ever made' to 'Anne Butts, widdowe' 1609, mother-in-law of Sir Nicholas Bacon, with the inscription: 'The weaker sexes strongest precedent, lyes here belowe; seaven fayer yeares she spent in wedlock sage; and since that merry age, sixty one yeares she lived a widdowe sage'; superb monument in black and white marble to Sir Nicholas Bacon, Knight 1616 and Anne his wife at E end of N aisle, and another, in white marble N of the chancel, to Lord Chief Justice Sir John Holt, Knight 1710, who it is said on asking an old adversary who had been brought before him what had become of certain wild fellows of the days of his youth, received the reply, "Ah, my lord, they are all hanged but myself and your lordship."

Cardinal Wolsey was rector here in 1506 before his rise to fame.

REDISHAM (formerly 'Great')

Location: 5 miles SW of Beccles.

Dedication: St Peter.

Description: Tiny church with only a nave and chancel. The W tower which fell over a hundred years ago, has been replaced by a little wooden belfry.

Periods: Probably Saxon in origin and altered in Norman times when the elaborate S door was inserted. The simple N doorway is also 12c, and the chancel 14c.

Features: 15c octagonal font; fine E window; some old carved benches; square pulpit dated 1619; Hanoverian Royal Arms; cup c1567.

REDLINGFIELD

Location: 3 miles SE of Eye.

Dedication: St Andrew.

Description: The small parish church stands within the precincts and originally formed the chapel of the old Priory of Benedictine Nuns founded in 1120. It consists of a brick nave (rendered over), chancel, S porch and what remains of the W tower in brick and wood, now reduced to the height of the nave and covered by a gabled roof.

Periods: Mainly Dec and Perp.

Features: 15c octagonal font; some old bench-ends; set of Royal Arms of George IV; cup and paten c1620. The village stocks, now preserved in tower.

RENDHAM

Location: 3 miles W of Saxmundham.

Dedication: St Michael.

Description: Nave and chancel with no chancel arch, N porch and W tower with bell-openings, and flint decorated battlements and buttresses.

Periods: The chancel is 14c with an E window of probably c1600. The tower is 15c, and the nave, which still retains one early lancet window and several Perp windows, was rebuilt in 1861.
Features: Good carved roof over nave and chancel; piscina and windowsill sedilia in chancel; rood-loft staircase, discovered c1870; fine pulpit, dated 1632; 18c screen in tower arch; 19c pews with doors; Royal Arms of Charles II; cup and paten 1567; a brass chalice to the memory of Thomas Kyng 1523, and a brass memorial to Richard Thurston 1616. The Register dates from 1550.

RENDLESHAM

Location: 5 miles NE of Woodbridge.
Dedication: St Gregory.
Description: Lofty church comprising a nave, aisle, chancel, S porch and tall W tower with flint decorated battlements.
Periods: The church is mainly 14c, but the S porch and most of the windows are later Perp.
Features: Interesting nave roof; stoup in S porch; 15c octagonal font; pretty 14c piscina in S wall of chancel; fine E window of 1783 with unusual wood tracery; mid-17c? communion rail; 19c box-pews; Royal Arms of George III; set of plate 1812-13; 14c recessed tomb in N chancel wall containing an effigy of probably Rev. John Chaperon 1349, and 19c monuments to the Rendlesham and Thellusson families.

REYDON

Location: 2 miles NW of Southwold.
Dedication: St Margaret.
Description: Nave, chancel, S porch and W tower with a stair turret projection. There was formerly a N aisle, said to have been destroyed when the S porch was built in the 15c (the foundations of a former N chapel were discovered in 1952). Part of the roof fell in on 7 December 1883.
Periods: The church is chiefly 15c Perp but the tower is early 14c.
Features: Altar stone with consecration crosses; piscinas in nave and chancel; Royal Arms of Queen Anne, dated 1713; Elizabethan cup and cover; inscribed 15c bell in the tower.

RICKINGHALL INFERIOR

Location: 8 miles NE of Ixworth.
Dedication: St Mary.
Description: Neatly attractive church comprising aisled nave, chancel, two-storeyed S porch and round tower with octagonal belfry.
Periods: Apart from the main body of the round Norman tower, restored in 1859), and possibly its Saxon foundations, and the aisle arcading which may be 13c, the church is today a good example of the early 14c style.
Features: Hammerbeam roof to nave; wall arcading to S porch; early 14c octagonal font; 14c piscinas and windowsill sedilias in both aisle and chancel; fragments of old stained glass in SE window, a magnificent five-light E window and fine side windows in S aisle; reredos, made with repainted panels from the 15c rood-loft; Elizabethan cup.

RICKINGHALL SUPERIOR

Location: 8 miles W of Eye.
Dedication: St Mary.
Description: The church, which lies half a mile S of the previous, on the E side of the road, stands on a slope overlooking a small hamlet known as Candle Street. It features very fine flint decoration and comprises a wide (30') but aisleless nave, chancel, S porch with vaulted room above, and W tower.
Periods: The chancel and tower are early 14c and the nave and S porch 15c. The church was restored in 1868.
Features: Octagonal 14c font; 15c piscina and windowsill sedilia in chancel; a stone bench runs the whole length of the N and S nave walls - a relic from the days before churches had pews and when 'the weak (or weariest) went to the wall'; some old glass and a delightful traceried chancel E window; 16c carved chest; the old bier, dated 1763; Elizabethan cup, paten 1710.

RINGSFIELD

Location: 2 miles SW of Beccles.
Dedication: All Saints.
Description: Until its complete rebuild in 1883, the church comprised a thatched nave and chancel, and a W tower. Still under a thatched roof, the nave has been extended by 20' and continues straight into a new chancel. A vestry has been added, and the whole interior virtually redesigned.
Periods: The elaborate W tower is now the oldest part of the church being of c1450 with a 17c top of flint and brick panelling; the S porch is 16c.
Features: Octagonal 15c font; much interior 17c woodwork includes pews, a square pulpit and a low screen; Elizabethan cup and paten; mural monument with brass plate to Nicholas Garnys 1599 and his wife Anne attached to S wall of chancel, a monument to Robert Shelford 1701, and outside and below the E window, a tablet to Rev. Nicholas Gosling 1663; In the churchyard, erected in 1902, is a memorial to Princess Caroline Murat, grand-daughter of Napoleon's sister.

Little Redisham or Redisham Parva was anciently a separate parish, but was long ago consolidated with Ringsfield, and the settlement which lies in the park of Little Redisham Hall has all but vanished. There are some remains of **All Saints**, its church, in the grounds of the Hall. They include part of the W wall of the nave, the S door and fragments of the chancel.

RINGSHALL

Location: 3 miles SW of Needham Market.
Dedication: St Katherine.
Description: The church, which stands elevated on a site, thought to be an early fortification, has a massive square Norman W tower, nave and chancel.
Periods: The tower was completed and remodelled c1300 when a belfry was added. The nave is also Norman but again there is evidence of modifications to some windows and doors around 1300. The chancel has late 15c brick.
Features: Kingpost roof to nave and a hammerbeam roof to chancel; 13c octagonal font of Purbeck marble; painting of the Seven Works of Mercy on S wall; Elizabethan cup and cover.

RISBY

Location: 4 miles NW of Bury St Edmunds.
Dedication: St Giles.
Description: Nave, chancel, S porch and round tower with two-tiers of circular-headed windows in the upper stages.
Periods: Norman tower and Norman nave with windows of mostly c1300. The tower arch and chancel arch are also of Norman date but the latter was taken down and rebuilt. The chancel is 14c and the porch built c1435. A new vestry was added in 1843, and the chancel restored in 1881.
Features: 15c octagonal font with panel depicting the Annunciation; piscina in chancel and another in the window of the S wall of nave; ; fragments of old 14c glass in windows; paintings on W and N walls of nave range from a large Ecclesiastic of c1200 or a little later, to 14c date; two large coloured niches in each side of the 15c screen, one depicting the church's patron, St Giles, with a fawn; some old benches; 17c pulpit; 14c iron-bound chest; Royal Arms of George III; paten c1580, chalice 1633.

RISHANGLES

Location: 4 miles S of Eye.
Dedication: St Margaret.
Description: Nave, chancel, and SW tower, its basement forming a porch.
Periods: Evidence of Norman work in the S doorway (Transitional), the plainer N doorway and some nave windows. The decorated and battlemented tower is 15c and the chancel has an E window of the same period.
Features: Carved font, dated 1599; some ancient glass in nave S window; old benches in nave; Elizabethan cup, paten c1610; three 15c bells in tower; two brasses in chancel, one to Edward Grimeston 1599, and another to his son of the same name 1610; memorial stone in front of chancel steps to two children, John and Alice Greene 1629. A smugglers' hiding place, along with several complete 18c Dutch bottles of spirit, was discovered near the pulpit in 1858 with a tunnel leading outside the church.

ROUGHAM

Location: 3 miles SE of Bury St Edmunds.
Dedication: St Mary.
Description: A large impressive church comprising an aisled nave with clerestory, chancel, and exceptionally fine S porch and W tower.
Periods: The church is mainly 14c but received a major facelift in the late 15c when a new roof was placed on the nave, a clerestory added, and the tower raised and embattled. The N aisle rebuild was a little later, in 1514, and the S porch was re-roofed in 1632.
Features: Beautiful late 15c? hammerbeam roof to nave; probable tomb recesses in S aisle wall; octagonal 14c font; piscina and triple sedilia in S wall of chancel and piscinas in both aisles; rood-loft turret and stairs on S of nave; five-light chancel E window with fine net tracery, and old stained glass in E window of N aisle; 15c carved bench-ends; set of plate 1683; fine large brass in N aisle to Sir Roger Drury 1400 and wife Margery 1405, and another to Robert Drury 1621. Two stone coffins containing the remains of probable founders were discovered in the S wall to the right of the porch during 1880 restoration, and have been reburied in the churchyard.

RUMBURGH

Location: 4 miles NW of Halesworth.
Dedication: St Michael and St Felix.
Description: Built as the priory church for the small Benedictine house founded c1065 and subsequently becoming the parish church. It is oblong, looking more Saxon than Norman in shape, and consists of a long aisleless building with nave and chancel, divided only by a wooden screen, and a squat oblong W tower of the same width which was never completed - the top storey being of wood, weatherboarded with an odd hipped roof. There is also a S porch.
Periods: The tower in its present form dates from the mid 13c, with the wooden belfry probably 18c. There are other traces of early work in the 13c doorways on the N side of the chancel and S side of the nave. In the S wall of the chancel is a Norman priest's door blocked by a late 15c buttress on the exterior.
Features: Fine nave roof; 14c font with 17c cover; carved pulpit, dated 1637; some old bench-ends; beautiful 15c screen; Hanoverian Royal Arms; cup and cover 1569, paten 1806.

RUSHBROOKE

Location: 3 miles SE of Bury St Edmunds.
Dedication: St Nicholas.
Description: A small church built mostly in brick and comprising nave with S aisle, chancel, S porch and W tower. The aisle is divided into three distinct sections, two being given over to a family pew and a funeral chapel.
Periods: With the exception of its plain Dec tower, the church appears to have been rebuilt in the late 16c.
Features: The nave was refurnished by a Col Rushbrooke (1779-1845) along the designs of a chancel with stalls facing each other instead of pews. Early 16c roofs to aisle and chapel; some old glass in E window; the Royal Arms of Henry VIII carved and displayed on a tympanum above the rood-beam were thought original and of c1540 which would have made it the only example in the country, but now considered another Rushbrooke 'creation'; modern wooden font and cover; set of plate 1661; brass inscription to Thomas Badby 1583 in chancel; In the chapel at the E end of the aisle is an appealing marble monument to 15 year old Thomas Jermyn, dressed as he may have been when killed by a falling mast in 1692, and there are other monuments to the Jermyn family, one of whom, Sir Robert, entertained Elizabeth I on two occasions at the now lost and long lamented Rushbrooke Hall, burned down during demolition in 1961. The Register dates from 1568.

RUSHMERE (nr. Beccles)

Location: 6 miles SE of Beccles.
Dedication: St Michael.
Description: Round W tower with thatched nave and chancel.
Periods: The nave is c1300 and the chancel a 14c rebuild. The bell-openings on the Norman tower are also c1300.
Features: 15c font; piscina and windowsill sedilia on S side of chancel, and another piscina in the N wall; 17c pulpit constructed from some old seats; banner stave cupboard in SW corner of nave; paten 1712, cup and pater 1715.

RUSHMERE ST ANDREW (nr. Ipswich)

Location: 2 miles NE of Ipswich.
Dedication: St Andrew.
Description: Nave and chancel with N and chancel aisles, S porch and W tower.
Periods: The church was rebuilt in Early English style in 1861 except for the tower, which had been rebuilt in the 16c under the provisions of a Will of 1521 'of like fashion with that at Tuddenham' (which it was), and the S doorway, which is Norman.
Features: The church has no furnishings of note.

SANTON DOWNHAM

Location: 2 miles NE of Brandon.
Dedication: St Mary.
Description: A small, neat flint building with nave, chancel and square W tower. There were formerly two chapels.
Periods: The church is of very early date with the priest's door in the chapel possibly pre-Conquest, though the arch was altered c1175; it formerly stood in the N wall where more carved stones of similar date may be seen. The main church is late Norman with original N and S doorways. The chancel was rebuilt in the 13c, and the section of pointed arch uncovered from the S chapel dates possibly to c1300. The N chapel was 14c and the tower is 15c.
Features: When uncovered, the pointed arch of the former S chapel revealed a 13c wall painting of thin scrolls; a piscina of the former N chapel may be seen in the exterior wall; several windows have modern stained glass; 17c font cover and pulpit; very early 14c rood-screen; old bench-ends; Elizabethan cup and cover. W of the tower is the base of a medieval churchyard cross.

SAPISTON

Location: 3 miles NW of Ixworth.
Dedication: St Andrew.
Description: Nave, chancel, S porch and W tower.
Periods: The remarkable S doorway is Norman, the rest of the church, c1300 and a little later.
Features: Doorway and stairs to the rood-loft remain in a very complete state; recess in N wall of nave; stoup near S door; early 13c font with 17c cover; interesting 14c piscina in chancel; painted consecration crosses on N and S nave walls; some old glass; adapted Hanoverian Royal Arms; 15c bell in tower. Some very early headstones in the churchyard, S of the nave.

SAXMUNDHAM

Dedication: St John the Baptist.
Description: Situated on the rise of a hill with nave, aisles and clerestory, chancel and W tower. There was formerly a S porch.
Periods: Despite much restoration it still retains a plain Norman S door from its earliest beginnings and the lower part of the 14c tower may be of the same period. The chancel, with its definite inclination to the S, is 14c, as is the S chancel aisle (1308), and the nave and clerestory 15c Perp. The N

aisle was erected in 1851, and part of the S clerestory has been rebuilt. The church was completely restored in 1873.

Features: Fine hammerbeam nave roof; octagonal font c1400; two piscinas in S wall of chancel and a mutilated piscina in the S chancel aisle; a number of Flemish 16c and 17c stained glass panels in S aisle E window; modern reredos; lower part of traceried screen is now the front of a table in the chancel; Annunciation discovered during 1873 restoration in a column behind the reading desk had been presented to the church in 1348 by Sir John Wingfield; cup and paten 1757; 15c inscribed bell; 18c and 19c monuments to the Long family of Hurt's Hall. The Register dates uninterruptedly from 1538.

SAXTEAD

Location: 2 miles NW of Framlingham.
Dedication: All Saints.
Description: Despite claims that the eminent personage of Thomas de Brotherton, Earl of Norfolk, who died in 1307, is supposed to have founded or rebuilt the church, it goes unnoticed by travellers along the busy A1120 Roman road. This is particularly so since the tower fell in 1805 leaving only nave, chancel and S porch hidden from view amongst the trees. Some of the material was used to build a vestry with a belfry above.
Periods: The earliest survival is the N door which appears to be Early English. The large chancel, inclining noticeably to the S, is Dec and the nave and S porch with its fine flint panelling, Perp.
Features: Hammerbeam roof to nave; simple 15c octagonal font; angle piscina in chancel; some old glass and three-light E window with flowing tracery; Creed, Lord's Prayer and Ten Commandments all painted 18c; a few old bench-ends; late 17c communion rail; reredos with parts of the rood-screen; Royal Arms of George II; Elizabethan cup. The village stocks and whipping post are preserved in the porch.

SEMER

Location: 3 miles NW of Hadleigh.
Dedication: All Saints.
Description: Isolated in a meadow by the river Brett and consisting of a nave, chancel, vestry, S porch and a W tower.
Periods: The nave and tower are Perp, the chancel was rebuilt and the vestry added in 1873, and the timber S porch rebuilt in 1899 using some of the old woodwork.
Features: Plain 14c font with 17c cover; 18c paintings of Moses and Aaron in chancel; Royal Arms of George II; Elizabethan cup and cover.

SHADINGFIELD

Location: 4 miles S of Beccles.
Dedication: St John the Baptist.
Description: Nave and chancel in one, brick S porch and lofty W tower.
Periods: The nave is Transitional Norman, as seen by the windows which date from c1200, as are the two doorways. The chancel, with one 13c lancet window, was rebuilt in 1879 when the mid-15c Perp tower was restored. The S porch is Tudor.

Features: The corbels by the chancel arch once supported the rood-beam and rood-loft; fine 15c font; banner-stave recess in NE buttress of tower; Carolean Royal Arms over chancel arch; linen altar-cloth edged with hand-made lace, presented 1632; late 18c organ case; almdish 1778, cup and paten 1780; brasses to Mary Cuddon 1586, Anne Harvey 1618, and Mary Cuddon 1640.

SHELLAND

Location: 4 miles NW of Stowmarket.
Dedication: King Charles the Martyr.
Description: A pretty little Gothic style church quietly situated at the end of the green with an unusual dedication acquired from the local Sulyard family, enthusiastic Royalists. It comprises a nave, chancel, porch and W turret all of one period.
Periods: Largely rebuilt 1767 but one Early English and one Dec window remain from earlier buildings.
Features: 14c octagonal font; 18c box-pews; three-decker pulpit; Royal Arms of Queen Victoria; old hand-operated barrel-organ with three drums containing thirty-six hymn tunes; the turret contains a bell of 1624; marble monument on N wall of chancel to William Cropley 1717, of Haughley Park.

SHELLEY

Location: 3 miles SE of Hadleigh.
Dedication: All Saints.
Description: Nave, S aisle, chancel, brick N chapel, and, unusually for Suffolk, a massive NW tower.
Periods: Mainly Dec but the chancel has two blocked Early English lancets in the S wall, whilst the E window is 15c. The Tilney Chapel which contains memorials of the family is 16c. The church was restored in 1882.
Features: Holy water stoup; double piscina in chancel and windowsill sedilia; wood panelling between the chancel and chapel with a rich canopy probably for the Easter Sepulchre, and later used as a manorial pew; chancel stalls bear the arms of the Tilneys; pulpit with 16c linen-fold panels; Royal Arms of George III; altar tomb to Dame Margaret Tilney 1592, a late Gothic tomb-chest in the chancel N wall, and a panel with the Tilney arms in the N chapel c1540-50.

SHIMPLING

Location: 4 miles NW of Lavenham.
Dedication: St George.
Description: Approached through an avenue of limes, the church comprises a nave with S aisle, chancel, S porch and W tower.
Periods: Mostly late 14c Dec epitomised in the E window with its flowing tracery, but some windows are 15c and the chancel S doorway may be earlier. The church was drastically restored in 1869 mainly through the donation of Helen Hallifax.
Features: Octagonal 14c font; piscinas in chancel and S aisle; old stained glass in some windows; monuments to Elizabeth Plampin 1774, and to Thomas Haillifax 1850. The Register dates from 1538.

SHIPMEADOW

Location: 3 miles E of Bungay.
Dedication: St Bartholomew.
Description: Nave, chancel, N porch and short W tower of flint and brick.
Periods: Although much restored in 1851, the windows are mostly of c1300 and there is one blocked Norman window in the N wall of the nave. The tower and porch are Tudor. The old thatched roof was replaced with slate in 1856.
Features: Late 15c octagonal font; lower part of 16c screen; Royal Arms of George III.

SHOTLEY

Location: 9 miles SE of Ipswich.
Dedication: St Mary.
Description: Standing in an elevated position on the Orwell-Stour peninsula it is, however, disappointingly mostly pebbledashed, except for the clerestory and ornate S porch, and has a squat W tower no taller than the aisled nave, giving vent to an old sailors' view of Shotley: 'Shotley church, without a steeple: Drunken parson, wicked people.
Periods: The church is Dec apart from the late Perp clerestory, the handsome chancel, rebuilt in 1745, and the modern tower.
Features: Fine double hammerbeam nave roof of 1473 with some remains of a painted Canopy of Honour to the rood at the E end; roof of N aisle with carved bosses and Tudor flowers; modern white marble font; chancel furnishings of c1745 well preserved and comprising carved oak panelling encasing the chancel arch with, above, the Royal Arms of George II; panelling of E wall with Creed, Lord's Prayer and Commandments; communion table and three-sided communion rail; set of plate 1744.

SHOTTISHAM

Location: 4 miles SE of Woodbridge.
Dedication: St Margaret.
Description: Nave with N and S aisles, chancel, porch and W tower.
Periods: The tower is 15c Perp and the N aisle and porch were added in 1868 when the church was restored, but the nave and chancel still retain their Early English origin with several early lancets.
Features: Octagonal 13c font in Purbeck marble; trefoil piscina in S wall of chancel; rood-loft staircase in S wall of nave; plate 1713; inscribed 15c bell in tower; brass inscription to Rose Glover, wife of the parson, 1620: 'As withered rose its fragrant scent retaines, So being dead her virtue still retaines. She is not dead but changed. Ye good ne'er dies, But rather she is sunlike set to rise.

SIBTON

Location: 2 miles W of Yoxford.
Dedication: St Peter.
Description: Nave with aisles, chancel and W tower.
Periods: The earliest parts of a building which was rebuilt c1450 are the S and N doorways of c1200 and the 13c N arcade. The tower remains from c1400. The late Perp S aisle has four arches supported on circular pillars of

much earlier date said to have come from the ruined abbey. The church was restored in 1872

Features: Single hammerbeam roof to nave with eastern bay panelled to form a Canopy of Honour to the rood; 15c font; 13c piscina and windowsill sedilia in chancel; screen made-up from the top panels of the original rood-screen; 17c pulpit; old altar rails; Elizabethan cup and cover 1572, flagon 1713; brasses to the Chapman family - John 1475; Robert 1501; Edmund 1574 and his wife, a later John (alias Barker) 1582 and his wife, and another Edmund 1626; mural monument on N side of chancel to Sir Edmund Barker, Knight, and his wife Mary, 1676. A series of delightful, if rather self-indulgent, 18c tablets form memorials to the Scrivener family.

SNAPE

Location: 5 miles NW of Aldeburgh.
Dedication: St John the Baptist.
Description: Standing on a bold eminence 1 mile N out of the village, the church has a nave, chancel, pretty S porch and fine W tower with brick and stone decoration.
Periods: The church is 15c Perp except for a blocked Norman N doorway.
Features: Ornate S doorway; beautifully carved 15c font; piscina and sedilia; recess in N wall of chancel, probably for Easter Sepulchre; 17c chest; Elizabethan cup, paten 1808.

SOMERLEYTON

Location: 5 miles NW of Lowestoft.
Dedication: St Mary.
Description: Nave, chancel, S porch and W tower.
Periods: Apart from the tower, which was restored and heightened, the church was entirely rebuilt in flint and stone by Sir Samuel Morton Peto in 1854. In 1871, the chancel was restored to its original Dec proportions.
Features: Octagonal 15c font with curious 17c cover; stone sculpture with the Signs of the Four Evangelists above S door, probably once forming a reredos; lovely rood-screen with sixteen painted figures of various saints in early 15c style; cup 1722, paten 1726; tomb-chest monument to Sir Thomas Jernegan 1446, inscribed 'Jesus Christ, both God and Man: Save thy Servant Jernegan', and a marble monument to John Wentworth who died in 1651.

SOMERSHAM

Location: 5 miles NW of Ipswich.
Dedication: St Mary.
Description: Nave, chancel, timber S porch and W tower.
Periods: The church is of c1300-40 and the porch, in its original form without the side openings, Cautley regards as possibly even earlier.
Features: Nave roof; delicate open tracery on roof; excellent paintings of Moses and Aaron with the Creed, Lord's Prayer, and Commandments, presented to the church in 1750; mid-17c communion rail and, above it, the support for the sanctus bell on S side of beam; Royal Arms of Charles II, and later Hanoverian set.

SOMERTON

Location: 7 miles NE of Clare.
Dedication: All Saints.
Description: Nave, chancel, a Lady Chapel (now used as a vestry), S porch and W tower.
Periods: The nave is Norman with a blocked N door, and the chancel and chancel chapel Early English, with one cusped lancet in the chapel and another to the W of it. The E window is Perp but retains its early 14c shafting. The S porch and tower are 15c.
Features: In the S wall of the nave is the respond of an arch for an aisle never built; S door with original ironwork; 16c octagonal font; two piscinas in the chancel, one with a squint from the S chapel; 17c Jacobean pulpit and communion rail; Royal Arms of George III; cup, paten and almsdish 1761; three 16c inscribed bells in tower; monument to Montague Blundell 1733.

SOTHERTON

Location: 4 miles NE of Halesworth.
Dedication: St Andrew.
Description: Small church of flint and stone comprising nave, chancel and stone bellcote.
Periods: Mostly rebuilt in 1854 in Dec style by Benjamin Ferrey, using much of the old 14c material.
Features: Good original nave roof; simple octagonal 15c font with interesting 17c cover; two painted panels from former rood-screen of c1500, now used in the vestry door; 17c poor-box; medieval lock and handle on S door; cup with Elizabethan stem and a bowl inscribed 'Sotherton 1668'; tomb recesses low in N and S walls of nave, one containing the life-size stone effigy of a Knight in armour, thought to be of Walter de Bernham and late 13c; magnificent bust of the first Earl of Stradbroke 1811.

SOTTERLEY

Location: 5 miles SE of Beccles.
Dedication: St Margaret.
Description: The church stands near the house in the park of Sotterley Hall. It comprises a nave, chancel, S porch and lofty, square but tapering W tower which is in two sections, the first to the roof level, and the second carrying the belfry.
Periods: Principally Perp but the nave has Norman walls.
Features: Fine traceried 15c S door; octagonal 15c font; cusped piscina and windowsill sedilia in chancel; large banner-stave locker in SW corner of nave; some original stained glass fragments in nave and 15c glass in the E window, one panel showing Sir William Playter, the Yorkist, in complete armour with his seven sons 1479; part of 15c rood-screen with twelve, much re-painted, figures; fine 15c choir stalls with traceried fronts; cup and paten 1568; brasses of a Knight c1470, Thomas Playter 1479 and wife, Christopher Playter 1547, plus two further Elizabethan brasses; tomb-chest monument to William Playter 1512 and wife, and a huge monument in black and white marble to Sir Thomas Playter, Knight, 1623, with his two wives and their family of twenty-two children below !

SOUTH COVE

Location: 3 miles N of Southwold.
Dedication: St Lawrence.
Description: Ancient thatched church with nave, chancel, porch and a decorated W tower.
Periods: The church still has Norman masonry and Norman N (plain) and S (decorated) doorways. The windows of nave and chancel are of c1300. The tower is Perp.
Features: Fine nave roof; carved N door with traceried panels; octagonal 15c font; interesting banner-stave locker in NW corner of nave; 15c painting of St Michael on a wooden board, now the door to the rood-loft stairs; Jacobean pulpit; part of the rood-screen with coloured panels; old benches with traceried ends; Elizabethan cup; 15c bell in tower.

SOUTH ELMHAM ALL SAINTS & ST NICHOLAS

Location: 5 miles SW of Bungay.
Dedication: All Saints and St Nicholas.
Description: An ancient church which took on the dedication to St Nicholas when that church closed several centuries ago. It has a nave, chancel and round tower. There is a curious series of moats in the vicinity of the church, one of which appears to surround the church itself.
Periods: The church was restored in 1870 when the Norman round tower was heightened but it still retains its nave from the same period. The remainder is 14c and 15c.
Features: Restored Norman S door; early windows in nave; 13c square Purbeck marble font; some old glass roundels representing St Dorothy and St Ursula; old benches; cup 1716.

Dedication: St Nicholas.
Description: The church was in ruins over three hundred and fifty years ago following its closure after the two parishes were united. A small portion of one of its walls was still standing a century ago and the site is now marked by a stone cross erected by Sir Shafto Adair.

SOUTH ELMHAM ST CROSS

Location: 5 miles SW of Bungay.
Dedication: St Cross (originally Sancroft St George).
Description: Standing on a mound with nave, brick clerestory, chancel, S porch and W tower. The dedication is to St George - St Cross being a mispronunciation of the name Sancroft - but the latter corruption has survived.
Periods: The building's early origins are noted in the ornate Norman S doorway and the simpler, blocked N doorway. The chancel, tower and S porch are 14c, and the brick clerestory 16c. The church was comprehensively restored in 1841.
Features: Traces of a former N aisle; remains of colour and sacred monograms on 15c roof; early 15c font; two repainted panels of the rood-screen, re-used as part of the reredos; 14c iron-bound chest; cup and paten 1638.

SOUTH ELMHAM ST JAMES

Location: 6 miles NW of Halesworth.
Dedication: St James.
Description: The church, which comprises aisled nave, chancel and W tower, stands on an elevated site, said to be the highest in the county.
Periods: The base of the tower is Norman, as are parts of the N doorway and N window. The chancel has one early 13c lancet window and the S arcade is 13c or early 14c. The church was restored in 1873.
Features: Square Norman font of Purbeck marble with 15c cover; 14c piscina and sedilia in chancel; square 17c pulpit; 14c chest; remains of a rather primitive 14c screen at the W end of the S aisle; brasses to Civilian and wife c1520, and inscriptions to Edmund de Frevyll c1500 and William Grudgfield 1601.

SOUTH ELMHAM ST MARGARET

Location: 5 miles SW of Bungay.
Dedication: St Margaret.
Description: Nave, chancel, N chapel and W tower.
Periods: The nave has a Norman S doorway and a Norman S window. The tower and N chapel of one bay appear early 14c. Most of the exterior is Perp and the church was completely restored in 1876.
Features: Attractive nave roof; 15c octagonal font; recess in N wall of sanctuary, probably for Easter Sepulcre; stained glass canopy in vestry window; lower part of painted rood-screen re-used in the sanctuary; hour glass stand by the pulpit; chalice and cover 1567, paten 1705; village stocks preserved in the porch, and an old barrel organ stored in the room above.

SOUTH ELMHAM ST MICHAEL

Location: 4 miles S of Bungay.
Dedication: St Michael.
Description: Small church of nave, chancel, timber porch and decorated W tower.
Periods: The church is mostly Perp except for the Norman S doorway and the 16c porch.
Features: 15c octagonal font; small piscina; simple 18c pulpit; cup and paten 1567-8, paten 1722.

SOUTH ELMHAM ST PETER

Location: 3 miles S of Bungay.
Dedication: St Peter.
Description: A very small church comprising nave, chancel and tall decorated W tower.
Periods: Again, as in all the South Elmham churches, there are Norman origins, seen here in the early Norman S doorway and the blocked N doorway. The chancel is 14c Dec, though much restored, and the nave and tower, Perp.
Features: Fine 14c chancel arch and a blocked arch which led to the former Tasburgh Chapel on N side of chancel; octagonal 15c font; well-carved screen of 1923; old chest dated 1758; cup 1567-8. Outside is a churchyard cross with a traceried base minus its shaft.

SOUTHOLT

Location: 5 miles SE of Eye.
Dedication: St Margaret.
Description: Flint decorated nave and S porch, new brick chancel, and bellcote; the W tower having fallen long ago.
Periods: 15c nave and porch. The chancel was rebuilt in 1907.
Features: 15c nave roof, the eastern bay boarded in to form a Canopy of Honour over the rood; octagonal 15c font with 17c cover; consecration cross at SE corner of nave; 15c stained glass in SE window of nave; mid-17c communion rail; Royal Arms of George III; paten 1696, two-handled cup 1802; brass to Robert (missing) and Margaret Armiger 1585.

SOUTHWOLD

Dedication: St Edmund.
Description: This mighty church, 144' long and 56' wide with a tower 100' tall, is 'the epitome of Suffolk flushwork' (Pevsner). The church was built after a fire of c1430 destroyed its predecessor, a simple chapel to the mother church at nearby Reydon. Amazingly, it continued in this lowly role until 1751, by which time the status of the neighbouring parishes had been reversed, Southwold becoming a prosperous town and port and Reydon reverting to a village. It comprises a nave with N and S aisles, each seven bays long - the S impressively battlemented, the N simpler - terminating in a stair turret at the W end. There is a clerestory of eighteen closely set windows interspersed with stone shafts, and a chancel with large windows culminating in the four-light E window. The two-storeyed S porch is encased in glorious flintwork (flushwork) and topped by an ornate parapet. The mighty tower is in four stages and needs no battlements or pinnacles to augment the quality of its flintwork decoration. Another special feature of the church is the exquisite French-looking fleche which once contained the sanctus bell; rebuilt in 1867, and positioned halfway along the ridge of a roof which runs in a continuous unbroken line from the tower to the E end of the building; it is an exact reproduction of the original.
Periods: The church was all rebuilt between 1460 and 1490, with the S porch added c1500.
Features: Vaulting on interior of S porch; the single hammerbeam roof faithfully reproduced in 1867, the bay above the rood being a Canopy of Honour; early Tudor S door; mutilated Seven Sacraments font with modern cover; remarkable piscina in chancel, with adjoining sedilia, designed more like a tomb chest, with a row of shields displayed against the front; 15c coloured pulpit; two old chests, one 13c the other 15c walnut; chancel choir stalls - among the richest in the county; tall rood-screen with thirty-six painted panels running right across nave and aisles; two 15c aisle screens - the Lady Chapel screen and the Holy Trinity screen; circular Elizabethan communion table; Royal Arms of George III, dated 1783; the 'Jack-in-Armour' by the tower arch of c1470, carved in oak and painted to represent a man-at-arms holding a battle-axe in his right hand, with which he strikes a bell; cup and cover 1661; three brasses to John Bischop c1500, Christopher Yonges 1626, and James Petre 1700. In the churchyard lies the noted antiquary and historian Thomas Gardner with his two wives, Honor and Virtue; his gravestone amusingly inscribed: 'Between Honor and Virtue, here doth lie, The remains of Old Antiquary.'

SPEXHALL

Location: 2 miles NW of Halesworth.
Dedication: St Peter.
Description: Nave, chancel and round tower.
Periods: The round tower, which fell in 1720, was rebuilt in 1910 on its very early Norman, or perhaps even late Saxon, base. The N doorway is also Norman and the S doorway late 13c. The chancel was rebuilt in c1250, altered c1450 - when the Perp windows were inserted - and the E end rebuilt again in 1713 with striking lattice-work panelling on the exterior; the S porch was also restored at this time. The whole church was restored in 1876.
Features: Octagonal 15c font; piscina and sedilia in chancel, and another piscina in nave; doorway and steps remain from vanished rood-loft; old bench-ends; Royal Arms of George II; Elizabethan cup; brass in chancel to John Browne 1591 and Silvester, his wife, 1593. A pre-Reformation Missal Prayer Book was found buried in sand during the 1876 restoration. The Register dates from 1557.

SPROUGHTON

Location: 2 miles NW of Ipswich.
Dedication: All Saints.
Description: Delightfully sited beside the Gipping, along with the hall and mill, the church comprises an aisled nave with clerestory, aisled chancel, and fine embattled W tower.
Periods: The building is a good example of 14c Dec style, though much altered in the 15c when the Perp windows were inserted and a clerestory built. It was thoroughly restored in 1863, and in 1870 aisles (or chapels) added to the chancel.
Features: 15c hammerbeam roof to nave; double piscina in chancel, and single in N aisle; squint in N chapel looking towards the high altar; window, inserted in 1922, shows St Christopher in dark purple; cup and cover 1568, flagon 1757, paten 1758; painted and carved mural monument to Elizabeth Bull 1634, a memorial to Metcalfe Russell 1785, and a tablet recording the death of three brothers on service in foreign lands - one dying of a wound suffered while storming an Indian fort in 1840, another of yellow fever the same year, and the third in China two years later.

STANNINGFIELD

Location: 5 miles SE of Bury St Edmunds.
Dedication: St Nicholas.
Description: An interesting church with nave, chancel and W tower which appears never to have been completed as there is no proper belfry.
Periods: The church dates from Norman times and the N doorway and some windows on both sides of the nave are from this period. The chancel was rebuilt c1300. The tower is 15c. The church was restored in 1881.
Features: Handsome 14c S doorway; 14c stoup inside the nave, E of the doorway; 15c octagonal font bearing the arms of the Rokewode family, builders of the chancel; piscina and windowsill sedilia in chancel; lovely Dec traceried chancel windows; magnificent 15c 'Doom' over chancel arch - the painting is one of the most complete representations of the Last Judgement surviving in Suffolk (Dickinson); simple 15c rood-screen; three early

hatchments over the E side of chancel arch of Rokewode and Gage families; their memorial stones in the floor of the sanctuary and a canopied altar tomb of Thomas Rokewode against the N wall of chancel.

STANSFIELD

Location: 5 miles NE of Clare.
Dedication: All Saints.
Description: Quite a large church comprising a nave, chancel, S porch and fine W tower and situated on the N slope of the valley aloof from the village to the S.
Periods: The tower and chancel are 14c, and the nave, while mainly of the same period, has earlier traces. The S porch is Perp.
Features: Rood-loft stair turret on N side of nave; old font; piscina in corner of chancel SE window; three painted consecration crosses on chancel wall; fragments of old stained glass in chancel windows; 17c Jacobean pulpit; base of 15c rood-screen; carved benches; 14c iron-bound chest; Elizabethan cup and cover, patens 1666 and 1685; 18c memorials to the Kedington and Plume families on chancel walls.

STANSTEAD

Location: 6 miles NW of Sudbury.
Dedication: St James.
Description: Small church of nave, chancel, fine S porch and W tower.
Periods: Mainly Perp, but the tower with its small lancets is earlier, while the N doorway and chancel doorway are early 14c. The chancel and roof were restored in 1865, and the church renovated in 1878 when the tower was opened into the church.
Features: Corbels of chancel roof; 15c font, the cover of which has some old ironwork; fragments of 15c glass in window tracery; Royal Arms of Queen Anne. The Register dates from 1570.

STANTON

Location: 3 miles NE of Ixworth.
Dedication: All Saints.
Description: Nave with ornate S aisle and low clerestory, chancel, and a S porch created from the basement of the SW tower which fell in 1906.
Periods: Almost entirely 14c with fine windows. Completely restored 1876.
Features: The NE buttress of the former tower projects into the aisle and has a large stoup; the rood-loft stairs with both doors remaining; 13c octagonal font; 14c piscina and windowsill sedilia in chancel, another 14c piscina and tomb-recess in S aisle, and a third in sill of NE window of nave; Royal Arms of George III; brass to John Parker 1575 and wife Elizabeth 1597.

Dedication: St John the Baptist.
Description: Standing in ruins on a hilltop above the village, half a mile NW of All Saints church.
Periods: Was a splendid early 14c building - possibly as early as c1300, with a chancel rebuilt in 1616. As its W wall stands on the boundary of conse-crated ground, the tall 15c W tower rises above two open arches to allow a Procession Way N-S. Surplus to requirements, the church was abandoned in

1876 when All Saints was thoroughly restored and reroofed. So it has remained except for a short period in 1906 when it stood in for St John after the latter's tower collapsed.

STERNFIELD

Location: 1 mile S of Saxmundham.
Dedication: St Mary Magdalene.
Description: Brick chancel and brick-faced nave, exceptionally long flint S porch and W tower. There was formerly a N chapel.
Periods: There may be Norman masonry in the nave. The S porch is early 14c and the 14c chancel was rebuilt and the nave restored, in brick, in 1766. The church was completely restored in 1879.
Features: Late 14c octagonal font; external early 14c piscina, on former wall of N chapel; some old glass in W window; painting by Benjamin West above the altar represents Christ healing a blind man; old bench-ends carved with strange animals; cup and paten 1568. The Register dates from 1558.

STOKE ASH

Location: 3 miles SW of Eye.
Dedication: All Saints.
Description: Aisled nave, chancel and W tower.
Periods: The building is mainly Dec and Perp apart from the two nave and one chancel plain, round-arched doorways probably of late 12c. The porch is late 15c. The church was restored in 1868.
Features: 14c font; fragments of old stained glass in the tracery of SE chancel window; 17c pulpit; paten 1628; 1718 and 1719; memorials to the Bedingfield family. The register claims that a Thomas Parr, 'that old, very old man', died in 1635 aged 152 !, and that the year previously a widow Reade had died aged 126 ! Unfortunately our assumption from this must be that many people in those days had little idea of their real age; neither did their appearance in the register mean they died here; in fact we know Thomas was buried in Westminster Abbey; in the days before newspapers, the register was often used to record national as well as local events.

STOKE BY CLARE

Location: 2 miles SW of Clare.
Dedication: St Augustine (often wrongly assigned to the collegiate church and given the dedication to St John the Baptist).
Description: The 14c W tower remains from a previous aisleless church which was considerably enlarged late in the 15c. It now comprises a new aisled nave with N and S porches, chancel with side chapels and a two-storeyed vestry.
Features: Fragments of 15c glass in S transept window, one panel of which has a representation of a post-mill; well-preserved mid-16c Doom on the E wall of the N chapel and a 17c? painting on W wall of the nave; very small pulpit c1498 - 'the richest in the county' (Pevsner); some old carved bench-ends in chancel; old chest with floriated ironwork; clock mechanism c1680; 15c sanctus bell in frame above the tower stair turret; flagon 1674; brass of Alice Talkarne 1605, another of a lady c1530, and an effigy, possibly of Edward Talkarne, 1597.

STOKE BY NAYLAND

Location: 6 miles SW of Hadleigh.
Dedication: St Mary.
Description: Standing beside the timber-framed guildhall, providing a memorable and much photographed picture, this is one of Suffolk's loveliest and most ornate churches. 168' long and standing on the summit of a hill, its 120' high warm brick tower can be seen for miles around. The church is large, with nave, N and S aisles, clerestory, chancel with N and S chapels, N and S porches and W tower, and money was left for its building by many wealthy local merchants who made constant donations between 1439-1462.
Periods: The main building is all Perp but earlier parts include the early 14c N chapel and vaulted two-storeyed S porch (with 19c alterations). Of a later period is the simple 16c brick N porch, and the clerestory windows, inserted in 1865.
Features: Good 15c nave roof; beautiful panelling and tracery on S and W doors; finely carved 15c octagonal font; late 13c piscina in the Maddock Chapel, and a 14c piscina in the chancel; modern stained glass W window, E window and N and S chapel windows; reredos of 1865; simple Perp screens to N and S chapels; old stalls in chancel chapel, the painted fronts of which probably came from the rood-screen; some misericords; Hanoverian Royal Arms adapted to Queen Victoria; cup and two patens 1774, cover 1791, flagon 1819; parish library on first floor of S porch containing 16c religious works; brasses in the S chapel - to Katherine Clopton 1403, Sir William Tendring, Knight 1408, Sir John Howard 1426 and his wife Alice, and Lady Katherine Howard 1452; in the N chancel aisle - to Dorothy Mannock 1632, Francis Mannock 1590, and William Mannock 1616; worn floorstones devoid of their brasses in the N chapel he built, mark the 14c resting place of Sir John de Peyton and his three wives, and there are fine tombs with alabaster effigies to Sir Francis Mannock of Giffords Hall 1634, and Lady Ann Windsor 1615. The Register dates from 1545.

STONHAM ASPAL

Location: 6 miles E of Stowmarket.
Dedication: St Mary and St Lambert.
Description: Beautiful church with many fine windows. It comprises an aisled nave with clerestory, chancel, and large S tower, the basement of which forms a porch. The tower is topped by a remarkable belfry with parapet and pinnacles, built in wood to lessen the danger of structural damage caused by the peals of the ten bells it was to house.
Periods: The church is mainly 14c, with the lovely chancel being early Dec, but most of the windows, later Perp. The belfry was erected in 1742 replacing an earlier one. The church was fully restored in 1873.
Features: Font of c1300; piscina and windowsill sedilia in chancel; sixty-six figures feature in the very fine five-light E window and there are fragments of stained glass in some windows; pulpit dated 1616; part of the rood-screen re-used in vestry; ten Jacobean benches at the W end; 15c iron-bound chest, 8' long with twelve locks; Royal Arms of George III; Elizabethan cup, paten 1676; brass of John Metcalfe, rector 1606; in a recess in the chancel N wall is a tomb of a Knight of c1330, probably one of the Aspalls, founders of the church. In the vestry hangs an odd assortment of curiosa - a village constable's handcuffs and truncheon, and a left-handed sickle.

STOVEN

Location: 5 miles NE of Halesworth.
Dedication: St Margaret.
Description: Nave, chancel and thin W tower rebuilt in neo-Norman style.
Periods: The church was totally rebuilt 1850-58 - a good example of the work of the early Victorian period. The S doorway and parts of the N doorway are the only original Norman remains.
Features: cup and cover 1562.

STOWLANGTOFT

Location: 2 miles SE of Ixworth.
Dedication: St George.
Description: Standing within an ancient camp surrounded by a double moat, and without aisles or clerestory, this is still one of the most beautiful churches in Suffolk, with a fine tower and impressive S porch of flint and stone. There is excellent panelled flintwork throughout and splendid windows.
Periods: Apart from the 13c N doorway, the church, said to have been built around 1370 by Robert Davey de Ashfield who died in 1401, 'a servant to the Black Prince', is a fine example of early Perp work.
Features: Interesting roofs of porch, and nave where the eastern bay is panelled and painted as a Canopy of Honour over the rood; iron-bound door to upper stages of tower; rood-loft stairs on N side of chancel arch; early 14c octagonal font; either side of reredos are nine early 16c Flemish reliefs; painting of St Christopher on N nave wall; the carved woodwork is an outstanding feature of the interior, especially the misericords and bench-ends featuring over sixty animal and other figures; repainted lower part of rood-screen; iron-bound chest in porch; Elizabethan cup 1562, salver 1740; brasses of Robert Ashfield and his two wives c1550, and Paul D'Ewes 1631; monuments in the tower to Sir William D'Ewes 1685, and Lady Anne Wombwell 1808, and in the chancel to Paul D'Ewes and his two wives 1618.

STOWMARKET

Dedication: St Peter (and St Mary).
Description: Standing in a delightfully peaceful churchyard, yet just off the market place, the church comprises a nave with N and S aisles, clerestory, chancel with N Tyrell Chapel, N and S porches, and a W tower with a new spire; it also has arches N and S for a Procession Way, where it abuts the boundary of the consecrated ground. The double dedication comes from the fact that a second church had been erected in the churchyard in 1086 - now long gone - to take the overspill from the mother church.
Periods: Except for the tower, clerestory and porches, the church is externally all Dec. The tower was new in 1453; its slim elegant spire of 1712 which rose to a height of 120' was taken down as unsafe several years ago and has recently been replaced by a new spire in similar style. The porches are also Perp. The church received drastic restoration in 1840 and again in 1867 when many ancient features including some interesting parclose screens were 'swept away'.
Features: 13c coped sepulchral slab in S aisle; 15c font; pulpit includes parts of rood-screen; a few old bench-ends; paten 1651, flagon 1698, almsdishes 1732 and 1791, spoon 1824; iron wig stand 1675; in the chancel

arch in the nave is a monument to Dr Thomas Young, vicar here 1628-1655, and tutor to John Milton and in the E bay of the N aisle (known as the Tyrell Chapel) is a brass to Ann Tyrell 1638 aged eight, a mutilated tomb-chest monument with indent of brass, probably of an abbot of St Osyth, (the priory owned the manor and had a grange here where Abbot's Hall stands), and monuments to Margaret English, daughter of Sir John Tyrell, and family 1604, and to William Tyrell 1641 and his wife. The Tyrells are a noted family in history, perhaps notorious is more apt, as it was a bowman of that name who accidently killed the Conqueror's successor, William Rufus, in the New Forest, and another, responsible for the murder of the 'Princes in the Tower'.

STOWUPLAND

Location: 1 mile NE of Stowmarket.
Dedication: Holy Trinity.
Description: The village was without a church until this attractive building was erected in 1843 in local 'Woolpit whites' (a brick with an unfortunate tendency to weather from a warm mellow ochre to dirty white). This interesting example of early Victorian ecclesiastical architecture has a wide nave, short chancel and a W tower with a wide broach spire.
Features: W gallery on cast-iron columns; font - brought from Creeting All Saints' Church when it was abandoned; modern pulpit incorporating c1600 Flemish panels depicting scenes from the life of Christ; cast-iron Royal Arms of George IV; cup 1732.

STRADBROKE

Location: 7 miles SE of Eye.
Dedication: All Saints.
Description: A large impressive church of brick and stone symbolising the village's former status as a small town. There is an aisled nave with clerestory, spacious chancel with one bay chapel, N and S porches and a fine W tower, 100' tall, with a stair turret, built from the donations of John de la Pole, Earl of Suffolk.
Periods: Mainly 15c Perp, apart from the Dec chancel and arcade. The church was completely restored in 1871 and the chancel in 1879.
Features: Nave roof with bosses and shields; carved stone corbels supporting the chancel roof; 15c font; canopied niche on N side of chancel, probably for the Easter Sepulchre; good four-light E window; two painted c1500 panels of rood-screen in vestry; cup and cover c1567, flagon 1696; monument of Elizabeth White 1840.

STRADISHALL

Location: 5 miles NW of Clare.
Dedication: St Margaret.
Description: A small church despite having N and S aisles to the nave and a clerestory. There is also a rustic timber S porch.
Periods: There are traces of Norman work but the church was practically rebuilt in the 14c and 15c. The W tower is of c1300.
Features: Octagonal 15c font; painting of St Christopher on N wall; lower part of 14c rood-screen; bench-ends; squire's pew in N aisle; 18c pulpit; ancient chest; two almsdishes 1638, paten 1694, cup 1799.

STRATFORD ST ANDREW

Location: 3 miles SW of Saxmundham.
Dedication: St Andrew.
Description: Nave, chancel, brick N porch, and W tower with a good parapet with flintwork.
Periods: The Nave has a Norman window, the chancel Dec, and the porch Tudor.
Features: Font - 'an imitation of the 13c Purbeck type' (Pevsner); the attractive but curious piscina in the chancel S wall has a Norman shaft one side and a 13c one the other; 17c pulpit; Elizabethan cup, 'one of finest pieces in the county', and paten inscribed 'Stratfurth 1583'.

STRATFORD ST MARY

Location: 11 miles SW of Ipswich.
Dedication: St Mary.
Description: The large impressive church is a wonder of carving and decoration. It comprises an aisled nave, tall clerestory, aisled chancel, N porch, and W tower with NW stair turret. Flintwork inscriptions include the whole alphabet while, as Arthur Mee puts it, 'carved figures riot over the building; faces peep and spy, some to welcome, some to amuse, some to intimidate; little men and little animals smirk and grimace over the windows and more alert heads on the pinnacles scrutinise those who pass...'
Periods: A mainly Perp church, though the chancel is Dec, except for the E window restored in the 19c. The Dec tower was partially taken down and rebuilt 'to bring it in harmony with the rest of the church' in 1878, and now incorporates an over-elaborate belfry. The S porch was built in 1532, and many of the windows replaced and made very ornate when the church was restored during 1876-9.
Features: Piscina in chancel; rood-stairs - now leading to the pulpit; fragments of original old stained glass collected in W window of N aisle, including a shield of the Black Prince who once probably owned the manor; original parts of the rood-screen preserved in vestry; cup and paten 1702-3, almsdish 1823; an old bassoon hangs in the S aisle; three inscribed bells in the tower, one dated 1589; brass to Edward Crane 1558 and wife; two ledger-stones in the N aisle probably mark the graves of the founders, and a coffin lid, now in the churchyard, which was found in the chancel upside down with a double cross in relief, is thought to have once covered the grave of either some ecclesiastical dignitary or a Crusader. To the W of the church, on the S side of the road, is the timber-framed Priest's House of c1500. William Dowsing, who did such irreparable damage to Suffolk churches, is said to have been born in the parish.

STUSTON

Location: 3 miles N of Eye.
Dedication: All Saints.
Description: Nave, over-restored chancel, modern N transept, N and S porches and round tower.
Periods: The nave and chancel are Perp, and the Norman tower has a 15c octagonal top, crowned by battlements. The N transept was added in 1860 when the church was restored and the old thatched roof replaced with tiles.

Features: 'Pevsner considers the chancel interior 'truly terrible, of yellow, red and blackish blue brick'. N and S porches both have stoups; Elizabethan cup 1582, flagon 1692, almsdish 1723?; handsome marble monument of Sir John Castleton 1727 and Bridget his wife, of Stueton Hall. William Broome was rector here. He helped translate Homer's Odyssey into English for the poet Pope; his contribution was such that it was said: *Pope came off clean with Homer but they say, Broom went before and kindly swept the way.*

STUTTON

Location: 7 miles S of Ipswich.
Dedication: St Peter.
Description: Nave, chancel, N transept, and large SW tower, its basement forming a porch with a tall entrance arch.
Periods: To the mainly Perp church was added a N transept in 1862, and a N aisle in 1875 when the chancel was rebuilt. Evidence of an earlier building can be seen in the Norman window reinserted into the E wall of the 19c vestry and some 12c stonework reworked into a modern buttress on the S of the nave.
Features: Original S door with simple modern metalwork; some attractive modern glass in chancel windows; some old bench-ends; Royal Arms of George IV; brass inscription to John Smyth 1534; two 17c monuments of 1623 and 1662 at the W end of the nave to members of the Jermy family.

SUDBOURNE

Location: 1 mile N of Orford.
Dedication: All Saints.
Description: The parish church (and one-time mother church of Orford) comprises a nave, chancel, N and S transepts, N and S porches and W tower with wooden needle-like spire.
Periods: The mostly early Perp church was rebuilt, except for the tower, in 1879 at the expense of Sir Richard Wallace, but a blocked Norman S doorway (uncovered during the restoration) and one Norman S window (with a 13c lancet close by) remain from the original church.
Features: Font c1200; piscina (also uncovered during restoration); very pretty early 18c pulpit; Sir Richard's private family pew occupies the S transept; damaged Royal Arms of George III; cup and two patens 1723; magnificent alabaster monument of Sir Michaell Stanhope 1619, against the N wall of chancel. When the church was restored, over 2,600 silver pennies were discovered under the floor of the N transept, covering the reigns of kings John, Henry II and III, and of William the Lion of Scotland.

SUDBURY

Location: To the NW of the town centre.
Dedication: St Gregory.
Description: With its ancient dedication, the mother church of Sudbury. An ancient Saxon church, almost certainly in wood, stood on the site when the Normans came. They built the first stone church, a few fragments of which were incorporated in the building you see today. This comprises an aisled nave with clerestory, tall chancel with brick vestry, S porch with a chapel dedicated to St Anne attached to its E side, and a flint W tower with SE

stair-turret. The church is unusually long to formerly accommodate a collegiate of priests.

Periods: The chancel was rebuilt in 1365 by Simon of Sudbury who founded a college here ten years later when Archbishop of Canterbury. The N aisle is of the same period and the rest, apart from the 16c clerestory, from a remodelling of c1485. The church was restored between 1860-74.

Features: Nave roof with re-coloured Canopy of Honour in eastern bay; 16c chancel roof; S door of nave with good tracery; an altar-tomb, standing against the external wall of the S tower, was formerly in the chancel and probably used as an Easter Sepulchre; late 14c Perp octagonal font with beautiful telescopic cover; one painted panel of rood-screen at W end of nave; twenty fine choir-stalls, and misericords in chancel; tomb of Thomas Carter 1706 in the S chapel with the inscription 'Traveller, I will relate a wondrous thing. On the day on which the aforesaid Thomas Carter breathed his last, a Sudbury camel passed through the eye of a needle; if thou hast wealth, go and do likewise, Farewell.', another monument, in the S chapel floor, bears an inscription to the wife of the Sieur de St Quenton c1325. A macabre curio is the preserved head of Archbishop Simon of Sudbury, Lord High Chancellor in 1380 and beheaded by the populace on Tower Hill a year later during Wat Tyler's insurrection - with the dignity of a martyr - despite the fact that it took eight blows of the axe. His head was fixed over Tower Bridge for six days before being returned to his home town, and his body eventually buried in Canterbury Cathedral.

Location: Market Hill.
Dedication: St Peter.
Description: A large church standing prominently at one end of Market Hill and unfortunately now redundant. It began as a chapel-of-ease to St Gregorys and took over the function of the parish church about the time of the Reformation. It comprises an aisled nave, clerestory, chancel with chapels, S porch, and W tower which had a pretty spirelet, taken down in 1968. The chancel was built at an angle with the nave (inclining to the right) to represent Christ's head leaning in that position on the cross.
Periods: The church is all Perp; the lofty tower, which stands on three great arches, being built c1460-85. The church was restored in 1853, and again in 1968.
Features: Underground vestry beneath N chancel chapel; fine nave and chancel roofs; S and N doors with tracery; carved Canopy of Honour over chancel arch; octagonal Perp font; paintings of Moses and Aaron c1730, which formed part of reredos in NW corner of church; some 15c choir-stalls; badly restored lower panels of rood-screen; excellent parclose screens; chest dated 1785; beautiful embroidered Alderman's Pall c1480.

Location: Church Street.
Dedication: All Saints.
Description: Situated not far from Ballingdon Bridge, it comprises nave with aisles and clerestory, chancel with Eden N chapel and Felton S chapel, and W tower with big angle buttresses and large SE stair-turret.
Periods: Claimed the best of the three fine Sudbury churches, All Saints belonged to St Albans Abbey from 1150 until the Reformation. Apart from the Dec chancel, it was mainly rebuilt in Perp style during the 15c and 16c.

Features: Dutch prisoners of war were held in the church during the first Dutch War of 1666 when much damage was done to the interior. Remains of colour in nave roof; tracery on N and S doors; simple octagonal 15c font; painted family tree of the Eden family c1622 on E wall of N chapel; superb Perp oak pulpit, and prayer desk made from panels of rood-screen; parclose screens to N and S chapels; Elizabethan cup and cover, flagon 1757, patens 1761. Three of the eight bells in the tower are of pre-Reformation date and includes the heaviest in Suffolk, weighing about a ton.

SUTTON

Location: 3 miles SE of Woodbridge.
Dedication: All Saints.
Description: Offering no competition to the prestigious Sutton Hoo burial site close by, the towerless church stands forlorn, now with only a nave, chancel and S porch.
Periods: The church was severely damaged by fire in 1616 and the S tower completed the misery by collapsing in 1642; a bell, dated 1713, hangs in a wooden frame in the churchyard, yet is still rung from within the church. The nave and chancel were mainly Dec but have been renewed, and the porch is of c1873.
Features: Exceptionally fine font of c1420; modern stained glass E window; traceried panels of rood-screen re-used in communion rail; small face mask graffiti on western jamb of SW window, created by craftsmen during construction; Elizabethan cup, paten 1569, flagon 1637; brass inscription to William Burwell 1596.

SWEFFLING

Location: 3 miles NW of Saxmundham.
Dedication: St Mary.
Description: Nave, chancel, fine flint-decorated S porch and relatively large W tower.
Periods: The church has Transitional Norman N and S doorways. The chancel is c1300, with renewed lancet windows, and the tower is Dec. The remainder is Perp.
Features: 13c octagonal font in Purbeck marble; Royal Arms of Queen Anne, and Lord's Prayer, Creed and Commandments; chancel chair dated 1622; Elizabethan cup and paten, paten 1761; very rare 14c leather chalice case.

SWILLAND

Location: 5 miles NE of Ipswich.
Dedication: St Mary.
Description: Nave, chancel, and brick W tower with strange half-timbered belfry.
Periods: The earliest part of the church is the lovely Norman S doorway. The nave and chancel are later, and the tower early 16c with a belfry added in 1897.
Features: Simple hammerbeam roof to nave; painted font with elegant wood cover; Jacobean pulpit; Royal Arms of Queen Anne carved in wood; fine and colourful modern reredos; Elizabethan cup, paten 1683; 15c inscribed bell in belfry.

SYLEHAM

Location: 6 miles E of Diss.
Dedication: St Mary.
Description: The church stands on an ancient site, beside the banks of the river Waveney, and at the end of a long causeway-like lane. This isolated, marshy and somewhat eerie place is where, it is said, Baron Hugh Bigod, the rebel Earl of Norfolk, swore submission to Henry II in 1174, surrendering his castles at Bungay and Framlingham; he later saved their demolition only by a fine of 1,000 marks. The building comprises a nave, chancel, S porch and round tower.
Periods: The 15c nave has traces of Anglo-Saxon long-and-short work at the NW angle, and the tower is early Norman - its base possibly even Saxon - with a belfry with brick battlements of much later date. The chancel has two 13c lancet windows; the S porch is 15c and the roof, Victorian.
Features: S door with 13c ironwork; font with Norman base and a cover dated 1667; 13c piscina in chancel; plain Jacobean pulpit and 17c communion rails; some old bench-ends; Elizabethan cup, Elizabethan paten dated 1605; brass inscription to William Fuller 1634 and Anne his wife 1619, and to Anthony Barry 1641 and Elizabeth his wife 1638.

TANNINGTON

Location: 4 miles NW of Framlingham.
Dedication: St Ethelbert.
Description: The church, with its rare dedication, comprises a nave, chancel, S porch and W tower.
Periods: Norman N doorway and a chancel of c1300, but the windows of the nave and chancel are Dec and Perp. The porch has good 15c flint panelling.
Features: Wagon-roof nave with panelled Canopy of Honour at the E end to the rood showing traces of original colour; 13c octagonal font of Purbeck marble on 12c shaft; 13c piscina and windowsill sedilia in chancel; 15c benches have interesting, though mutilated, carvings; brasses to Anne Dade 1612, Thomas Dade 1619, and Mary Dade 1624.

TATTINGSTONE

Location: 5 miles SW of Ipswich.
Dedication: St Mary.
Description: Nave, chancel, N and S porches and W tower. The church has been unsympathetically restored in brick, especially the E wall of the tower.
Periods: The nave, tower and S porch are 14c Dec, the chancel and N porch 15c Perp. The church was restored in 1872.
Features: Late Perp double hammerbeam roof to nave; octagonal 13c font in Purbeck marble; piscinas in chancel and nave; cup 1791; marble monument of Thomas Western 1814.

THEBERTON

Location: 2 miles NE of Leiston.
Dedication: St Peter.
Description: Thatched nave and chancel in one, with a S porch attached to the S aisle, and a round W tower with octagonal belfry.

Periods: N side of the Nave is Norman as is the lower part of the tower with masonry six feet thick. The chancel was lengthened c1300 and a short S aisle (rebuilt 1848) with attached S porch were added in the 15c. Also of this time is the octagonal tower belfry.

Features: Fine decorated Norman N doorway; S door with tracery and delicately carved niche above; consecration cross in tower; interesting corbel table with small semi-circular arches under the chancel eaves; 15c octagonal font with 17c cover; early 14c piscina and windowsill sedilia in chancel; late 15c pulpit with fine traceried panels; panels of the rood-screen used in the modern choir stalls; an aumbry in N wall of chancel; old crude chest; Elizabethan chalice; brass to Katherine Pays c1500; Gothic monument to Frederica Doughty 1843. In the churchyard is the grave of the sixteen German crew of the Zeppelin L48 brought down in flames nearby on 17 June 1917 during the First World War. Locals had good cause to be unforgiving, yet their actions in providing this final resting place are epitomised in the inscription which says: 'Who art thou that judgest another man's servant? To his own master he standeth or falleth.'

THELNETHAM

Location: 3 miles NW of Botesdale.
Dedication: St Nicholas.
Description: Thatched nave, chancel, S aisle with chapel, and W tower.
Periods: All c1300 and a little later, with some later Dec and Perp windows. The S chapel was built by Edmund Gonville, rector here c1340, and founder of Gonville and Caius College, Cambridge. The church was restored in 1872.
Features: Stone altars in chancel and S aisle (now framed in oak) found in the church and churchyard, their consecration crosses recut; angle piscina and sedilia in chancel, and another piscina in the S chapel; lovely traceried windows in S aisle, old fragments of stained glass in S aisle E window and chancel S window, and unusual five-light E window in chancel; 18c Italian? relief of the Flight into Egypt; set of plate 1744; brass inscription to Anne Caley c1500 below squint at E end of nave; alabaster and marble monument to Henry Bokenham 1648 and wife 1654. The Register dates from 1538.

THORINGTON

Location: 4 miles SE of Halesworth.
Dedication: St Peter.
Description: Set on rising ground, this very early church has one of the most interesting round towers in East Anglia. Half way up is the unusual decoration of a band of tall blank arches; there is a belfry with two-light windows topped by a 16c octagonal brick parapet. The rest of the building comprises a nave, chancel and S porch.
Periods: The main tower may be late Anglo-Saxon and, whilst the tower arch has been restored, the original Norman arch can still be seen outside above the roof of the S porch. The nave is also Norman but was widened at a later date by scooping out the lower walls and supporting the thicker walls above with a continuous corbel table. The chancel was rebuilt in the 14c.
Features: Early c13 octagonal Purbeck marble font; 14c piscina in chancel; some old bench-ends; finely carved oak reredos; 17c chests; Royal Arms of George II; cup and paten 1652, flagon and almsdish 1660; bell, given by the Attorney-General, Sir Edward Coke in 1598; brass to Richard Gould 1626.

THORNDON

Location: 3 miles SW of Eye.
Dedication: All Saints.
Description: Nave and chancel of same dimensions with no chancel arch, and S tower, the basement of which forms a porch.
Periods: This interesting church dates from c1270, but an extensive fire appears to have occurred in the middle of the 14c after which the nave was rebuilt and extended, and the S tower built. Evidence of the earlier building can be seen in the N doorway. The nave and chancel were over-restored in 1866-7.
Features: 13c S door, and good W doorway with niche on either side; stoup by tower entrance; arched tomb recess in nave; 15c octagonal font; trefoiled piscina in chancel; fragments of the original and Flemish stained glass in chancel NW window; Jacobean pulpit; fine modern reredos representing the Last Supper and given in 1866; Elizabethan cup; massive stone slab of c1250 covers 16c tomb of Bishop Bale.

THORNHAM MAGNA

Location: 3 miles SW of Eye.
Dedication: St Mary.
Description: This small but attractive church stands in the park of Thornham Hall and comprises a nave, chancel, fine flint panelled S porch and W tower.
Periods: The chancel and tower are Dec, and the rest Perp, but much restored by the Hennikers.
Features: Late 15c hammerbeam roof to nave; 14c angle-piscina in chancel; fine series of hatchments; Royal Arms of George II; cup c1630, paten 1726, flagon 1731, almsdish 1807; brass inscription to Edmund Bokenham 1620 and his wife Barbara 1618, fixed to a chancel stall; monument to Lord and Lady Henniker 1821.

THORNHAM PARVA

Location: 3 miles SW of Eye.
Dedication: St Mary.
Description: To the NE of Thornham Park and representing a very tiny village, this little thatched church has a nave, chancel and low W tower with pyramidal roof, built up against what seems to be the W wall of a Saxon church (see below*). Attempts in the early 14c to complete the tower ended with the new walls "fallen dowen".
Periods: Plain Norman N, and decorated S doorways, and one Norman S window. The circular W window, high up*, may be Saxon (Cautley). The nave and chancel appear Dec.
Features: Octagonal 14c font; faint traces of 14c wall paintings on N and S walls - a king wearing a crown and a part of St Catherine's wheel still visible; remarkable painted retable of c1300, discovered in 1927 and wonderfully preserved - it is not known by whom or for whom it was painted; 17c pulpit; altar back with Jacobean panelling; early 15c rood-screen with the cut-off ends of rood loft beam remaining in the wall; Elizabethan cup, paten c1675, flagon 1715, almsdish 1825.

THORPE MORIEUX

Location: 5 miles NW of Bildeston.
Dedication: St Mary.
Description: Nave with unusual V-shaped side buttresses, chancel with curious angle-buttresses, fine timbered S porch, and W tower.
Periods: The church is all of 13c and 14c. The nave, chancel and tower possibly c1300, and the porch c1400. The church was restored in 1869.
Features: Ancient panelled S door and original carved oak W door; part of altar stone in chancel; rood-loft stairs on N of nave; plain 13c square font; 13c piscina in chancel, another in the N vestry, and a third of 14c date in the nave in which was found the elaborately carved late Perp bracket now on the S wall; paten 1708, flagon 1751, cup 1765; marble monument to John Fiske 1764, and others to the Fiske and Harrison families. The Register dates from 1538.

THRANDESTON

Location: 3 miles NW of Eye.
Dedication: St Margaret.
Description: Impressive church comprising an aisled nave, fine clerestory, chancel with a two-storeyed N vestry, S porch, and flint decorated W tower rising in three reducing stages with three-light bell-openings.
Periods: Early English chancel and 14c nave remodelled in Perp style to match the 15c tower.
Features: Nave roof of tiebeams alternating with hammerbeams; octagonal restored 15c font with cover; 14c piscina from the earlier nave, now in S aisle; 15c niche in N aisle; E window with unusual tracery, stained glass canopies in N aisle window and some old glass in a nave window; late 15c rood-screen, and a good screen in the tower arch; 15c choir stalls with traceried fronts; old bench-ends; Royal Arms of Queen Victoria; Elizabethan cup, paten inscribed 1568 and 1674; brass inscription to 'Mastrys Elsabeth Cornewaleys' 1537, and another to Prudence Cuppledicke 1619; handsome stone reredos commemorating the French family, one of whom, Thomas Lee, was rector here for 64 years; two square stones in chancel without brasses but said to cover the vault of Judge Reynolds.

THURSTON

Location: 5 miles E of Bury St Edmunds.
Dedication: St Peter.
Description: The church consists of a nave with N and S aisles and clerestory, chancel and modern W tower.
Periods: The chancel and arcade are original Perp. In March 1860 the tower fell, destroying much of the nave. The next year the church was creditably rebuilt, apart from the chancel and arcade, in the same Perp style.
Features: Chancel roof with modern woodwork; 14c font; double piscina and triple sedilia in the S wall; fragments of old stained glass in aisle and chancel windows, some good modern glass in chancel and S aisle, and fine E window in chancel presented by Sir Walter Greene of Nether Hall; old benches with traceried ends; rood-screen, choir stalls with traceried fronts, and reredos; cup 1675; memorial tablets to the Bright, Oakes, Smith, and Stedman families.

THWAITE

Location: 5 miles SW of Eye.
Dedication: St George.
Description: The little church in the small hamlet of Thwaite is now threatened with redundancy. The W tower fell about 1800 leaving a nave, chancel, brick S porch and bell-cote.
Periods: Almost entirely rebuilt, the chancel still has one slit lancet of c1200. The porch is early 16c and the bell-cote 19c. The church was much restored in 1846 and again in 1870.
Features: The hammerbeam roof to the nave may in fact be cut-off tie-beams; 14c octagonal font; piscina and windowsill sedilia; some fragments of 14c stained glass in several windows which still retain their Dec tracery; excellent 15c pulpit with elaborate traceried panels; 17c reading-desk; very unusual Elizabethan cup. In the churchyard is a tombstone to Orlando Whistlecraft 1810-1883, weather prophet and poet.

TIMWORTH

Location: 3 miles N of Bury St Edmunds.
Dedication: St Andrew.
Description: Standing in a secluded position at the end of a narrow lane, this small church comprises a nave, chancel and S tower, its basement forming a porch.
Periods: The church was virtually rebuilt in 1868, but the chancel retains two lancets in the N wall - part of the old 13c church. The nave is Dec as is the S doorway.
Features: Mass-dial on piece of stone high up on SE buttress; 18c pulpit with earlier panels from St James Church, Bury St Edmunds; 17c communion rail; Royal Arms of William III. The Register dates from 1538.

TOSTOCK

Location: 7 miles E of Bury St Edmunds.
Dedication: St Andrew.
Description: Aisled nave, narrow chancel, S porch and W tower.
Periods: The chancel is of late 13c-early 14c date, the tower and S porch 14c, and nave and N and S aisles are Perp. The nave was restored in 1872.
Features: Nave roof with alternating double hammerbeams; ; unusual rood-loft access on S of nave; early 14c octagonal font; partly blocked tracery in S porch windows and fragments of original stained glass in E window; 15c carved benches; communion rail of c1660; Elizabethan cup, paten 1558. The Register dates from 1675. In the churchyard is the tombstone of Thomas Chapman, reputed to have been 111 years old when he died in 1756, and his wife who died in 1753 aged 93. (ages quoted in those days need be taken with a certain amount of caution.)

TRIMLEY

Location: 9 miles SE of Ipswich.
Dedication: St Martin.
Description: The two churches of St Martin and St Mary lie on the edge of their respective parishes and share the same churchyard. St Martin

consists of a modern nave, mainly brick chancel and N chapel, and low W tower with brick parapet.

Periods: Basically 14c Dec, but was 'thoroughly repaired' 1850. Early survivals are the Dec S doorway, Perp N doorway, and tower erected 1432, its brick top rebuilt in 1949. The charming chapel was built in 1405 as a chantry to the Will of Roger Cavendish, whose descendant, the Elizabethan Thomas Cavendish, became only the second Englishman to circumnavigate the globe.

Features: 12c font; Royal Arms of George I.

Dedication: St Mary.

Description: The more interesting church of the two despite its ruinous W tower, it is said to have been first built by Thomas de Brotherton, natural son of Edward I, whose arms are over the door. It now consists of a nave, chancel and S porch.

Periods: The present ruined tower is of c1430-50, but it still has a row of shields above the doorway which can be dated by their heraldry to the late 13c. The N and S doorways are 14c, and the chancel arch clearly Dec. The church was restored in 1854-5.

Features: In the lower stage of the tower is a fine doorway with a window above; 14c piscina in chancel; cup and paten 1793.

Attempstone, formerly a parish here, was consolidated with Trimley in 1362. Its church is supposed to have stood near Grimstone Hall where many human bones were dug up in 1720.

TROSTON

Location: 3 miles NW of Ixworth.

Dedication: St Mary.

Description: A fine church comprising a nave, chancel, lovely decorated S porch and lofty W tower.

Periods: The chancel is Early English with N and S lancet windows and an E window with three stepped lancet lights. The tower is c1300, the nave Dec. and the S porch Perp. The church was restored in 1869.

Features: Four painted consecration crosses; 13c font; double piscina and original credence shelf; front of old rood-loft behind altar - a rare survival; some old stained glass; wall paintings in N of nave comprise a small St George of c1250, a large 15c St George, a large 15c St Christopher, and a Martyrdom of St Edmund, and a fragment of a Doom over the chancel arch; three-decker Jacobean pulpit with reading desk; panels of 15c painted rood-screen; 17c communion rail; old benches; Royal Arms of James I, altered to a George; almsdish 1715, set of plate 1778. The Register dates from 1558.

TUDDENHAM ST MARTIN (nr. Ipswich)

Location: 3 miles NE of Ipswich

Dedication: St Martin.

Description: Picturesquely sited on the top of a hill overlooking the village and the Finn valley, the church comprises nave, chancel, and W tower with fine flint-panelled parapet and buttresses.

Periods: The N doorway is Norman, chancel Dec, nave and tower Perp - the latter of 1452-60.

Features: Hammerbeam roof to nave; fine N door; font, dated 1443; ; Perp pulpit 'one of best examples of the period remaining in England' (Dickinson); good 15c carved bench-ends; well-restored screen; fine modern Kempe window.

TUDDENHAM ST MARY (nr. Mildenhall)

Location: 3 miles SE of Mildenhall.
Dedication: St Mary.
Description: Aisled and clerestoried nave, chancel, S porch and W tower.
Periods: Mostly 14c Dec, but the clerestory and hammerbeam roof are Perp. The church was restored in 1876.
Features: Much restored hammerbeam roof to nave; W door with niches either side; S door has lock with ancient key; statue niche on S side of S aisle E window; Norman font; circular window in W wall of tower, and excellent window tracery, especially the E window; 14c tomb recess in N wall of nave; 18c pulpit; cup and paten 1626; memorials to Davies, Goldwell and Shelley families including a fine black marble memorial stone in nave.

TUNSTALL (with Dunningworth)

Location: 7 miles NE of Woodbridge.
Dedication: St Michael.
Description: Nave, chancel, flint decorated S porch and tall W tower.
Periods: The church, which has been severely restored, has a Dec nave with tall three-light Perp windows, Dec chancel and Perp porch and tower.
Features: Priest's door in chancel; late Norman octagonal font in Purbeck marble on 15c stem; 17c altar rails now built into front of choir stalls; 18c pulpit; 18c box pews with W end gallery dated 1831; Royal Arms of George III, dated 1764; brass to John Haughfen and his wife Mary 1618; large floor slab to Elizabeth, Countess of Rochford 1746. The Register dates from 1539.

Dunningworth was formerly a separate parish with a church which went into decay in the latter part of the 16c. In Chapel Field, where the church was supposed to have stood, several skeletons were unearthed in 1841.

UBBESTON

Location: 6 miles SW of Halesworth.
Dedication: St Peter.
Description: The church stands on what is thought to be a Roman site near Ubbeston Wood. It has a nave, chancel, brick S porch and W tower.
Periods: A Norman building from about 1140, of which the nave with its fine S doorway remains - though all the windows are Dec and Perp insertions. The chancel was enlarged in the 13c, but again the windows are later. Porch and early brick tower are Tudor of c1500.
Features: Fine 15c roofs to nave and chancel, and the wooden pulley in the former probably used for raising the lamp that burned before the altar; octagonal Perp font; 14c chest; Elizabethan cup and paten, paten 1721; a wooden collecting shoe dated 1683; monument to Francis Legg 1671 and a coffin slab of c1200 carved with a cross in the nave. The Register dates from 1555.

UFFORD

Location: 2 miles NE of Woodbridge.

Dedication: St Mary.

Description: A fine and interesting building with nave, S aisle, clerestory, chancel, flint-panelled S porch and lofty W tower.

Periods: The N wall of the nave is Norman, as is the re-used doorway in the chancel, and the two E bays of the arcade which are c1200. The main nave and S aisle are 14c but with Perp windows; the clerestory, porch and tower, transitional Dec to Perp, and the chancel 15c Perp.

Features: The interior, once much more ornamented than today, suffered greatly during the civil war when Dowsing's men took up 6 brasses, broke 30 pictures and gave instructions for the destruction of a further 37, plus 40 'cherubin of wood'. When these instructions were disobeyed they returned to complete the job themselves, leaving only the church's crowning jewel, a spire-like cover over the 15c font, 18' tall and reaching to the roof - claimed by Cautley to be 'the most beautiful in the world'. So overawed were they by its magnificence it was mercifully left untouched for future generations to enjoy. Fine nave and chancel roofs retaining much original colouring, the former with alternating tiebeams and hammerbeams; S door with early 14c ironwork; piscina and aumbry on S wall of chancel; wall painting on the N wall of St Christopher, now virtually lost; lower part of screen with painted figures representing SS. Agnes, Cecilia, Agatha and Brigid; very fine benches with much tracery and carving, and two original choir stalls with misericords; processional cross, thought to be 17c Flemish; candlesticks and crucifix on the high altar are said to be Italian and to date from 1707; cup and paten 1671; bell of c1400 on the floor at the W end; brass memorials in nave floor to Symon Brooke 1483 and his three wives, on N wall of nave to Richard Ballett 1598, and an inscription to Henry Groome 1634; memorial to members of the Onebye family, former owners of Loudham Hall in Pettistree, and a curious marble monument of another owner, Sir Henry Wood 1671 at the W end of the S aisle. The S aisle chapel was restored by Sir J.N.Comper as a memorial to those who fell during the First World War. Richard Lovekin, a former rector here from 1621-1678, is said to have lived to be 111 and preached to the people the Sunday before he died. The village stocks and whipping post stand close by the churchyard gates.

UGGESHALL

Location: 5 miles NE of Halesworth.

Dedication: St Mary.

Description: The church has a thatched nave and chancel, and weatherboarded truncated tower with a thatched wooden belfry only slightly higher than the nave.

Periods: Norman nave with blocked N doorway. The chancel, which was rebuilt c1300, now has an 18c E wall of flint and brick. The tower is 15c - a modern belfry replacing the top which fell in the mid 18c. Most of the windows are Dec and Perp insertions.

Features: Handsome nave roof with remains of original colour on the Canopy of Honour above the rood in the E bay; priest's doorway in chancel; excellent octagonal Perp font with a canopy surmounted with a pelican; Jacobean pulpit; cup and cover 1568, almsdish 1682, credence 1808.

WALBERSWICK

Location: 4 miles NE of Dunwich.
Dedication: St Andrew.
Description: Originally built to represent the wealth and status of this onetime medieval port, it must have been one of the most splendid churches in Suffolk, 126' long and 60' broad with a tower 90' tall. Though today it is the parish church of what is now merely a small coastal village, it remains impressive in its ruins. The plan comprised a nave with aisles and clerestory, chancel, N chapel, N and S porches and lofty W tower with spire.
Periods: The church was rebuilt between 1473 and 1493 on to a tower of c1426 to replace a smaller edifice which stood on the marshes some 600 yards to the S. To this building a N aisle was added c1507. It suffered considerably during the civil unrest in the 17c, but managed to continue until 1695 when, unable to afford its repair, the townspeople petitioned to have the greater part of it taken down in order to make a portion of the S aisle fit for worship. This they did, constructing a small chapel in the SW corner and leaving the tower and some of the outer walls of the chancel standing. The tower was partly blown down in 1839 but repaired the following year.
Features: Two-storeyed porch with good flint panelling and vaulted roof; 15c font; 15c pulpit; lower part of late 15c rood-screen; beautiful incised medieval floor slabs bearing merchants' marks; communion table in which is set the medieval altar stone found in the ruins.

WALDRINGFIELD

Location: 4 miles S of Woodbridge.
Dedication: All Saints.
Description: Nave and chancel in one, S porch and red brick W tower.
Periods: The nave is Dec, the chancel modern and the tower Perp, but the church was over-restored in 1865.
Features: Fine 15c decorated font; stained glass E window representing the Baptism of Christ, the Crucifixion and the Last Supper; cup c1567.

WALPOLE

Location: 2 miles SW of Halesworth.
Dedication: St Mary.
Description: In an elevated position above the village, the church consists of a nave, chancel, N aisle and W tower, with an octagonal wooden spire.
Periods: Although externally all of 1878 when the church was restored and the N aisle and spire added, it occupies a very early site and has Saxon work in the nave and chancel. The S doorway is Norman as are the broad flint buttresses of the chancel.
Features: Octagonal Perp font; piscina and windowsill sedilia in chancel; stoup inside S door; Hanoverian Royal Arms; Elizabethan cup, paten 1576.

WALSHAM-LE-WILLOWS

Location: 5 miles E of Ixworth.
Dedication: St Mary.
Description: Large church with fine flint decoration and comprising a nave with seven-bay aisles, very fine clerestory, chancel, N porch and W tower.

Periods: The church is a fine example of 15c Perp work. The porch is of 1541. The church was comprehensively restored in 1878.

Features: The beautiful nave roof of alternating tiebeams and short hammer-beams has some original colouring; iron leather-bound inner door to vestry, probably one time used as a treasury; 14c font; piscina; fragments of old stained glass in E window, rediscovered and inserted in 1805; remains of paintings uncovered on the S wall during 1843 restoration; rood-screen, re-coloured and dated 1441; some bench-ends; reredos dated 1883 features The Last Supper, in terracotta; 13c iron-bound chest; panelling in the aisles, one dated 1620; restored Royal Arms of George III; Elizabethan cup; bell in tower dated 1576; pendant memorial hanging from the end of an iron rod projecting from the S wall of the nave and called a 'virgin crant', bears the name of Mary Boyce, aged 20 who 'died of a broken heart' 15 November 1685. It was often the custom on the untimely death of any young unmarried girl, to erect these above their seat upon the anniversary. The 'Garland' as it was often called was hung with wreaths by the village boys and girls; brass to Jane Smalpece 1602; unusually narrow stone coffin at the E end of the S aisle bearing emblems of a prior, possibly that of Richard Gotte who occupied the the Vicerage, a monastic country retreat for the canons of Ixworth, in the early part of the 16c.

WALTON

Location: 1 mile NW of Felixstowe.

Dedication: St Mary.

Description: The church has a nave, chancel, S aisle, and SW tower the basement of which forms a porch. A septaria fragment of the SW corner of an earlier church is in the churchyard.

Periods: The chancel and the N side of the nave are mainly 14c. The S aisle was built in 1860 and the chancel in 1899.

Features: Octagonal 15c font; lower part of rood-screen with blank tracery; Elizabethan cup and paten; brasses to William and Agnes Tabard 1459, and to William Simond 1612. The old village lock-up cage has been re-erected beside churchyard as a bus-shelter.

WANGFORD (nr. Brandon)

Location: 3 miles SW of Brandon.

Dedication: St Denis.

Description: This small church, situated in isolated wasteland beside U.S. airfield, has a rare dedication and comprises a nave, chancel and W tower.

Periods: The nave and chancel are Norman and the tower 14c.

Features: Pretty niche in N wall; stoup in porch; early 13c font; handsome E window of c1300; silver-gilt cup and paten c1680; brass inscription to Dorothy Franklyn 1596, sister of Sir Edward Coke, Attorney-General to Queen Elizabeth I.

WANGFORD (Nr. Southwold)

Location: 3 miles NW of Southwold.

Dedication: St Peter and St Paul.

Description: A large church with nave, N aisle, chancel, N porch, and a tower with a pinnacled parapet standing at the E end of the aisle. The W end of the nave has two heavy octagonal turrets with short spires.

Periods: The church was much altered and rebuilt between 1865 and 1875 when a new tower, chancel and vestry were built. The N aisle and N porch are Perp and escaped any severe restoration.

Features: The N arcade of the nave; simple octagonal 15c font; very ornate piscina, sedilia and reredos; pulpit and reading desk made from fine examples of 17c Flemish inlaid woodwork from the chapel at Henham Hall; cup and paten 1694; brass to Christopher Rous 1635; monuments of Sir John Rous 1730, Sir John Rous 1771 and John, first Earl of Stradbroke, 1827.

WANTISDEN

Location: 7 miles NE of Woodbridge.
Dedication: St John.
Description: A small church comprising nave, chancel, and a W tower built entirely of loacl coralline crag. It has an isolated situation on the edge of Woodbridge airfield and only approached via fields and footpaths.
Periods: The S doorway, one window in the chancel, and the chancel arch are Norman. The church was restored in 1864 and the chancel rebuilt.
Features: Crude Norman font; 14c piscina and sedilia in S chancel wall, and another piscina of similar date in the nave; old carved benches with holes for rushlight holders; small priest's door in chancel; Creed, Georgian Lord's Prayer and Commandments hang above chancel arch; brass inscriptions to Mary Wingfeilde 1582, and to Robert and Marian Harvie 1633.

WASHBROOK

Location: 3 miles SW of Ipswich.
Dedication: St Mary.
Description: Tucked away in the valley and quietly secluded despite its proximity to Ipswich, the church consists of a nave, chancel, N porch and massive brick W tower.
Periods: Norman nave, ornate chancel of c1340-50, and late Perp low W tower which still retains two old lancets. The church was restored in 1864.
Features: Good 14c nave with kingpost roof; 14c 6-bay stone arcading forming a series of recessed stalls along N and S sides of chancel; octagonal 14c font; piscina and sedilia in chancel; opposite, an Easter Sepulchre; table in vestry formed from the 17c tester of the former pulpit; fine iron hour-glass stand on bracket above pulpit; iron-bound chest; Royal Arms of Queen Victoria in plaster; brass inscriptions to Edmund Knappe 1609, and to Rev. Joseph Clarke 1653; a large Sarsen stone at the base of the tower.

WATTISFIELD

Location: 6 miles NE of Ixworth.
Dedication: St Margaret.
Description: Consisting of nave, chancel, timber N porch, ornate, though considerably repatched S porch, and W tower.
Periods: The tower arch is c1300 or earlier, and the N porch 14c, but the church is generally Perp throughout.
Features: Terracotta arms of the De la Poles over S porch; octagonal Perp font with 17c cover; lovely 14c piscina and a windowsill sedilia in chancel;

modern stained glass in E window; old chest; some panels of former rood-screen made into a prayer-desk and lectern; bell in tower dated 1584; two Elizabethan cups. The Register dates from 1540.

WATTISHAM

Location: 6 miles SW of Needham Market.
Dedication: St Nicholas.
Description: This small church, in a village dominated by its important airfield, comprises a nave, chancel, S porch and W tower with good flint decorated parapets.
Periods: Mostly 14c and 15c, the church was restored and 'beautified' in 1847 when stained glass was inserted in eleven windows; this has unfortunately resulted in a dark and gloomy interior.
Features: Statue niche on E wall with modern statue; piece of old glass in NW window of chancel features an armorial shield; old bench-ends; lower part of rood-screen with modern painted figures; a mural tablet dated 1762 on S side of tower records how eight members of one family lost their feet by mortification (gangrene).

WENHASTON

Location: 3 miles SE of Halesworth.
Dedication: St Peter.
Description: Situated on high ground with a nave, N aisle, chancel, porch and W tower, 62' tall.
Periods: Rebuilt in the 15c shortly after the transition from Dec to Perp style. The nave still retains two Norman windows, and the chancel two 13c lancet windows. When the latter was restored in 1892 traces of a former Saxon building were discovered. The tower and S nave arcade are c1400, the porch and S nave windows 15c, and the N aisle added c1530.
Features: The church contains one of the most important specimens of late 15c art now remaining, a wonderful 'Doom' or Last Judgement which formerly filled the chancel arch above the screen. It was painted c1500 on a board 17' long and 8'6" high, probably by a monk from Blythburgh Priory. In the reign of Edward VI, the rood and attendant figures were removed, and the painted board taken down and whitewashed. During the 1892 restoration, the boarding was placed in the churchyard where a rain storm removed some of the whitewash to reveal the painting underneath. 15c roof to nave; badly mutilated Seven Sacraments font; banner-stave locker, W of the S doorway; Jacobean pulpit; some 15c bench-ends; Royal Arms of George III; cup and paten 1567, flagon 1690; several monumental inscriptions to the Leman family and a monument of Philippa Leman 1757; a truncheon adorned with the royal arms, and a set of irons and handcuffs.

WESTERFIELD

Location: 2 miles NE of Ipswich.
Dedication: St Mary Magdalene.
Description: The small church consists of a nave, chancel and massive W tower with flint panelled parapet. The former N porch was converted to a Sunday School.
Periods: Norman S doorway replaced by a window which retains fragments

of former. Most windows suggest a date of c1300. The tower is 15c but contains Norman stones.

Features: Continuous hammerbeam roof over nave and chancel; 15c octagonal font; piscina and aumbry in chancel; modern stained glass in chancel E and S windows; Royal Arms of George III; Elizabethan cup and paten. The Register dates from 1538.

WESTHALL

Location: 3 miles NE of Halesworth.

Dedication: St Andrew.

Description: A large, well-proportioned and interesting building. It comprises a small thatched Norman church to which the present nave and chancel have been added. The old nave survives as the S aisle.

Period: In the early 13c the N wall of the old Norman nave was pierced with arches and a northern extension built. The old nave then became the S aisle, its W end richly ornamented and containing the original Norman doorway and arcading, a window above, together with the S door and part of another Norman window. The E window of the S aisle fills what was formerly the Norman chancel arch, and to the E, the foundations of the former Norman apsed chancel have been found. A fine new chancel and the lower part of the W tower were erected c1370 and the N porch added c1460. The narrow N aisle was rebuilt in the 14c, and in the 15c the walls of the nave and N aisle were heightened and Perp windows inserted. A belfry was added to the tower in the 17c. The chancel was restored in 1882.

Features: Lovely ornate Norman S doorway; good roofs to nave and chancel; fine Seven Sacraments font with much original colouring; 14c piscina and windowsill sedilia with a locker for the napkins; consecration cross on S wall; fragments of original mid-14c stained glass in E window; Jacobean pulpit; lower part of fine 15c rood-screen of sixteen painted panels; cup 1567, almsdish 1811; altar tomb of Nicholas Bohun 1602 and brass genealogical table of the family going back to Thomas Plantagenet and Eleanor Bohun.

WESTHORPE

Location: 8 miles N of Stowmarket.

Dedication: St Margaret.

Description: Large, beautifully unrestored building, the former parish church to the Queen of France. It consists of a nave with N and S aisles and clerestory, chancel, brick N Barrow Chapel, S porch and W tower.

Period: The church is a rarity, being unrestored and virtually undisturbed since it was last built during the 14c and 15c.

Features: Fine roof to nave of alternating tiebeams and hammerbeams; 14c S door with tracery and iron-ring; stoup in S porch; tower-stair door with iron protection; medieval altar stone retaining its consecration crosses; modern font with Stuart cover; 14c piscina and mutilated triple sedilia in chancel; good Dec window tracery; traces of wall paintings; 14c parclose screen with original colouring and some panels of the rood-screen; 15c pulpit with 17c top; 17c pew; Royal Arms of George III dated 1765; cup 1631; 14c tomb recess in S aisle with marble slab thought to be to Henry of Elmham c1330; monument to Maurice Barrow 1666 in Barrow Chapel, and a tablet in

S aisle in memory of Mary Tudor, sister of Henry VIII, widow of Louis XII of France (she was 18, and he 52, when he died), and wife of Charles Brandon, Duke of Suffolk, who lived and died at nearby Westhorpe Hall - her tomb is by the altar in St Marys Church, Bury St Edmunds, having been moved from the Abbey after the Dissolution.

WESTLETON

Location: 6 miles NE of Saxmundham.
Dedication: St Peter.
Description: The large W tower fell in 1770 leaving only a low tower built later on the foundations, and a long thatched nave and chancel.
Periods: Nave and chancel are early Dec though no original windows survive.
Features: Octagonal Perp font; fine piscina and triple sedilia of c1300 in chancel; striking five-light E window with intersecting tracery; choir stalls with good 15c tracery; cup and cover 1570, flagon 1709.

WESTLEY

Location: 2 miles W of Bury St Edmunds.
Dedication: St Mary.
Description: The Marquis of Bristol gave this site overlooking the Linnett valley for a new church with nave, chancel, and SW tower with 'crude' spire.
Periods: Built in Early English style of Roman cement in 1836 to replace the old church dedicated to Thomas a Becket.
Features: Paten 1564, flagon 1703.

Location: Along a lane, a quarter of a mile W of the village and St Marys.
Dedication: St Thoms a Becket.
Description: The E wall of the mainly 14c medieval church stands in a field along with the void of the E window. There are also remains of the NW corner of the nave, foundations of the porch and a buttress on the S.

WESTON

Location: 2 miles S of Beccles.
Dedication: St Peter.
Description: Built in flint and septaria, the church consists of a nave, long chancel, N porch and W tower.
Periods: The church, which was thatched until 1848, has a late Norman N door and a blocked N window in the nave. The chancel is 13c with blocked N lancet windows and other lancets re-used, and the rest mainly 14c.
Features: Nave roof with arched braces; lovely, though mutilated Seven Sacrament font; c1300 painting, showing through later 16c painted text, of Christ's Entry into Jerusulem; fine 15c carved benches; parts of rood-loft incorporated in reading desk; rare Royal Arms of Jame II; Elizabethan cup, paten 1694. The Register dates from 1560.

WEST STOW

Location: 5 miles NW of Bury St Edmunds.
Dedication: St Mary.
Description: The church of flint and stone consists of a nave, chancel and

W tower with large buttresses at the NE and SE.
Periods: The nave and chancel are 14c Dec, but there is an early 12c Norman N doorway. The windows are mainly Perp and the tower also of this later period.
Features: Fine chancel roof; plain font with rich oak cover; interesting canopied piscina and windowsill sedilia in chancel; aumbrey by the altar; paten 1710. The Register dates from 1558.

WETHERDEN

Location: 4 miles NW of Stowmarket.
Dedication: St Mary.
Description: The church is dominated by its splendid S aisle and S porch (at one time with an upper floor) bearing the arms of its great benefactor Sir John Sulyard, Chief Justice of England. The porch is attached to the W end of the aisle and forms part of it. There is also a nave with brick buttresses, a chancel, N vestry (once a chapel), and W tower with belfry.
Periods: Dec chancel and W tower, and a Perp nave. The S aisle and porch which were begun by Sir John in the 1480s were temporarily halted following his death in 1484. The work was completed after his widow Ann's remarriage in 1490. The church was restored in 1864.
Features: Beautiful double hammerbeam roof to nave and excellent S aisle roof; 15c carved font; 14c piscina and windowsill sedilia in chancel, and another piscina in the N chapel which has an unusual vaulted stone roof; an Easter Sepulchre recess in chancel; fine 14c E window with poor modern stained glass; modern pulpit incorporating some 15c panels; fragments of lower part of rood-screen re-used behind the altar; good carved bench-ends; box-pews in S aisle; cup and cover c1680, set of 18c; the S aisle contains - the tomb of Sir John Sulyard 1484, the tomb-chest monument of his grandson Sir John Sulyard 1574, and other memorials to the family from 1400 to 1800. Dowsing claimed to have removed nineteen superstitious brass inscriptions weighing 65 lb, broken 100 pictures (window glass) and ordered the destruction of sixty more.

WETHERINGSETT (cum Brockford)

Location: 6 miles SW of Eye.
Dedication: All Saints.
Description: A stately church, delightfully situated in an enchanting village with nave, aisles (the N a memorial to the Revett family, seated here for four centuries), superb clerestory, chancel, S porch and lofty W tower.
Periods: Fine late 13c arcades with large Dec and Perp windows. 13c S doorway protected by 15c porch. Dec S aisle and tower, and a much rebuilt chancel, restored in 1851.
Features: Fine nave roof; octagonal font c1660-5; early 13c angle-piscina in N vestry, and sedilia in chancel; panels of rood-screen used in choir stalls and on top of organ; two simple misericords; an old benefaction board; two flagons and almsdish 1743, cup and paten 1745, cup 1816. Richard Hakluyt, born in London about 1552 and rector here for 26 years from 1590, collected records of sea history and published his notable work *Principal Navigations of the English Nation*. The Register dates from 1534 - one of the earliest in the county.

WEYBREAD

Location: 9 miles NE of Eye.
Dedication: St Andrew.
Description: Aisled nave and clerestory, chancel, panelled S porch and lovely tapering round W tower.
Periods: The church was over-restored in 1864, but the tower is very early Norman in its lower parts with Dec windows in the belfry. 14c Dec also the aisled nave and chancel, while the clerestory and S porch are early Perp.
Features: Damaged font not in use and standing at E end of the nave; 14c piscinas in chancel and S aisle; statue niche S of chancel arch; much colourful stained glass; large modern painting on W wall of the nave of Our Lord with angels; fine c15? almsdish.

WHATFIELD

Location: 3 miles NE of Hadleigh.
Dedication: St Margaret.
Description: On high ground overlooking the Brett valley with nave, chancel, S porch and low broad W tower.
Periods: The tower (with later pyramidal roof) and nave are c1300, chancel 14c (with signs of its c1300 origin), and the simple brick porch late 16c.
Features: Fine 14c tiebeam with crownpost roof to nave and beautiful wagon roof to chancel; stoup of c1300 just inside S door; 15c font with 18c cover; some good window tracery; some old benches - one inscribed 1589; late 17c pulpit with sounding-board; squire's(?) pew by altar rails; communion rail and west gallery c1700; Hanoverian Royal Arms; men's hat-pegs on N wall of nave; Elizabethan cup, paten 1691, fine Dutch paten 1715; two large 13c coffin slabs with carved crosses in chancel; marble monument to William Versey 1699. The Register dates from 1558.

WHEPSTEAD

Location: 5 miles S of Bury St Edmunds.
Dedication: St Petronilla.
Description: The church, which comprises a nave, chancel and W tower, is the only one in England with a dedication to Petronilla. At the time, it was believed she was the daughter of St Peter, but in 1873 her sarcophagus was found under a half-buried church in Rome with an inscription showing her to be the daughter of a Roman noble. She was, however, re-buried in St Peter's in Rome.
Periods: The Norman nave retains the original jambs of the chancel arch, though the present arch is modern 'Norman' style. The chancel is Early English c1300. The lead-covered spire of the Perp tower was blown down during the memorable storm which raged the night Oliver Cromwell died (as was also that of Dalham church tower). The church was thoroughly restored in 1869.
Features: Rood-stair climbs up in window recess; fragments of old stained glass in a chancel S window, heraldic glass in SE window of the nave, and modern glass shows St Petronilla in green and red with St Peter in blue; pulpit made-up of Elizabethan carved panels; paten 1725, Parisian(?) cup c1810; coffin slab to 14c priest near altar. The Register dates from 1538.

WHERSTEAD

Location: 2 miles S of Ipswich.
Dedication: St Mary.
Description: Situated away from the village with fine views over the river Orwell. It has a nave, chancel and a fine W tower of flint septaria and brick with a pinnacled parapet.
Periods: Very thick walls remain from the old Norman nave plus a decorated S door and plainer N door. The chancel is mainly 14c Dec, though also still retaining parts of its original 4' thick walls and two small lancets on either side. The rest of the church is Perp, including the tower. The church was restored in 1864.
Features: Hammerbeam roof to chancel; piscina in chancel; Caen stone pulpit; modern carved benches; much modern stained glass in windows; paten 1735, almsdish c1742, cup 1751; marble monument to Sir Robert Harland 1848. In the churchyard is a memorial to Robert Gooding, a 'salt-finer' who died in the early 17c. The process of obtaining rough salt through the evaporation of sea-water was once a major industry along the tidal river where remains of the old salt-pans still exist.

WHITTON

Location: 1 mile NW of Ipswich.
Dedication: St Mary.
Description: Now a suburb of Ipswich, Whitton's modern church comprises nave, S aisle, chancel and SW tower.
Periods: Built in 1851, the church was enlarged in 1862 by the addition of a S aisle and tower using materials from Thurleton old church. The only remains of the previous medieval building which stood on the site is the late 13c S doorway into the tower.
Features: Piscina (removed from old church); Elizabethan cup. The Register dates from 1585.

The small village of **Thurleton** now forms part of Whitton. The old church of St Botolph was in use in 1500 but after being amalgamated with Whitton was long used as a barn and then fell into ruin. It was taken down in 1862 and the material that remained used in the building of a S aisle and tower for Whitton church (see above). Some cottages now stand on the site.

WICKHAMBROOK

Location: 10 miles SW of Bury St Edmunds.
Dedication: All Saints.
Description: A large church with aisled nave, clerestory, fine chancel, N chapel (now used as a vestry), N porch and W tower.
Periods: Principally 13c and 14c, but the richly decorated N doorway dates from c1240.
Features: Small Saxon figure with shield recently discovered outside in S wall; large blocked arch in N wall of chancel formerly leading to N chapel; Jacobean hammerbeam-type roof to nave and archbraced roof to chancel; stoup in porch; 13c font, with pyramidal cover dated 1943; piscina of c1240 in vestry; a portion of the rood-stair remains and is used to ascend the pulpit; unusually small but fine E window; 16c - 17c benches of an unusual

shape; 17c altar rails; flagon 1740; fine brass of Thomas Burrough 1597, his two wives Elizabeth and Bridgett, and their nine children; marble altar tomb and effigy of Sir Thomas Heigham, Knight 1630, on S side of sanctuary with interesting inscription.

WICKHAM MARKET

Dedication: All Saints.

Description: The church is dominated by its graceful S tower with belfry and landmark lead spire, 140' high, from the top of which it is said that up to 30 other churches can be seen; it is unusual in being octagonal all the way up from the base which orginally formed a porch but now contains the font. One third way up the W side of the spire is a small external cage containing the clock bell, formerly the sanctus bell. The western part of the nave is unaisled, but the eastern part opens to chapels which are continued along the chancel.

Periods: The main body of the church is of c1339 except for the Perp tower, and the Tudor brick S aisle erected by Walter Fulburn (who died in 1489) as a burial chapel for himself and family. A N aisle was added during complete restoration in 1870 at which time the S aisle was given new windows.

Features: Large squint in chancel arch gives a view of the high altar from the S aisle chapel; 14c octagonal font; 14c triple sedilia and piscina with credence shelf in chancel (discovered during the 1847 restoration), and a piscina and windowsill sedilia in S chapel; the NW window of the N chapel has very fine Dec tracery; pulpit bearing small figure of St John, said to have come from the Savoy Chapel in London and to be the work of Grinling Gibbons; base of much altered rood-screen in the chancel arch; finely carved 14c oak reredos, fashioned in Bruges and acquired in 1881; Elizabethan cup, paten 1567, paten 1685, flagon 1737.

At Domesday, a church with 20 acres of land stood in Harpole, a hamlet of Wickham Market now known as **Thorpe Hall** and situated 1 mile W of the town. Possibly originating from a Danish settlement, Thorpe Hall, which formed a separate manor until the 17c, was held by the Hovel family from 1225 until 1389 when it was granted to Campsea Abbey. The site of the church is unknown.

WICKHAM SKEITH

Location: 5 miles SW of Eye.

Dedication: St Andrew.

Description: Nave and chancel, N porch and two-storeyed S porch, and massive W tower.

Periods: The church is all Perp period except for the Dec W tower. Monies were left for the building of the S porch in 1459.

Features: Hammerbeam roof to nave; W door with tracery and S door with linenfold; large niche S of chancel arch and three more on the N side; badly preserved font; small piscina in S wall of chancel; fine nave windows; three massive dials on SE nave buttress; mid-17c communion rail; fine set of old carved bench-ends; part of brass effigy shows kneeling Lady in widow's dress with her daughters c1530; three ledger stones of the Harvey family in the chancel lying side by side. The Register dates from 1558.

WILBY

Location: 2 miles SE of Stradbroke
Dedication: St Mary.
Description: Lovely little church comprising a nave with S aisle only, clerestory, large chancel with good windows, and lofty flint-panelled W tower. There is a very good panelled S porch which must at one time have been even more ornate than now.
Periods: Almost entirely Perp, but standing on the site of an earlier Norman building, the material of which was re-used in the new church. The tower was "new" in 1459.
Features: Rich carving to vaulted nave roof and roofs of aisle and chancel; nine canopied statue niches over the S porch entrance, and others in the angle buttresses; altar stone in S aisle; pretty font; piscina in S wall of the chancel; lovely 15c stained glass in nave windows; wall painting of St Christopher on N wall, and an inscription on S wall; elaborate early 17c canopied pulpit; 13c chest - now cut in half; beautifully carved 15c benches with armrests representing the Seven Sacraments, the Seven Acts of Mercy and the Seven Deadly Sins; statue of the Virgin and Child c1500 on a bracket in chancel; Elizabethan cup and cover, almsdish 1630, flagon 1638; medieval inscribed bell in the tower; brasses to Elizabeth Bayles 1588, Joane Bayles 1620, and others of the same family, inscription to Rev. Joseph Fletcher 1637, and another brass to a Civilian c1530 on nave floor; 18c Rococo monument to the Green family.

WILLINGHAM

Location: 4 miles S of Beccles.
Dedication: St Mary.
Description: The church has been in ruin since the 17c and the benefice now united with Sotterley. Only a small section of its west wall remained at the end of the 19c and today this has been reduced to a small scatter of flints - their position marked by a young oak tree. The parish church of Ellough, itself only a hamlet of Willingham at Domesday, stands across the narrow valley. (see Ellough).

WILLISHAM

Location: 4 miles SW of Needham Market.
Dedication: St Mary.
Description: Tiny church of nave, chancel and W bellcote.
Periods: Rebuilt on old Norman foundations in 1878.
Features: Preserved 14c font; Elizabethan(?) cup, paten 1647.

WINGFIELD

Location: 7 miles NE of Eye.
Dedication: St Andrew.
Description: Magnificent collegiate church of flint and stone comprising a nave with N and S aisles and clerestory, beautiful clerestoried chancel with side chapels, S porch and a low W tower, never completed to its full height.
Periods: The earliest part of the church is the 14c W tower and the S aisle windows of 1362 with their beautiful tracery. The N chapel is also Dec. The

remainder, including the S porch and clerestory, is 15c Perp, the chancel being lengthened in 1430 when the very rich arcade on the S side was erected by William de la Pole. The church was restored in 1866 and 1880. *Features:* Fine nave roof, and the Trinity Chapel roof retains painted eastern bay; good doorway leads to Trinity Chapel, now the vestry; mutilated canopy niches in the S chancel aisle i.e. the Lady Chapel; rood-loft stairs included in the thickness of the walls and rising from the windowsills; 15c font and cover; mutilated piscina at the E end of the N aisle - what was St Margaret's Chapel; some old glass in E window and N chapel, and beautiful window tracery in chancel E window; pulpit comprising some old panels adorned with the De la Pole arms; ancient chest; old carved benches; choir stalls with simple misericords; excellent parclose screens to N and S chapels; lower part of rood-screen; Elizabethan cup and cover; 18c graveside shelter - looking like a sedan chair - for the parson to conduct funerals in wet weather. The church contains a series of fine monuments to the Wingfield and De la Pole families including: the only survival of a series of fine brasses is one of 1303 to Richard de la Pole; a piscina and wooden sedilia is incorporated with the altar-tomb with wooden effigies of Michael de la Pole, builder of neighbouring Wingfield Castle, and his wife Katherine 1415, which stands between the chancel and the lavish S chapel for which he must also have been responsible; an elaborate canopied recess and altar tomb on the N side now contains the stone effigy of Sir John Wingfield 1361, founder of the college; on the N side of the sanctuary is a canopied altar-tomb with the exceptionally fine alabaster effigies of John de la Pole, Duke of Suffolk 1491, and his wife Elizabeth Plantagenet, sister of Edward IV; William de la Pole, created first Duke of Suffolk in 1448, lies alone in his altar-tomb - his Duchess buried in Oxfordshire. He became the most powerful man in England and led the siege of Orleons; the city saved by the appearance of Joan of Arc, and the Duke forced to surrender to the woman he called "the bravest on earth". He survived this reverse but was 'executed' in horrible fashion whilst on his way into exile for later misdemeanours, his head being chopped off, after several attempts with a blunt axe, on the gunwale of a boat and hurled into the sea. It was later washed ashore and returned to Wingfield for burial in 1450. In the churchyard is a mounting step for horsemen, and on the S side, College Farm incorporates the remains of the college.

WINSTON

Location: 2 miles SE of Debenham.
Dedication: St Andrew.
Description: Nave, chancel, brick S porch with unusual arch, and W tower.
Periods: Fine Norman S door with rich carvings. The rest is Dec or Perp except for the Tudor S porch and the chancel which is mostly of 1907.
Features: 13c piscina in chancel and another in the nave; 18c pulpit; Royal Arms of George III; 15c carved bench-ends in chancel.

WISSETT

Location: 2 miles NW of Halesworth.
Dedication: St Andrew.
Description: Nave, chancel, handsome S porch and ancient round W tower with narrow windows in the middle stages and battlemented belfry.

Periods: The tower is late 11c Norman with its original tower arch towards the Perp nave where there remains N and S Norman doorways - the N being especially elaborate. The porch is 14c and the chancel arch of c1470, but the Dec chancel was rebuilt c1800.

Features: Good nave roof with alternating tiebeams and arched braces; N doorway with splendid early Norman arch; octagonal font painted 1491-2; curious niche on N side of nave and another niche in E jamb of S nave window; rood-loft staircase with wooden stairs which commence high up in the jamb of a window; some fragments of 15c stained glass in S nave tracery and one N window; Elizabethan cup and paten; brass to Stephen Blomfeld 1638.

WISSINGTON

Location: 1 miles W of Nayland.

Dedication: St Mary.

Description: Nave, chancel with apse, and pretty weatherboarded bell-turret. It is a rare example in Suffolk of a Norman tripartite plan, practically unaltered, and consisting of an apsed sanctuary, choir, nave with a modern S porch, and a wooden bell-turret at the W end (Dickinson). There are signs the church orginally had a central tower.

Periods: The church is all of Norman date except for the porch and bell-turret, but in 1853 the chancel, which had for some time been 'squared off', had the apse rebuilt on its old foundations and given rib-vaulting, and 'modern Norman' substituted for the old tracery windows.

Features: Tall, sumptuous S doorway and simpler N doorway; kingpost roof to nave; 15c octagonal font; modern stained glass E window; series of very interesting wall paintings c1250-75, in the nave, restored but now again somewhat faded: - on the N wall is St Francis preaching to the birds, and two women gossiping, attended by devils - W of the N doorway is a painted consecration cross - and on the S side are eight subjects, The Magi asleep warned by angels, King Herod, The Presentation in the Temple, The Archangel Michael, The Nativity, The Angels appearing to the shepherds, The Adoration of the Magi, and The Miracle of St Nicholas; two good 17c chests; two choir stalls with misericords; Royal Arms of George III; Elizabethan chalice, paten 1697. The Register dates from 1538.

WITHERSDALE

Location: 6 miles NE of Stradbroke.

Dedication: St Mary Magdalene.

Description: Tiny isolated church consisting of a narrow nave, chancel, wooden S porch and weatherboarded belfry.

Periods: Largely 12c with two Norman windows and a plain blocked early Norman doorway. The chancel is of c1300, but most of the windows are later.

Features: Unrestored interior with square Norman font; three-decker pulpit; box-pews; Jacobean communion rail; 17c carved benches; 18c western gallery; beam over sanctuary which goes right through the walls to the exterior, probably for lentern veil; Royal Arms of George III; cup and paten in leather case 1680, given by Archbishop Sancroft, a Suffolk man, who also financed the porch and belfry.

WITHERSFIELD

Location: 2 miles NW of Haverhill.
Dedication: St Mary.
Description: Situated in a pretty valley near the stream, with clerestoried nave with N and S aisles, chancel with S chapel, and fine W tower with higher SE stair turret. The tower received bomb damage during the last war but has been well restored.
Periods: Perp nave, Dec but rebuilt S chapel. N aisle built by Robert Wyburgh c1480. The Perp chancel was rebuilt, and the S aisle added, in 1868.
Features: Fine 15c roof over N aisle; octagonal 17c font; good 15c rood-screen, poorly repainted; Jacobean pulpit; interesting carved bench-ends in nave; iron ring-handle of S door formed from two salamanders; cup and paten 1701.

WITNESHAM

Location: 4 miles NE of Ipswich.
Dedication: St Mary.
Description: Nave with S aisle and clerestory, chancel, vestry, and S tower, the base of which forms a porch.
Periods: Apart from the Perp S aisle and clerestory, mostly late 13c (chancel) and early 14c. The vestry was added in 1868.
Features: 15c hammerbeam roof to nave; sundial on tower erected 1729; re-cut 15c octagonal font; 13c piscina in chancel; 13c priest's door; S chapel with good Dec E window, some old glass and a modern stained glass chancel E window; late 17c painted texts; Jacobean pulpit; carved bench-ends; reredos, presented in 1868; Royal Arms of Charles II; Elizabethan cup; monument to R.C.King 1842. The Register dates from 1538.

WIXOE

Location: 4 miles SE of Haverhill.
Dedication: St Leonard.
Description: Small church with the nave and chancel in one, S porch and a weatherboarded bell-turret.
Periods: The nave and chancel are Norman, but all the windows are Dec and Perp restored in the 19c and 20c. It has an original ornamented S door and a plain N door, now blocked.
Features: Good modern stained glass E window of c1892; Elizabethan cup and paten, cup 1728; bell-turret contains bell dated 1460; an inscription on a plaque in the chancel floor informs us that this is 'The Entrance into the Vault of Henry Berkeley Esq. and Dorothy his wife containing Ten Foot Square.'

WOODBRIDGE

Location: Church Street, off Market Hill.
Dedication: St Mary.
Description: The parish church, large, impressive and decorated in black flints, comprises an aisled nave, clerestory, chancel with N and S chapels, and a lavish N porch, and W tower 108' tall. The S chapel is of brick, rendered over. There is no division between the nave and chancel which gives

the interior a very spacious and imposing appearance.

Periods: The church is thought to have been built in the reign of Edward III (1327-77) by Lord John Segrave and his wife Margaret de Brotherton whose arms were over the door of the tower until the mid 19c, but benefactors in the mid 15c saw much of the church rebuilt and restored, including the tower (1444-56) and the N porch (1455). Thomas Seckford, a later benefactor, built the N chapel which is named after him, in 1587.

Features: The 5c roof extending over nave and chancel has alternating tie-beams and hammerbeams; niches over the porch contain the figures of the Madonna, St Anne and St Cecilia, and in the spandrels of the doorway, St Michael with the dragon; lovely, but damaged late 15c Seven Sacraments font with modern tabernacled cover; restored piscina and triple sedilia in chancel; modern 20c stained glass in E window; lower half of 15c rood-screen, erected by John and Agnes Albrede, now used as parclose screen between S chapel and chancel, and also in the N aisle; old chest dated 1672; 16c cupboard with linen-fold door panels in vestry; brass chandelier given in 1676; Royal Arms of George III dated 1744; two cups 1636, paten 1683, paten and two flagons 1752; the various brasses and inscriptions include one on the N wall of the sanctuary to John Shorland, a child of seven who died in 1601, the marks of a lost brass possibly one commemorating John Albrede and his wife, and another to John Sayre, who has in his epitaph these amusing lines: 'Reader, thou shalt find, Heaven takes the best, still leaves the worst behind'; tomb-chest monument on N side of chancel to Thomas Seckford, the town's great benefactor, who built the N chapel 1587, and another fine, impressive marble monument at E end of S aisle to Geoffrey Pitman, Sheriff of Suffolk, 1627, his two lawyer sons and two wives.

Location: St Johns Hill.

Dedication: St John.

Description: A modern church built in yellow brick in Early English style, and an interesting example of the ecclesiastical architecture of the period. It has a most curious tower spire rising 138' which, as White describes: 'terminates in two caen stone crosses intersecting each other diagonally and decorated with foliage thrown out in bold relief'.

Periods: The foundation stone was laid in 1842 and the church consecrated in 1846.

WOOLPIT

Location: 6 miles NW of Stowmarket.

Dedication: St Mary.

Description: A beautiful church dominated by its wonderful spire, held by flying buttresses and rising to a total height of 135'. And this is not the only jewel, for the N porch, with its flint decoration and lovely stone tracery, is described by Dickinson as 'probably the best in Suffolk'. The building also has an aisled nave, clerestory, chancel and W tower. The S aisle originally contained the Chapel and shrine of Our Lady of Woolpit. In a meadow E of the church is Lady Well, the water of which was said to be beneficial for sore eyes. In the Middle Ages it became a favourite resort of pilgrims. One of the niches in the outer wall of the church is said to have once contained a famous Madonna by which they prayed before passing to the well.

Periods: The chancel and S aisle are Dec, but the bulk of the church is Perp including the tall 15c clerestory. The S porch can be dated to c1430-55, a period when the church received many donations. It was thoroughly restored during 1843, but on July 17 1852, the tower and spire were destroyed by lightning. Within two years they were rebuilt in the spectacular, if rather Nene Valley rather than Suffolk (Pevsner) style, seen today.

Features: Wooden vault of 1854; double hammerbeam roof to nave 'one of finest in Suffolk' (Dickinson), plus fine 15c aisle roofs; five niches over the porch; Canopy of Honour over the chancel arch on the E wall of the nave, erected 1875, and presumably from another church; double piscina and windowsill sedilia in S wall of chancel, and a damaged piscina and windowsill sedilia in the former medieval S aisle chapel (now the vestry); excellent five-light E window containing some old glass; 15c rood-screen in chancel arch with repainted panels; series of fine carved 15c bench-ends; fine brass eagle lectern c1525, traditionally said to be the gift of Queen Elizabeth I; cup and paten 1576, cup 1776. The Register dates from 1558.

WOOLVERSTONE

Location: 4 miles SE of Ipswich.
Dedication: St Michael.
Description: Situated in the grounds of Woolverstone Hall on the S bank of the river Orwell, and comprising a nave, chancel, brick S porch and W tower.
Periods: The church was largely rebuilt in 1862 and extensively restored in 1889, leaving only the porch, S doorway and the tower from the old medieval church. The old chancel and nave now form the S aisle and chapel of a modern nave and chancel to which have been added new vestries on the S side.
Features: Octagonal Perp font; 14c piscina and windowsill sedilia in former chancel; Berners family memorial windows; paten 1697; brass at the base of the chancel steps, with inscription to a former rector Thomas Runtyng 1399; a number of memorials to the Berner family including Henry Denny Berners 1839, and others to Philip Bacon 1635 and Daniel Smart 1689.

WORDWELL

Location: 5 miles NW of Bury St Edmunds.
Dedication: All Saints.
Description: Small, neat church of nave, chancel, S porch and bell-cote.
Periods: Of Saxon or very early Norman origin. The N wall is 11c, and there are N and S doorways, each with an unusual tympanum, and a chancel arch of the same period. The church was restored in 1827 (and again in 1868) after being used for many years as a granary.
Features: Large 11c font; 13c double piscina in sill of SE window of nave; 14c canopied priest's door; 14c E window; fine set of 15c carved and traceried bench-ends. In the churchyard an ancient well was discovered during the 1868 restoration.

WORLINGHAM

Location: 2 miles SE of Beccles.
Dedication: All Saints.
Description: Nave, chancel with two-bay S chapel, N porch and W tower.
Periods: Although traces of Dec and Perp work remain, the church was

considerably restored in 1608 and in 1876 and has mostly modern windows.
Features: 15c octagonal font; piscina in chancel; rood-loft stairs; seven
modern stained glass windows; six carved benches; cup 1568, paten 1807;
brasses to Nicholas and Mary Wrenne 1511, and an inscription to Walter
Lecberd c1500; wooden panel memorial to the Duke family 1637, a monument by Chantrey to General Sparrow and his son 1809 and 1818 in chancel,
and a wall monument to Mrs Parnell Duke with an epitaph beginning: A Rous
by birth, by marriage made a Duke, Christened Parnell, she lived without
rebuke. Outside against the S wall is a large tomb to John Felton 1703.

WORLINGTON

Location: 1 mile SW of Mildenhall.
Dedication: All Saints.
Description: Aisled nave, clerestory, chancel, yellow-brick S porch and W
tower with belfry. The W end of the S aisle is now a vestry.
Periods: Early English chancel with a lancet on the N side and Dec windows
on S. The nave has Early English N and S doorways but the arcades are Dec,
as is the tower. The aisles and clerestory are 15c Perp, and the porch 18c.
Features: Over the E gable of the nave is the sanctus bell-cote; ancient
stoup and niche in S porch; handsome W door; 15c roof to nave of tiebeams
alternating with hammerbeams; Perp font; rood-loft stairs complete; good
three-light 14c E window in the chancel, and old glass in several windows;
preserved rood-beam above chancel arch; several old bench-ends; late 17c
pulpit; Royal Arms of George III; cup and paten 1669; 14c bell in belfry, the
only one in Suffolk from the well-known Lynn foundry of Johannes Godynge;
brass inscription to John Mortlock 1620. In the churchyard is the base of a
medieval cross.

WORLINGWORTH

Location: 6 miles NW of Framlingham.
Dedication: St Mary.
Description: The church comprises nave, wide chancel, S porch and W tower.
Periods: The chancel is c1300, the nave and tower 15c Perp.
Features: Impressive double hammerbeam roof 30' wide and 100' long
spans nave; good carving on N and S doors; mutilated gable-cross over E
wall of nave; inscribed 15c octagonal font has a lofty cover some 20' high,
with beautiful tabernacle work which is said to have come from Bury Abbey;
piscina and tiny aumbry; medieval altar-stone fitted upside down to 17c
communion table; much old glass in chancel; traces of wall paintings in
chancel; St Michael and the Dragon in spandrels of the entrance arch of the
S porch; canopied 17c pulpit; poor-box dated 1699, and collecting shoe of
1622; complete set of nave pews of 1630; lower part of screen; modern
reredos carved in 13c style; Hanoverian Royal Arms over chancel arch; 15'
spit in belfry, with inscription dated 1810, on which a whole ox was roasted
to celebrate the Jubilee of George III (see picture in tower); manual fire-
engine inscribed 'The Gift of John Major Esq., to ye Parish of Worlingworth,
1760'; Elizabethan cup, paten 1699, flagon 1720; brasses to Susanna
Barker 1622, Jaspar Hussie 1624, and another of c1525 to four sons and
seven daughters with no inscription; very fine marble monument to Sir John
Major 1781, and others to Dame Ann Henniker 1793 and Elizabeth, Duchess
of Chandos 1817.

WORTHAM

Location: 6 miles NW of Eye.
Dedication: St Mary.
Description: A structure which may once have provided a watch tower for the abbots of Bury, now provides the largest round church tower in England, almost 30' in diameter and about 62' high. The top collapsed in 1780 and it has since remained open to the sky, the bell now placed in a quaint weatherboarded turret that peeps out from behind the tower. Inside are two arched recesses believed to be fireplaces. The remainder of the church consists of nave, aisles, clerestory, chancel and S porch.
Periods: Whilst generally considered Norman, Cautley regards it as a Saxon watchtower. The main building, which if Cautley is right, would initially have been of wood, is now mostly Perp, the aisles early, of c1360, and the clerestory c1430, but the chancel S doorway is Dec. The N aisle was rebuilt in 1731 ,the church restored in 1868 and the S porch rebuilt in 1908.
Features: Hammerbeam nave roof and fine modern archbraced chancel roof; 14c octagonal font; 14c canopied piscina and sedilia in chancel, and another small trefoiled piscina; blocked recess on N side of chancel for the Easter Sepulchre; two-storeyed sacristy on N of chancel; fragments of old stained glass in E window; re-used parts of rood-screen by the altar; oval Royal Arms of Charles I carved in oak; cup 1567-8, paten 1776.
Richard Cobbold, whose Suffolk tales during the 19c included a notable work on Margaret Catchpole, was rector here for 52 years.

WRENTHAM

Location: 5 miles N of Southwold.
Dedication: St Nicholas.
Description: Wide nave, N and S aisles, wide chancel, S porch, and lofty flint panelled and embattled W tower with traceried belfry which can be seen from the sea. It was used in 1804 during the Napoleonic wars as a signal station.
Periods: The chancel, with lancet windows, was extended c1260 and is the earliest work. All the rest is Perp, except the N aisle which was added in 1842 when the church was renovated and the chancel 'beautified'.
Features: Fine S arcade; W door with canopied niche on either side; octagonal Perp font on later shaft; altar-stone with elaborate consecration crosses; modern carved oak altar screen; old stained glass in N aisle featuring St Nicholas; two Jacobean candlesticks; cup 1660; brass to Ele Bowet c1400, and another to Humphrye Brewster, Knight, 1593.

WYVERSTONE

Location: 7 miles N of Stowmarket.
Dedication: St George.
Description: Nave, clerestory, chancel, timber S porch and W tower.
Periods: The church is basically Dec. When the hammerbeam roof was built in the 15c, the Dec nave walls were raised by a clerestory.
Features: Good 15c hammerbeam roofs to nave and S porch; octagonal 15c font with 17c cover; some old 15c stained glass in NE and NW nave windows; some carved bench-ends, one dated 1616; lower part of rood-screen with remains of scenes carved, not merely painted; early 16c pulpit with linenfold panelling; 17c communion rails; sanctuary knocker on S door; Royal Arms of

William and Mary; wooden pulley in nave roof for raising the rowell lights in front of the rood; paten and almsdish 1724, flagon 1729.

YAXLEY

Location: 2 miles W of Eye.
Dedication: St Mary.
Description: Nave, chancel, clerestory, superb two-storey vaulted N porch with very fine flint panelling, and W tower.
Periods: The church is mainly of Dec and Perp period. The tower is early 14c. and the nave, clerestory and N porch are 15c, but the nave has a Dec S doorway and arcade. The chancel was rebuilt on its old foundations in 1868 except for the E wall and window.
Features: Interesting 14c door to S porch; ornamented nave roof, the eastern bay of which retains colour from a former Canopy of Honour; in the chancel a flying buttress forms a little porch over the priest's door; old fragments of stained glass said to range from 1199 to 1549 made up into a pattern in the E window in the 19c; a virtually unrecognisable painting of a Doom over the chancel arch; fine 15c rood-screen in chancel arch, the panels of which are painted with the figures of saints including St Ursula, St Katherine, St Barbara, St Dorothy, and Mary Magdalene; beautiful pulpit with canopy dated 1635, and said to be best in Suffolk; sexton's wheel over S door consisting of two iron wheels from which could be determined fast days (only one other example in England, at Long Stratton in Norfolk); brasses to Andrew Felgate 1598, Margaret wife of Robert Felgate 1596, and inscriptions to Alice Yaxley 1474, Alice Pulvertoft 1511, and Joan Yaxley 1517; tomb in the chancel of a 14c priest.

YOXFORD

Location: 4 miles NE of Saxmundham.
Dedication: St Peter.
Description: Aisled nave, chancel with chapel, and W tower with lead spire.
Periods: Though chiefly of 14c and 15c date, the church has been much restored. The tower is Dec. Most of the windows are Perp insertions and the E window is modern. The N aisle was added in 1837 and altered again when the church was restored in 1868.
Features: Octagonal 15c font; piscina in S aisle; old glass in window of S aisle; Jacobean pulpit; good helmet in the Cockfield Chapel; cup and cover 1580, flagon 1720. The church is known for the number of its memorials which include: fragments of the tomb of Nicholas Sydney 1513, and a hatchment of Elizabeth Mann 1691 hanging over N door. In the aisle are memorials to William Betts an early 17c lawyer, Eleazer Davy, and a small brass of John Skottow and Agnes his wife 1511. In the chancel are John Copeland 1758, and William Bernard 1660, and there are brasses to John Norwiche 1428 and Maud his wife 1418, and opposite, an unusual brass of Tomasine Tendring 1485 shown as a corpe in a shroud, with a number of her children - five in shrouds died in infancy. In the S aisle of the chancel, known as the Cockfield Chapel and built c1520, are a number of memorials to the Hopton family: on the S wall the monument of Sir Robert Brooke 1646, and at the E end a brass to Dame Joan Brooke 1618, together with a number of memorials to the Blois family. In the S aisle are various Foxe brasses and a monument to Sir Charles Blois 1850, and other members of that family.

Glossary

Ambulatory: The semi-circular or polygonal aisle enclosing an apse.

Apse: Vaulted semi-circular end of a chancel (sometimes polygonal).

Arcade: Range of freestanding arches supported on piers or columns (Blind Arches are attached to the wall).

Aumbry: Cupboard or recess to hold sacred vessels.

Box Pew: Pew with a high wooden enclosure.

Canopy: Hood or projection over an altar, pulpit, niche or statue.

Capital: Head or top part of a column.

Castellated: Decorated with battlements.

Chancel: That part of the E end of a church in which the altar is placed.

Chancel Arch: Arch at the W end of the chancel usually forming a division from the nave.

Chantry Chapel: A chapel within or attached to a church for saying Mass for the soul of an individual, usually the founder.

Clerestory: Upper storey of the nave walls of a church pierced by windows.

Collar Beam: Tie-beam applied higher up the slope of the roof.

Collar Purlins: A lengthwise beam supporting the collar-beams, found in the context of crownpost roofs, which do not have a ridge-piece.

Corbel: Block of stone projecting from a wall to support some horizontal feature.

Crownpost: An upright timber carried on a tiebeam and supporting a collar purlin braced to it and the collar-beam with 4-way struts.

Dec: Period of architecture known as Decorated and covering the period

from c1290 to c1350.

Early English: Architectural period roughly covering the 13c.

Easter Sepulchre: Recess with tomb-chest to receive an effigy of Christ for Easter celebrations, usually in the wall of a chancel.

Flushwork: Decorative use of flint in conjunction with dressed stone to form patterns.

Foil: Lobe formed by the cusping of a circle or an arch. Trefoil, quatrafoil, express number of leaf shapes seen.

Hammerbeam: Beam projecting at right angles, usually from the top of a wall, to carry arched braces or struts and arched braces.

Herringbone Work: Where brick, stone or tile used in construction is laid diagonally instead of flat. Alternative courses lie in opposing directions to form zig-zag pattern.

Jamb: Staright side of an archway, doorway or window.

Kingpost: An upright timber carried on a tie-beam and suporting the ridge-beam.

Lancet Window: Slender pointed-arched window usually signifying Early English period of architecture.

Linenfold: Tudor panelling ornamented with a representation of a piece of linen laid in vertical folds.

Long and Short Work: Saxon quoins consisting of stones placed with the long side alternately vertical and horizontal, usually providing corners on flint buildings.

Lychgate: Wooden gate structure with a roof and open sides placed at the churchyard entrance for the reception of a coffin. (Saxon: lych - corpse).

Glossary

Misericord: Bracket placed on the underside of a hinged choir stall seat which, when turned up, provides the occupant of the seat with a support during long periods of standing.

Norman: Covering the period from 1066 until the end of the 12c.

Parapet: Low wall placed to protect any spot where there is a sudden drop.

Parclose Screen: Screen separating a chapel from the rest of a church.

Paten: Plate to hold the bread at Communion or Mass.

Perp: Period of architecture known as Perpendicular and covering the period from c1335-50 to c1530.

Piscina: Basin for washing the Communion or Mass vessels, provided with a drain and generally set against the wall. A Pillar Piscina is free-standing on a pillar.

Purlins: Longitudinal members laid parallel with wall-plate and apex some way up the slope of a roof.

Queenposts: Two upright timbers placed symetrically on a tie-beam and supporting purline.

Reredos: Structure behind and above an altar.

Rood: Cross or Crucifix.

Rood Loft: Singing gallery on the top of the rood-screen.

Rood Screen: Screen below the rood usually at the W end of the chancel.

Rood Stairs: Stairs to give access to the rood loft.

Rubble: Rough building stone not squared or hewn, nor laid in regular courses.

Sanctuary: Area around the main altar of a church.

Sarcophagus: Elaborately carved coffin.

Saxon: Covering from the end of the Roman period (5c) to 1066.

Sedilia: Seat for the priests on the S side of the chancel.

Sounding Board: Horizontal board or canopy over a pulpit - also called a Tester.

Squint: A hole cut in a wall to allow a view of the main altar from places where it could not otherwise be seen.

Stoup: Vessel for the reception of holy water, usually placed near the door.

Terracotta: Burnt unglazed clay.

Tie-Beam: Beam connecting the two slopes of a roof at the height of the wall-plate, to prevent the roof from spreading.

Tomb-Chest: Chest-shaped stone coffin; the most usual form of funeral monument in Medieval times.

Tracery: Intersecting ribwork in the upper part of a window - or used decoratively in blank arches, on vaults, etc.

Transept: Transverse portion of a cross-shaped church.

Transom: Horizontal bar across the openings of a window.

Tympanum: Space between the lintel of a doorway and the arch above it.

Wagon Roof: (also called Candle Roof) Roof in which the closely set rafters with arched braces give the appearance of the inside of a canvas tilt over a waggon.

Notes